Interpersonal Conflict

Second Edition

Interpersonal Conflict

Second Edition

Joyce L. Hocker
University of Montana

William W. Wilmot
University of Montana

ᴡᴄb

Wm. C. Brown Publishers
Dubuque, Iowa

To Janice Hocker Rushing

cherished sister,
gentle peacemaker,
scholarly reviewer,

who knows what she knows.

Contents

Preface   xi

Acknowledgments   xv

Part 1
Conflict Components

Chapter 1   Assumptions about Conflict   4
The Nature of Conflict Dysfunctional Perspectives on
                             Conflict   6
                           Metaphors and the Conflict
                             Process   9
                           Common Images of Conflict   12
                             Conflict Is War   *13*
                             Conflict Is Explosive   *15*
                             Conflict Is an Upward
                               Struggle   *15*
                             Conflict Is a Trial   *15*
                             Conflict Is a Mess   *16*
                             Conflict Is a Ball Game   *16*
                             Conflict Requires a Hero   *16*
                             Conflict Is a Bargaining Table *17*
                           Communication: The Essence of
                             Conflict Expression   19
                           The Elements of Conflict   22
                             An Expressed Struggle   *23*
                             Perceived Incompatible Goals   *24*
                             Perceived Scarce Rewards   *25*
                             Interference   *26*
                             Interdependence   *26*

Destructive Conflict   29
Productive Conflict   32
The Need for Productive
   Management   34
Summary   35

Chapter 2
Conflict Styles

Individual Conflict Styles   37
Identifying Personal Styles   *39*
Limitations of Individual Style
   Approaches   *49*
System Styles   53
Identifying System Styles   *53*
Limitations of System Styles   *59*
Adapting and Unfreezing   60
Individual Styles   *60*
System Styles   *64*
Summary   66

Chapter 3
Power in Interpersonal Conflict

Orientations toward Power   67
The Prevalence of Power   71
Power Currencies   72
A Relational View of Power   76
Assessing Power   79
Power Imbalances   83
Power Balancing   86
Summary   90

Chapter 4
Clarifying Goals

Advantages of Goal Clarity   92
Goals Change over Time   94
Prospective Goals   *94*
Transactive Goals   *95*
Retrospective Goals   *98*
Content and Relationship Goals   99
Building Collaborative Goals   102
People: Separate the People
   from the Problem   *102*
Interests: Focus on Interests,
   Not Positions   *102*
Options: Generate a Variety of
   Possibilities before Deciding
   What to Do   *103*
Criteria: Insist That the Result
   Be Based on Some Objective
   Standard   *103*

	Action Planning	104
	Summary	106
Chapter 5	The Process of Strategizing	107
Conflict Tactics	The Choice to Avoid or Engage	109
	Tactical Options	111
	Avoidance Tactics	*112*
	Engagement Tactics	*115*
	Conflict Directions and Tactical	
	Patterns	123
	Summary	126

Part 2
Conflict Intervention

Chapter 6	Systems Theory: An Organizing	
Conflict Assessment	Framework	130
	Identifying Conflict Patterns	133
	Metaphoric/Dramatic	*133*
	Conflict Triangles	*136*
	Sculpting or Choreographing	*139*
	System Rules	*140*
	Microevents	*142*
	Quantitative Assessment	145
	Comprehensive Assessment	
	Guides	149
	Wehr's Conflict Map	*150*
	The Hocker-Wilmot Conflict	
	Assessment Guide	*153*
	Summary	156
Chapter 7	Options for Change	157
Self-Regulation: Changing Conflict	Midrange Conflict	159
from the Inside Out	Types of Self-Regulation	161
	Regulation through Belief in	
	Nonviolence	*161*
	Interpersonal Nonviolence	*162*
	Techniques for Self-Regulation	166
	Fractionation	*166*
	GRIT	*168*
	Stuart's Conflict Containment	
	Model	*169*
	Negotiation: Agreeing to Rules	
	of Process	*172*

Negotiating Interpersonal
Agreements   *173*
Handling Crises (Editing)   *175*
Leveling   *176*
A Postscript on Further
Education   177
Summary   178

Chapter 8   The Intervention Continuum   180
Third Party Intervention: Changing   *Formal Intervention:*
Conflict from the Outside In   *Consultation*   *180*
Informal Intervention   *182*
The Intervention Process   184
Identify Intervention Needs   *184*
Decide to Intervene   *186*
Negotiate a Role   *187*
Assess the Conflict   *190*
Design the Intervention   *191*
Intervention Tactics   *191*
Assess the Intervention and
Exit from the System   *198*
Formal Intervention Modes   199
Adjudication   *199*
Arbitration   *203*
Mediation   *204*
Summary   208

Epilogue   209
Appendix: Conflict Resources   211
References   215
Author Index   231
Subject Index   235

Preface

This is a book about interpersonal conflict—an activity that requires energy, wisdom, and creativity. Our approach to conflict is that "we do not have to stay the way we are"; we all have more choices in conflicts that we assume. Many people have changed the destructive patterns of their conflicts to productive, creative new approaches. A thorough understanding of the factors that contribute to the entire conflict process can lead to more successful conflict management. This book is a systematic examination of those factors, with a focus on the communication behavior of the conflict participants. This communication approach assumes that conflict and communication are intrinsically related; this work is an attempt to clarify that notion.

In this second edition of *Interpersonal Conflict,* we kept the general approach that we used in the first edition, while expanding our scope with a new part II, "Conflict Intervention." Part I, "Conflict Components," treats the same topics as did the first edition but with updated research and greater depth. We deleted the chapter on structure, developing a new approach to structure in chapter 6, "Conflict Assessment."

Chapter 1, "The Nature of Conflict," provides a comprehensive view of the conflict process. The widely quoted definition of conflict from the first edition was revised in a minor way. Two new sections illustrate how metaphors for conflict can be used for an understanding of conflict. We added a new section on the nature of interference between parties. Throughout, we expanded our treatment of the role of communication in conflict.

Chapter 2, "Conflict Styles," presents both individual styles and a new section on system styles. Information on identifying both personal and system styles is presented, along with an expanded treatment of how styles interact to create a new approach, and suggestions about how to change styles are given.

Chapter 3, "Power In Interpersonal Conflict," benefits from a greatly expanded research base. New sections on power assessment and power currencies have been added. We retain, however, the previous relational perspective on power dynamics. Finally, new sections on "power imbalances" and "power balancing" conclude the chapter by arguing that people in conflict will balance their power either productively or destructively. When parties openly discuss their power perceptions, they are able to collaborate in balancing power.

Chapter 4, "Clarifying Goals," keeps the same philosophy of goal development but drops the distinction between goals and issues, which proved difficult for students. Specific suggestions for building collaborative goals are advanced. We have added a new section on putting goals into action, a step of goal development routinely neglected by conflict parties. Throughout this chapter and the entire book, we present a more consistent argument for the use of collaboration than we did in the first edition. The keystone could be stated as "When in doubt, collaborate."

Chapter 5, "Conflict Tactics," has been completely rewritten. At the time of the first edition, research on conflict tactics was almost nonexistent. Since that time, significant research has become available. The new list of tactics is conceptually and empirically grounded. We have illustrated how tactics combine conjointly to escalate, maintain, or reduce conflict.

Part II, "Conflict Intervention," is new. Chapter 6, "Conflict Assessment," uses eclectic approaches to assessment, ranging from metaphoric/dramatic approaches to the latest in quantitative devices. We present two overall assessment guides to help you organize the information needed for a thorough conflict assessment. The Hocker-Wilmot guide has been used by our students and has proved useful as a teaching tool.

Chapter 7, "Self Regulation: Managing Conflict from the Inside Out," is a new chapter that flows from our conviction that the single most effective way to change a conflict is to alter one's own values and behavior. We offer a philosophy of midrange conflict, an overview of how one's belief structure can be used to regulate conflict, suggestions for practical nonviolence, and many techniques for regulating one's own conflicts.

The final chapter, "Third Party Intervention: Managing Conflict from the Outside In," is a greatly expanded version of our previous treatment. We have added new sections on formal intervention modes: adjudication, arbitration, and mediation, so you can be an informed consumer of conflict services. Specific steps in the informal intervention process are set forth; they may be used as an intervention guide for formal or informal third parties.

We conclude the book with a new appendix of conflict resources. Here you will find addresses for many of the scales and exercises mentioned in the text.

We feel privileged to be in this field of study. This revision has been difficult and rewarding—much as productive conflicts are. The changes in the book are products of our continuing process of learning about interpersonal conflict. We hope you find the book useful and challenging and that your own conflicts are made more creative and productive through the principles presented. We invite your correspondence and comments about the ideas in the book.

Joyce L. Hocker
William W. Wilmot

Acknowledgments

Joyce and Bill thank their students in Communication 485 at the University of Montana who have given helpful responses to new ideas and have put up with Bill's creative lecture style and Joyce's impromptu dramatizations. They remain the sounding board and inspiration for the book. Carl and Rosie Schroer were close to us for our wedding and fifth anniversary—times of writing both editions. Their friendship, Carl's sermons, and Rosie's outrageously tempting meals paralled the growth of the ideas in this book. Special role models show us how to embody conflict skills: Earl Koile, Richard Douthitt, Elise Boulding, Elaine Yarbrough, Sam Keltner, Lois Gold, and Will Neville. Our faculty appointments at the University of Montana continue to provide us with a healthful environment for our work in the Department of Interpersonal Communication. We thank our colleagues there. Former students give us support and confirmation enabling us to feel connected to a larger community. Finally, Jan Perrin, Norma McSloy, Karen Clark, and Sally Kingston typed numerous pages and helped us complete this book while we were away from our home. Jacqueline Gibson proofread the galleys with good humor and expertise.

We were fortunate to have excellent reviewers for our work on this revision. Many valuable suggestions were made, and we appreciate your work. Thanks to William P. Cahill, Janice Hocker Rushing, John Stewart, and Paul Yelsma.

To those of you who wondered whether we would get our work times together for this project—no, we didn't. But we learned to manage the conflict about it more productively!

From Joyce:

I thank the staff of the Morrison Center for Youth and Family Services in Portland, Oregon, for teaching me so much and providing a caring, supportive, and challenging environment for my internship in clinical psychology. Dr. Julian Taplin directs a dedicated and talented group of professionals who daily respond to the need for practical conflict management. Thank you to my clinical colleagues Orin Bolstad, Anne Van Dusen, Phyllis Jossy, Margaret Labby, Judy Steinberger, Jack Michels, Pauline Furness, the IFI group, Connie McCutcheon, Meg Eastman, Gail Armstrong, Peggy Rudolph, Bob Thompson, Mary Thompson, Pam Patton, Henry Miller, and all the rest of the Morrison Center staff. The office admistrators, headed by Sondra Perlman and Cheryl Glazer, made the work environment an experience of collaboration. The children and families at the center challenged everything I know about conflict management. Counseling days and writing nights and weekends would have been impossible without my special group of interns: Eric Johnson, Robin McCalister, Emilie Myers, and Aymee Torres-Michels. During rainy mornings at the Wooden Spoons and an intensive year's worth of multifaceted interactions, we developed the gifts of friendship and support. We made it! My heartfelt thanks and love to you all.

In Missoula and by long-distance, Lesley Guthrie provided me with confidence and friendship over the course of this project. She helped me through my conflict with statistics. Mike Burr and Elaine Yarbrough, supportive friends of long standing, included me in the birth of Lindsay. Lindsay, may you live in peace. My family continues to be the crucible for all my ideas on conflict; welcome to Tom Frentz and Jon and Annie Hocker. Anne DeVore still guides my spirit and helps me stay in touch with the feminine. My aunt, Edwina Roark, is one of the healing women in the family; my love and thanks for her early modeling. I thank my grandmother, Freddie Lightfoot, who died at 93 as these acknowledgments were being written, who believed in me as a writer and who has helped to teach me the spirit of healing. To you go love and celebration for your life.

Finally, to Bill, coauthor, colleague across the hall, energizer, initiator of this project, spirited supporter, friend, and husband, thank you for being my partner. Without your animus, this revision would still be undone.

From Bill:

I would like to thank the faculty of the Department of Communications at Lewis and Clark College, Portland, Oregon, for providing office space and access to campus resources. I recall with fondness "Billie's Bunker." I would like especially to thank Dr. Leslie Baxter, colleague and friend, for her supportive discussions about communication and her dedication to high levels of scholarship. Many years ago, Dr. Orville Pence at the University of Washington treated some of my earliest writing with brutal frankness and loving spirit. His comments on my convention paper have provided many minutes of humor. The officers and executive council members of the Western Speech Communication Association helped me manage a couple of conflicts and provided some valuable learning. John Hammerback was especially important for our long-distance talks and his encouragement. Finally, my children, Jason and Carina, deserve a special note. They have maintained close connections with me across many miles and months, always ready to begin anew. In answer to their recurring question, YES, we have finally finished the book.

Sometimes places, as well as people, are important. West Fork Butte is my place of contemplation and groundedness. Portland's occasional rain kept me inside working, and the Tri-Met bus system provided many opportunities for reflection while I was waiting for the next bus.

Joyce, my coauthor, spouse, and closest confidante, exemplified the principles set forth in this book. She actually *does* engage in collaborative, constructive conflict. She provides me with loving support coupled with intellectual challenge—an unbeatable combination. Without her interest in improving interpersonal relationships, this work never would have been initated.

Part 1 Conflict Components

Interpersonal conflicts share underlying similarities, and Part 1 examines those components. The first chapter, "The Nature of Conflict," gives an overview of the conflict process and examines conflict elements. Chapter 2 presents classifications of conflict styles on both individual and system levels. The third chapter illuminates the central role power has in conflict, while participant goals in conflicts are discussed in chapter 5. The final chapter overviews tactics used in conflicts. Part 2 of the book builds on the components of part I and applies them to intervention in conflicts.

No two people are exactly alike, think alike, or totally share the same interests. How then are order, harmony, and peace between men possible? (Rummel, 1976, 35)

1 The Nature of Conflict

Wife: I just came back from campus, and I've found that I can still register for fall quarter. I want to send the forms in tonight.

Husband: I don't think we can afford it. You agreed that my new business had to take priority, and we need your income. You could go back to school in two or three years.

Wife: When we agreed that you would start the business, we never mentioned my not being able to go back to school! You know I've been counting on it, and now you're backing out. I've been working at this boring job since we got married, and it's time for me to do something more rewarding.

Husband: Fine time you pick to better yourself! What are we supposed to use for money while you're becoming a coed again?

The husband and wife are engaged in a pervasive human activity—interpersonal conflict. Their conflict is a product of the communication behavior they use. The couple faces the problem of reconciling their individual goals with their shared goals as a couple. Individually, they work toward power, success in their work and personal lives, goal attainment, and a positive self-concept. Relationally, they work toward trust, affection, collective benefits, and mutual growth. Different goals all too often lead people into seemingly impossible dilemmas. However, people who are interdependent find, when they learn new skills and channel energy toward productive management of conflicts, that unforeseen options appear when conflict is treated as a problem to be solved instead of a battle to be won. Individual and relational goals *can* be met.

This book on interpersonal conflict is written to help people manage conflict in helpful and productive ways. The Chinese character for conflict is made up of two different symbols superimposed: one indicates *danger* while the other signifies *opportunity*. Conflict is often felt as a crisis, whether the crisis appears internally, in a two-person relationship, in a small group's work, or in an organization. Conflict presents a chance for growth, new life, and change at the same time that it affords potential destruction, death, and stagnation. We hope that by reading this book, you will be able to understand your present conflict behavior and make informed choices about how you might want to change your own conflicts and the conflicts of others. We have observed hundreds of people in families, work environments, and small groups who have been able to change their approach to conflict. They have demonstrated to us and to those around them that conflict behavior can change; it is not an inborn set of responses, but rather a developed repertoire of communication skills that can be learned, refined, and put into action in everyday life. You don't have to stay the way you are!

To begin our study of conflict, we will discuss assumptions about conflict that you may have learned. Then we will explore images and explanations of conflict through ordinary language, which offers clues about how conflict is commonly understood.

Assumptions about Conflict

In a training session held for a large computer corporation, a revealing dialogue ensued. The agreed-upon topic was "Conflict on the Job: Making It Work Productively." Three days before the training was to take place, a worried vice-president called. He said the proposed topic "certainly sounded interesting," and he was "sure everyone needed help in the area," but wondered if the leader would take a more "positive" approach to the subject. He urged a title change to "Better Communication in Business," and explained that his company didn't really have "conflicts," just problems in communicating. He felt conflict was such a negative subject that spending concentrated time on it might make matters worse. The executive's apprehensions about conflict were mirrored by a participant in a recent course, called "Managing Conflicts Productively," who said she came to the course because she had never seen a productive conflict—all the conflicts she had witnessed were destructive. Further, her statement suggested that such a thing as a helpful conflict probably did not exist.

If you were asked to list the words that come to your mind when you hear the word "conflict," what would you list? Common responses people have given us when we asked them to do this were:

destruction	anxiety	threat
anger	tension	heartache
disagreement	alienation	pain
hostility	violence	hopelessness
war	competition	

Many people view conflict as an activity that is almost totally negative and has no redeeming qualities. They take the attitude that "what the world needs now is love"; that if people just could understand each other better, they wouldn't have to have conflicts. Some people do not go that far, but they still see nothing particularly good about conflict, either. Would you list such words as the following when you hear the word "conflict"?

exciting	intimate
strengthening	courageous
helpful	clarifying
stimulating	opportune
growth-producing	enriching
creative	

One of the assumptions we hold is that conflict can be associated with all of the above words, both the negative ones and the positive ones.

People in Western culture have, however, developed a way of communicating about conflict that is almost completely negative. A notable exception is in the way competitive games are discussed—one of the few areas of conflict that commonly receives positive description. In games, children learn that "hitting hard" and "fighting to win" are positive virtues. Strategizing, scheming, and maximizing your gains are also necessary, as is playing as a team member. Few other positive viewpoints about the value of conflict creep into everyday conversation.

Several well-known cultural clichés present a fairly clear picture of how many of us were raised to think about conflict. Parents may tell their children, "If you can't say anything nice, don't say anything at all"; "Pick on somebody your own size"; "Don't hit girls"; "Don't rock the boat"; "Children should be seen and not heard"; "Act your age!" (which means act *my* age, not yours); "Be a man, fight back"; and "Sticks and stones may break my bones, but words will never hurt me!" All of these sayings give a bit of philosophy about conflict: with whom to fight, permissible conflict behavior, injunctions about when to engage in conflict, and the power of words in conflict behavior. All of the sayings make assumptions that we think are not helpful to persons who want to learn to carry out productive conflict behavior.

Social scientists explain the emergence of conflict in human behavior in various ways. Wehr presents some of the most common assumptions:

1. Conflict and fighting is innate in all social animals including humans.

2. Social conflict originates in the nature of certain societies and how they are constructed.

3. Conflict is an aberration, a dysfunctional process in social systems.

4. Conflict occurs because it is functional for social systems.

5. Conflict between societies occurs because each, as a nation-state, pursues often incompatible national interests.

6. Conflict is a consequence of poor communication, misperception, miscalculation, socialization, and other unconscious processes.

7. Conflict is a natural process common to all societies, with predictable dynamics and amenable to constructive regulation.

(Wehr 1979, 1–8)

One judges conflict behavior based on principles such as those just listed. For instance, if you believe that conflict is a dysfunctional process in social systems, then individuals who are out of power (in the nation, in the family, in the work place) are engaging in unacceptable acts when they engage in conflict activities. On the other hand, if you think that the root cause of conflict is in the structure of society (or any other entity), then you might find any means that restructures power to be desirable.

Our own position about conflict is similar to Wehr's (1979). We see it as a natural process, inherent in the nature of all important relationships and amenable to constructive regulation through communication.

Dysfunctional Perspectives on Conflict

Many societies, including our own, express contradictory views of conflict—sometimes it is bad, sometimes it is good. Therefore, we grow up with a confusing perspective on when conflict is helpful and OK or when it should be avoided. We learn few strategies for changing situations from harmful ones into productive ones. In a study of how children initiate and terminate friendships, Bell and Hadas (1977) found that children had twice as many ideas for how to get other children to be friends ("ask where they sit so you can sit next to them," "just walk up and say that you want to play!") than they did about how to end a friendship. The ending strategies relied heavily on such ideas as "ignore them," "you tell them to go away, or you move," and "beat them up." They also noticed uneasy silences when children were asked to tell how they ended friendships, or what they did when they wanted to make up after an argument. A poignant comment was made by one youngster who commented that friendships were over at the end of the school year anyway, so you did not have to make up.

Children receive confusing messages about their conduct of conflict. Sports are all right, random violence is not. Conflicts with peers are all right if you have been stepped on and you are a boy, but talking back to parents when they step on you is not all right. Having a conflict over a promotion is acceptable, but openly vying for recognition is not. Competing over a girl (if you're a boy) is admirable, but having a conflict over a boy (if you're a girl) is catty. And on and on. Double message situations are set up in which persons in power send two different messages: (1) fight and stand up for yourself, but (2) only when it is acceptable (Bateson 1972). Thus, persons emerge with a mixed feeling about conflict, and many simply learn to avoid the whole subject. Clearly, one of the dysfunctional teachings about conflict is that you need to check with those in power to determine if you should have a conflict and, if so, how to carry it out.

Until a decade or so ago, scholars usually presented conflict as negative, something to be avoided, a process that was altogether undesirable (Simons 1972). Recent studies and texts have begun to present conflict as helpful under certain circumstances. We agree with this reevaluation. But many assumptions that work against a potentially positive view of conflict still seem to be widely accepted. Some of the most common are presented here.

1. One of the most common dysfunctional teachings about conflict is that *harmony is normal and conflict is abnormal.* Hawes and Smith (1973) refer to this treatment of conflict as the *time* disruption in an otherwise peaceful system, whether the system be interpersonal or a large organization. In other words, conflict is temporary, while harmony is the usual lasting status of affairs. Coser (1967) and Simmel (1953) support the idea that conflict is the normal state of affairs in a relationship that endures over time. They describe conflict as cyclical, or rising and falling. No one expects relationships to be in a constant state of upheaval, or they would reach the "critical limit in a regressive communication spiral and disintegrate" (Wilmot 1979). Observation of people in relationships shows that conflict is not a temporary aberration. *It alternates with harmony in an ebb and flow pattern.* But common expressions such as "I'm glad things are back to normal around here" or "Let's get back on track" express the assumption that conflict is not the norm.

2. Another popular assumption is that *conflicts and disagreements are the same phenomena.* Often people in conflicts assure each other "This is really just a disagreement." Simons (1972) notes the extensive use of the term "communication breakdown" to describe conflict situations. This term seems to mean that in conflict, one is not communicating. A problem with referring to conflicts and disagreements as being the same is that people assume that if a discussion is "just a disagreement," it can and should be solved by reaching a better understanding or by communicating better. As we argue later in this chapter, conflicts are more serious than disagreements. They require more than a clarification of terms or more careful listening, although

those two communication skills greatly speed the process of conflict management.

3. Another common conception is that *conflict is pathological.* People who exhibit conflict behavior in a group, for instance, may be seen as "hostile," "neurotic," "paranoid," "oppositional," "anti-social," or "deviant." This view of conflict as being pathological ignores the phenomenological experience of the person expressing the conflict. Pathology, in this case, is in the eye of the beholder. The label substitutes for an understanding that a real conflict exists. Too often, the label vividly describes not the other party, but the power relationship between the parties. The high-power person can, by getting a label applied to the low-power person, avoid dealing with or engaging in the conflict, since the person is "sick" or has a personality problem. Low-power persons use the concept of pathological conflict by calling the high-power person(s) "authoritarian," "rigid," "defensive," "closed," or other terms that describe the current relationship instead of only the other person.

4. Many believe that *conflict should be reduced or avoided, never escalated.* Often, the term "conflict resolution" is used to describe the process of dealing with conflict. We prefer "conflict management," since sometimes the most productive direction to take is to make the conflict bigger, more important, or more crucial so that it can be dealt with. Ultimately, conflict ought to be reduced—possibly after a long and intense period of escalation. During the 1960s, when academic and popular attention were given to the needs of the oppressed minorities in the United States and when social protest movements were part of the everyday lives of many people, more attention was given to bringing up issues, getting attention paid to injustices, and challenging authority. Even in interpersonal relationships, some attention needs to be given to making enough "noise" to be heard, without the person's being perceived as a trouble-maker or a malcontent.

5. Conflict is sometimes assumed to be the result of *clashes of personalities.* Managers are often advised to handle conflicts in a parental way, assuming that some people just can't get along, as is suggested in this section from a management text:

There are some people who just cannot get along with each other. If, after trying such techniques as counseling and discipline, you still find two people battling with each other, physically separate them. . . . It's usually futile to try to convert such people to cooperative relations with others. On-the-job counseling can never be intensive enough and the effects of discipline will be short-lived at best. Do keep them away from the rest of your subordinates to the greatest extent possible. You will be doing everyone—including the battler himself—a favor (Weiss 1974, 33).

"Personality clashes" are the result of learned human behavior; therefore, they can be changed. People are creatures of their environment, which they can usually affect to some degree. As Fisher (1974, 104) has noted, "personalities don't conflict—behaviors that people *do* conflict."

6. A final misconception of conflict is the notion that *emotions are different from genuine conflict.* Common distinctions between kinds of conflict delineate "substantive" or "affective" conflicts, "real" and "phony" conflicts, or "genuine" and "pseudo" conflicts. Unreal conflicts, following this distinction, are always associated with emotional biases, feelings, ego investment, or prejudice, while real conflicts are associated with differences of policy, resource allocation, different goals, and rational analysis. A similar problem arises when some conflicts are referred to as "subjectively based," while others are "objectively based." Some conflict situations carry intense emotional involvement; others do not. The presence of feelings adds information about the intensity of the conflict, not about whether the conflict is genuine or phony. As we will discuss further, feelings are facts. They exist, must be reckoned with, and are potentially as useful as rational analysis for managing conflict. Jung has commented that no great change occurs without strong feelings. Emotional energy may indeed fuel collaborative efforts.

Metaphors and the Conflict Process

A Shady Deal

We're playing poker at a card table covered with green baize cloth, which is hanging down so no one can see under the table. Kevin is the dealer, and he also plays against me. He has the right to change the rules; sometimes I don't even know the game we're playing. The stakes are high; my tension mounts as the game progresses. Kevin smiles mysteriously; I hide my feelings, trying to bluff. An audience gathers, encouraging me to get out of such a lopsided game. I always stay for another hand, thinking that *this time* I'll understand the rules and be able to have a fair chance. My tension mounts again."

The shady deal mentioned above is an elaboration of a comment made by a female student in a conflict class. Frustrated with a romantic relationship, she said that sometimes it seemed to her that Kevin "dealt all the cards." In class, her discussion group expanded this description of the "shady deal" and provided imaginary ways the game could be changed. People often use metaphorical language to communicate about the pattern of interaction they experience in a conflict. Many times, the person generating the metaphor is amazed at the precise insights strangers can gather about the elements of an interpersonal conflict, based on the metaphor alone.

Metaphors? you may be wondering. Aren't those the literary things we had to learn in eleventh grade about poetry we didn't understand? The metaphoric process does interest students and teachers of literature, but its utility does not stop there. Metaphoric descriptions of conflict provide us with rich sources of insight about the conflict process.

A metaphor is a way of comparing one thing to another by speaking of it as if it were the other, for example, calling the world a stage. A metaphorical representation of conflict uses figurative *and* literal information. Kevin, in the above metaphorical description, is invested by the storyteller with some of the rich images associated with a shady riverboat gambler, while the hapless female student takes on the meodramatic aura of the confused and unfortunate player, caught in a game she is too innocent to understand.

Simons (1979) notes that the study of metaphor is enjoying a newfound respectability these days. Few scholars relegate metaphor to the role of mere ornamentation, as many have in the past. You may be used to thinking of metaphors as "pretty speech" added to poems and stories. Listening to yourself and your friends will convince you, we suspect, that metaphorical language is pervasive in everyday life, thought, and action. In fact, several authors argue that our thinking system is itself metaphoric in its fundamental nature (Lakoff and Johnson 1980; Hayakawa 1978; Ortony 1975; Weick 1979). Ortony (1979) asserts that metaphors are *necessary* for communication, not just a nice addition to language. Hayakawa (1978, 109) writes that metaphors are not "ornaments of discourse," but are "direct expressions of evaluation and are bound to occur whenever we have strong feelings to express."

Conflict management can be served by using the insights created by metaphoric speech. Rushing (1983) reminds readers that Aristotle saw analogy or metaphor as the source of nondeduced truths. Aristotle considers the use of metaphor to be a mark of genius:

> ". . . the greatest thing by far is to be a master of metaphor. It is the one thing that cannot be learnt from others; and it is also a sign of genius, since a good metaphor implies an intuitive perception of the similarity in dissimilars" (1941, 186).

Aristotle's evaluation of the importance of metaphor applies to our search for creative conflict management. Language choices about conflict may suggest some of the problems that are at issue, the view the parties maintain of what conflict is, and how they think conflict might be managed. A metaphor or analogy "can take its creator, as well as its hearers, quite by surprise" (Rushing 1983). Burke provides insight about the function of metaphor when he notes "It appeals by exemplifying relationships between objects which our customary rational vocabulary has ignored" (1968, 90).

In addition to offering insights about the structure of a particular conflict, one's metaphor or analogy of the experience may be closer than literal descriptions to one's perceptions of and feelings about a conflict (Ortony 1975). Metaphors evoke vivid emotions and sensory and cognitive images. Overhearing your friend say "I was devastated by his anger" gives a much more immediate perception of her response to the conflict than if she had said "I found myself feeling disconfirmed. He showed no regard for what I was trying to say." "Devastation" calls up images of tornadoes ripping through a town, of rubbish strewn about, and of destruction and violence. "Devastation" may also suggest that your friend saw herself as helpless in the face of the whirlwind of anger, or it may suggest many other feelings. Metaphors can make the experience of the conflict immediate and clear. Bochner (1978, 83) states that "Metaphor is a fertile and, as yet, unexplored aspect of interpersonal communication." In the last few years, scholars have turned attention again to human analogic processes, attention that can be expanded to the study of conflict.

Two further examples will, perhaps, set you thinking about how you would describe your own experience of conflict.

(1) A colonel in the army described his office as a windmill, with people going around in circles, finding no way to reach the general who sat in the center of the windmill. Worse, they were unaware that the pipe connecting the mechanism with the underground well had been disconnected.

(2) Karen described her family as a painting, in which a train rushed across a bridge about to collapse. The driver of the train, her father, was unaware of danger, since no lookouts were posted along the way to warn of hazards.

In the first image, one feels the exhausting and purposeless confusion; the second evokes a sense of impending disaster and speed. From these brief descriptions, an agency staff group was able to create conflict management approaches that emerged from the participants' full sense of the conflict. (This process will be described in chapter 4).

Recurring conflicts often symbolize core relationship issues (Haley 1976). When conflicts happen over and over, the content of the conflict may not be the most important issue of distress. Haley (1976) uses the example of a couple haggling over their budget time after time. The conflict may represent their basic relationship, in which resources are viewed as too scarce. They may view marriage as a balance sheet, requiring subtotals along the way to be sure no one is getting the better of the other. Children who squabble all the time about who gets the best gifts at birthday time or on holidays may be signaling that they are not sure there is enough love to go around.

Metaphors help us become aware of how the whole system works to-gether—or does not work together. Hansen's (1981) study of families in their homes generated the idea that families have a rhythm of interaction. "Each family conveys an impression of rhythm much like a group of figure skaters. Those groups that work together with unusual skill . . . give impressions of smoothness and ease; those . . . that are unskilled, give an impression of jerk-iness and tension. Rhythm provides the first indicator of how successfully the family is functioning" (p. 57). Hansen communicates impressions of well-functioning families without technical language, giving the reader a fluid ver-bal picture that suggests visual images of the family's interaction.

In conclusion, metaphors function in the following ways:

1. They provide a compact version of an event without the need for the message to spell out all the details (Ortony 1975; Weick 1979).

2. They enable people to describe characteristics that are unnamable. They allow an expression of a reality when words can't be found to give meaning to the event (Ortony 1975; Weick 1979).

3. Metaphors give a vivid, immediate version of a process that evokes strong, intuitive responses.

Metaphors provide compact versions of conflict, describe unnameable characteristics, and promote vivid response even when they are not in an elab-orated form. Participants in conflicts rarely provide a complete metaphorical analysis; they provide clues about their metaphors. For example, a vice-pres-ident of a technological firm would not say to another vice-president, "Look, Jack, you and I are just like opposing generals in a war; each of us is trying to wipe the other off the map. So let's just say that all's fair, and don't expect any cooperation from me, since I'd like nothing better than to run over you and take away your territory." Rather, the person would subtly cue the other to perceive their relationship in military terms. For instance, she might say, "We need to get together and check signals about what your troops are doing with this new R&D offensive." A student in class said, "My brother is about to bail out!" The class responded with a sense of urgency to the situation in the family, since Stan had elicited the image of a parachutist with his meta-phor.

Common Images of Conflict

In the previous section, we discussed how metaphors can be used to suggest creative conflict management possibilities. We recommended taking advan-tage of the intuitively communicated information stored in analogical descrip-tions of particular conflicts. Additionally, we urged both a rational and a metaphorical approach to analysis of conflicts. In the following section, we will discuss the most common images for the *process of conflict itself.* These images form one's philosophy of conflict. The metaphors were gathered by carefully listening to the way interviewees and people in families, groups, and organizations spontaneously speak of conflict. A not-so-surprising result emerged from our study of how people talk about conflict as a process. Negative metaphors that limit collaborative management greatly predominate over positive metaphors for conflict. You will undoubtedly be able to add to this list as you listen to yourself and others talk about conflict.

Conflict Is War

The military image is the central metaphor of conflict. Osborn refers to the image of brute force as the "bedrock of symbolism" (1967). Burke (1968) discusses the pattern of *victimage,* in which nations or individuals blame others for their troubles, as being a constant temptation in a hierarchy. Since an order exists, people naturally fall short of expectations, thus calling for a victim to pay for social or individual sins.[1] Conflict is often characterized as an *argument* or *battle.* Either way, the process is viewed as warlike, with all the attendant images. Key terms that indicate the existence of a warlike metaphor for argument are exemplified by Lakoff and Johnson (1980, 4):

Your claims are *indefensible.*

He *attacked every weak point* in my argument.

His criticisms were right on target.

I *demolished* his argument.

Okay, *shoot!*

He *shot down* all my arguments.

If argument is envisioned as a war, certain warlike actions are natural. Many debaters, political figures, legislators, public officials, speakers at public forums, and couples having an argument perceive themselves to be at war with their opponents. The original purpose of argument, the discovery of truth, is forgotten.

In a staff meeting, for instance, if accusations are "hurled back and forth" as if by primitives bashing each other with stones, if arguments are felt to be "right on target," then the whole melee is structured as a battle. The *scene* is that of a battlefield; the *actors* are people of warring tribes or clans who are committed to wiping each other out since the other is perceived as threatening. The *acts* are those that aim to produce an advantage by killing or reducing

1. See Ivie, 1982, for a discussion of this blaming process as it is applied to nations.

the effectiveness of the opponent. The *resolution possibilities* are reduced to offense and defense, and the *purpose* or outcome is inevitably a reduction of players, harm, desire for vengeance, and a repetition of the argument/battle.[2] The war metaphor influences the entire perception of the conflict. Both winning and losing sides feel incomplete; victors desire more power, and losers shore up their defenses for the next attack.

Perhaps you work in an organization whose workers act as if conflicts were large or small wars and fights were battles in the ongoing war. If your organization uses a "chain of command," gives people "orders," "attacks competitors," "wages advertising or public relations campaigns," "fires traitors," "employs diversionary tactics," or "launches assaults," then the organization may well have evolved a military metaphor for conflict management (Weick 1979). If so, when goal struggles or a perception of a scarce resource are identified, the conflict is likely to be solved the way it would be if one were on a battlefield. We actually heard one man say he was going to "marshal my troops for a counterattack." He was referring to another department's plan for a reduction in personnel (usually called a reduction in *force!*).

Couples talk in warlike terms, too. We have recorded conflict descriptions such as:

> I just retreat. I fall back and regroup. Then I wait for an opening. . . .
>
> He slaughters me when I cry and get confused.
>
> When I don't want it to come to blows (laughs), I launch a diversionary attack, like telling him the kids are calling me.
>
> That line rips me up!

Chronic use of the military metaphor severely limits creative problem solving. People overlook improvisation, devising new actions, and the opportunity to contradict the norms instead of following orders. The military image saves us the trouble of inventing new ones. However, "other metaphors are needed to capture different realities that exist right alongside those military realities" (Weick 1979, 51).

To illustrate a challenge to this habitual way of acting, see if you can do what Lakoff and Johnson (1980, 5) suggest:

> Imagine a culture where an argument is viewed as a dance, the participants are seen as performers and the goal is to perform in a balanced and aesthetically pleasing way. In such a culture people would view arguments differently, experience them differently, carry them out differently, and talk about them differently. . . . Perhaps the most neutral way of describing this difference between their culture and ours would be to say that we have a discourse form structured in terms of battle and they have one structured in terms of dance.

2. The scheme is adapted from Kenneth Burke, *A Grammar of Motives,* (Berkely & London: University of California Press, 1969).

Conflict Is Explosive

Perhaps you experience "explosive" conflicts, using phrases like the following to describe the process:

> He's about to blow up. Any little thing will set him off.
>
> Larry's got a short fuse.
>
> The pressure's building up so fast that something's gotta give soon!

Phrases like these may indicate a perception of conflict as being made up of flammable materials (feelings), trigger issues, and an ignition of the explosion that, once started, can't be stopped. Maybe the pressure builds "under the surface," like Mount Saint Helens, or "in a hotbox," such as an overcrowded office. We often hear folks say they "blew their stacks" in response to an event.

If people act out explosive conflicts, they often see them as somehow out of their control ("He touched it off, not me"). Explosions blow away familiar structures, often requiring a period of rebuilding and cleanup. The "exploder" may feel better after a release of pressure; the people living in the vicinity may not feel so relieved.

Conflict Is an Upward Struggle

Many people think of conflict as an *upward struggle.* If they can get high enough, or "on top of things," they will then exercise control *over* their opponents. Being "one down" is experienced as a loser's position; "one-upping" has come to signify a constant struggle for bettering oneself in relationship to someone else. Most people holding this image in mind would assume there is not room at the top for very many people and that being "down" means being vulnerable. Some key phrases you may notice are "superior," "rising power," and "low man on the totem pole." If conflict participants think of the process as one of gaining height over others, they are likely to be locked into a competitive spiral.

Conflict Is a Trial

The *trial* image is another common vision of the process. If you hear "He's got the best case," "The jury is still out on that one," "He's going to judge the outcome of the discussion," "You're accusing me of *what?*", or "She's clearly the guilty party this time," the speakers may see the conflict process as a sort of trial. Courts maintain clearly delineated processes, with a judge and jury who will make the ultimate decisions based on law and precedent. Many organizations set up quasi-judicidal systems of hearings to manage conflict. Parents may ask the adolescent to "make a case for yourself," assigning the judge (and jury!) role to one or both parents. Brothers and sisters may present evidence against the accused. The trial image affords a decision about the outcome of the conflict. Unfortunately, the decision is facilitated by the determination of guilt or innocence. Few trials settle the underlying issues in the conflict, especially "trials" in ongoing relationships. Parties keep going back to court to try again.

Conflict Is a Mess

An intriguing image that has come from our study is that of conflict as a *mess,* usually a hidden mess that is uncovered. You'll hear "Let's not open up that can of worms," "We uncovered a real mess," "They got it all out in the open," or "Let's try to tie up some loose ends at this meeting." The latter phrase actually refers to continued decision making and seems to assume that conflict is messy. The clearest reflections of this image are the exclamations "What a mess!" or "This is a messy, sticky situation." Messes, of course, are difficult to manage because they spill over into other areas. A messy conflict usually means one that is full of personal emotional attachments, often implying that someone has done something that is judged to be wrong. Sometimes it's even seen as *witches' brew* ("Something's brewing at home. I can smell it").

Conflict Is a Ball Game

The *ball-game* image is popular. People "bat around" ideas, "toss the ball in his court," "strike out," go "back and forth," and are "team players." The image assumes the existence of rules defining the game, thus defining the interaction among the participants. There are fouls, expected behavior, and even referees.

Conflict Requires a Hero

The *hero* image is also endemic to conflict images. The superheroes of Western movies, science fiction, myths, and of our own childhood are used even into adult life. This archetypal imagery describes a process in which slightly scared people appoint a leader who is "bigger" and better than they are, and then they pledge allegiance to that leader, who will protect them. This may come from the "My dad is bigger than your dad" syndrome of childhood.

Myths of the champion or the hero come from every culture. When a hero (occasionally a heroine) emerges from the group, other predictable roles usually are taken by other people. There is a helper or lieutenant of the hero, there are kings who reward the hero, and there are ordinary people who come to be dependent on the hero for their protection. The movie *High Noon* portrays the decadent effect that relying on a hero may have on people who perceive themselves as weak and dependent on someone else. In transactional analysis terms, the game is "Let's you and him fight!" (Berne 1964).

Conflict Is a Bargaining Table

A more collaborative approach to conflict is exemplified by the common metaphor of the *table*. Diplomacy, labor negotiations, and parliamentary procedure all use this image. The conflict structure and procedure depend on the table as a central feature.

Families are urged to sit down to dinner together, labor and management officials "come to the table," and diplomats struggle over physical dimensions of tables at conferences. These real or imagined tables communicate information about who the conflict participants will be, how they will act, and what their placement will be in relationship to each other. The table is a spatial metaphor defining the relationships.

King Arthur, in historical legend, created a round table to symbolize equal discussion, with each king having one vote. The idea of "Right makes might" substituted, for a time, for "Might makes right." When the federation disintegrated, a symbol of the disintegration became the round table, smashed to pieces by dissident knights. Following are other examples of "table" imagery in conflict management.

In parliamentary procedure, "tabling a motion" stops movement toward a decision; "bringing a motion off the table" indicates a readiness to decide.

"Under the table" refers to hidden or secretive agreements.

"Turning the tables" comes from a medieval custom of turning from one dinner partner to another to begin conversation. It was done in response to the king or queen's gesture. If the "tables are turned," a person feels an unexpected lack of support.

Clearly, people hold various images of the conflict process. Others that you may hear are that conflict is "a drain" a "storm," "hot," "a process of vengeance," a "heavy burden," "a lot of grief," or "poison." If you write down what you hear yourself and others saying about conflict, you will begin to understand the various ways in which people express their meaning for the process.

Problems occur in relationships when people envision conflict in completely different ways. One person may think of conflict as war, with all the images previously described, while the other assumes that conflict is more like diplomacy. Much confusion results from playing the game by different rules.

Not only do parties engage in conflict over the content and relationship issues involved, but they also struggle over what it is that they are doing together.

Two examples of the problems arising from different images follow:

Lynn and Bart are married to each other. Lynn sees conflict as a mess, something sticky and uncomfortable, even slightly shady or dirty. People in her family believed that husbands and wives who love each other don't have conflict very often. It is distasteful to her. She is likely to say,

"I don't want to talk about it now. Let's just leave the whole mess until this weekend. I can't handle it tonight."

Bart sees conflict as an explosion. He feels conflict as an explosion—his stomach tightens, his pulse races, his heart begins to pound. He likes to reduce the pressure of all this emotion. He's a feelings-oriented person, while Lynn is more likely to use a reasoning process if she has to deal with an issue. He is likely to say,

"I am not going to sit on this until Saturday morning. I'll burst. You can't expect me to hold all this in. It's not fair, you always. . . ."

In addition to their specific conflict, Bart and Lynn are fighting over how to fight; indeed, they are fighting over what conflict is and how they experience it. Each assumes that the other thinks about the conflict the way he or she does. They could not be farther from the truth, as they probably will find out.

Another example of different views of conflict occurred in an organization:

Charlotte, the district manager, sees conflict as a trial. She plays various roles when she is in conflict with the assistant managers. Sometimes she asks them to bring in facts to back up their opinion; sometimes she accuses them of not doing their homework. Sue is assistant district manager. She sees conflict as a process of bargaining around an imaginary table. She keeps trying to find areas of compromise, while Charlotte acts as judge or jury, deciding which ideas are best supported. Charlotte later fires Sue for not being able to take a stand, for being indecisive, and for not being agressive enough in developing her own program. The two managers thought conflict was a different kind of process, and they made no provisions for their differing expectations.

Initiating some process of talking about *what is happening* in a small group, *how decisions are going to be made,* and *how conflicts will be managed* gives potential opponents a chance to understand that their friends or coworkers may have a completely different idea about what is appropriate. One way to generate creative ideas about the management of conflict is to understand what it is that the people with whom you conflict think conflict *is*. Their metaphors and your own language and images will help you learn more about the task of conflict management.

Communication: The Essence of Conflict Expression

When is a conflict really a conflict? An interpersonal approach to conflict focuses on the communicative interchanges that make up the conflict episode. While it is worthwhile to examine the *intra*personal, internal nature of an individual's conflict, such as one's anger or fear, our approach incorporates internal conflict only to the extent that the thought or feeling has communicative force. For example, if you are angry at your father yet do not write less often nor divulge your concern, he will not know that the two of you have a "conflict." People in conflicts have (a) perceptions about their *own* thoughts and feelings and (b) perceptions about the *other's* thoughts and feelings. Examine table 1 for a moment to see some of the more basic possibilities of whether people are "in conflict" or not.

One could argue indefinitely about the starting point of an "interpersonal conflict." For example, does an "interpersonal conflict" occur in situation three in table 1? Each person knows of his or her own interpersonal conflict about the other. Yet neither A nor B sees that the other has a conflict with him or her. For our purposes in this book, *conflict is present when there are communicative representations of it.*

The communication may be subtle indeed—a slight shift in body placement by Jill and a hurried greeting by Susan—but it communicatively demonstrates the conflict. Intrapersonal perceptions are the bedrocks upon which conflicts are built, but only when there are communicative manifestations of them will we consider an "interpersonal conflict" to be in operation.

Table 1. Recognition of Conflict

Person A		Person B	
Recognizes his/ her conflict with B	Recognizes B's conflict with A	Recognizes A's conflict with B	Recognizes her/ his conflict with A
1. yes	yes	yes	yes
2. yes	yes	no	no
3. yes	no	no	yes
4. no	yes	yes	no

Communication is the central element in all interpersonal conflict. Communication and conflict are related in the following ways:

- Communication behavior often *creates* conflict.

- Communication behavior *reflects* conflict.

- Communication is the *vehicle* for the productive or destructive management of conflict.

Thus, communication and conflict are inextricably tied. For example, the most distinguishing characteristic of happily married couples is their ability to reach consensus on conflict issues (Mettetal and Gottman 1980). How one communicates in a conflict situation has profound implications for the residual impact of that conflict. If two work associates are vying for the same position, they can handle the competition in a variety of ways. They may engage in repetitive rounds of damaging one another, or they may successfully manage the conflict. The successful management of a conflict of interest can leave the parties without lasting enmity.

The expression of conflict through the communication process is carried out through both *content* and *relationship* information (Haley 1963). Every communicative message, both verbal and nonverbal, creates meaning through sharing specific content information, such as, "We cannot afford to grant your request for a raise," and information about how the relationship is being defined at that time (Haley 1963). In this example of a communicative message, the supervisor may be warning, on an unstated relational level, "Don't push too far. I will tell you what we can afford and what we cannot afford." If the employee says "Why not? This is the best year we have ever had!" the relational message might be, from the employee's perspective, "I have a right to challenge what you say." Each person defines the relationship in every communication transaction and communicates that relational definition to the other, along with specific content. Seldom does the relational definition become an open, spoken message (Wilmot 1979). Relational definitions can be communicated by "who talks first, who talks the most, nonverbal cues, eye contact," and many other factors (Wilmot 1979). Many times, the distinction between content and relationship levels of the communication is blurred. In addition, it is often the case that (1) a relationship disagreement will emerge as a conflict over content, and (2) a content disagreement may emerge as a relational conflict. Of these two, the most common is a relational disagreement acted out via a content issue.

The following simple example will give an indication of how content information and relationship information are communicated.

"Whose Food Is It?"

Connie, Sharon, and Janene share an old house near the campus where they are
seniors at a university. They have known each other for years; they grew up in
the same town. Their roommate relationship has, thus far, been fairly smooth,
although recently an issue has emerged. Janene eats two meals a day on campus
at the food service. Connie and Sharon like to cook, so they prepare their meals
at home. They have invited Janene to share their evening meal several times,
and Janene has accepted. It's Thursday night, Janene is rushing to get to the
food service before it closes, and the following dialogue ensues:

Connie: Hey Janene, you might as well stay and eat with us. It's late—
you'll never make it.

Janene: No big deal, if I miss it, I'll get a hamburger or something.

Janene rushes out the door.

Connie to Sharon: That's the last time I'm going to ask her to eat with
us. She thinks she is too good to be bothered with staying around here
with us.

Later Janene informs the other two women that she will be moving out because
she feels that she has been excluded and that Connie and Sharon would rather
not have her around. They begin to try to talk about the decision, since each
person interprets the events of the last few weeks differently.

When Janene said, "No big deal. . . ." the content was fairly clear: "No,
I'll go ahead, and if I miss the food service, I'll get a hamburger." However,
the content was not the problem. Instead, various relational meanings were
communicated by the two women—meanings that led them into a protracted
conflict. Connie might have been communicating any of the following relationship messages:

"We feel sorry for you. Please stay."

"I feel guilty when you might miss dinner. I don't want you to stay, but
I'd rather you stay than I continue feeling guilty."

"I never get to see you. I miss you. Please stay."

"You don't eat right. I'm worried about you."

Obviously, Janene and Connie needed to clarify the relational level of their
communication about food. Without discussing what is meant, on the relationship level, this particular conflict will not be resolved in a productive manner.

One cannot avoid giving relationship information. One's choice of words and nonverbal actions communicate a definition of the relationship, which may be in conflict with the other's definition of the relationship. For instance, a student visited a professor to explain her many absences from class. At the end of the explanation, the student said, "What is your personal opinion of me?" The professor replied, "I don't have a personal opinion." By refusing to give content information about the "personal opinion," the professor was communicating that the question was inappropriate, that she wished to avoid commenting, or that she disliked the student. Many other meanings are possible. The student was communicating that she wished to personalize the interview or perhaps simply that she wanted to know where she stood as a result of the explanation of the absences. It is impossible to stay on the factual level, even though we may try. Relationship definitons are always communicated, giving information about how each conflict participant views his or her relative power, closeness, level of intimacy, affection, or emotional state in relation to the other.

Both the content and the relational meanings of communication transactions are important. Conflict management often requires that participants deal with both, since no "purely content" conflict exists. Who we are to each other is at least as important as the facts and information being communicated.[3]

Common elements present in all conflicts will be discussed in the next section. Conflict is reflected in communication behavior, but it is also more than communication. Underlying conflict elements are required before "problematic" communication is truly "conflict" communication.

The Elements of Conflict

All interpersonal conflicts, whether they occur in a family, between student and teacher, between worker and supervisor, or between groups, have elements in common. We will illustrate what those underlying elements are, first by providing a definition of conflict, then by systematically examining the central elements.

Not surprisingly, scholars disagree about what conflict is (Fink 1968). One of the most popular definitions of conflict is Coser's (1967, 8), who says conflict is "a struggle over values and claims to scarce status, power and resources in which the aims of the opponents are to neutralize, injure, or eliminate the rivals." Deutsch (1973, 156) maintains that *"conflict* exists whenever *incompatible* activities occur. . . . An action which is incompatible with another action prevents, obstructs, interferes with, injures, or in some way makes

---

3. For further discussion of this issue, see William W. Wilmot, *Dyadic Communication.* 2nd ed. (Reading, MA: Addison-Wesley,. 1979), chapter 4.

it less likely or less effective." Mack and Snyder (1973) say that two or more parties must be present, there must be "position scarcity" or "resource scarcity," and conflictual behaviors "destroy, injure, thwart, or otherwise control another party or parties, and a conflict relationship is one in which the parties can gain (relatively) only at each other's expense." They further state that conflict requires interaction and always involves attempts to acquire or exercise power. All of these definitions contribute important elements to a process definition of conflict and properly avoid the overly simple identification of conflict with "strain," "disagreement," or "controversy" (Simons 1972; Schmidt and Kochan 1972). A key element in all conflicts is the recognition that the parties are interdependent; they have some degree of mutual interest. As a result a perceived opportunity exists for interfering with the other's goal attainment (Schmidt and Kochan 1972). Parties who perceive that the other can interfere with their goal attainment likewise perceive that there are scarce resources—money, land, status, power, or others. From a communication perspective, *conflict is an expressed struggle between at least two interdependent parties who perceive incompatible goals, scarce rewards, and interference from the other party in achieving their goals.*

An Expressed Struggle

People often say, "I'm in a conflict, but the other person doesn't know it." Sometimes they leave home, resign, get divorces, or change professions without other people close to them knowing that they were "having a conflict." In Bergmann's film, *Scenes From a Marriage,* for instance, Johann came home one night and told his wife of ten years that he had fallen in love with another woman and was leaving the next morning. He then related "conflicts" in their marriage that had built up to an intolerable level, while Marianne watched, shocked, trying to absorb the new reality of Johann's definition of their relationship as a relationship of conflict. Internal, one-person conflicts certainly exist. We have all experienced them—agonizing choices that have to be weighed carefully before life can go on. But as communication scholars, we are not primarily interested in these inner conflicts, important as they are. This book deals with *expressed* conflicts between at least two people. It is impossible to have conflict without either verbal or nonverbal communication behavior, or both. The "expression" may be very subtle, but it must be present for the activity to be interpersonal conflict. Therefore, although other conditions must exist also before we label an activity "conflict," we agree with Jandt (1973, 2) when he asserts, "Conflict exists when the parties involved agree in some way that the behaviors associated with their relationship are labelled as 'conflict' behavior." Often, the communicative behavior is easily identified with conflict, such as when one party openly disagrees with the other. Other times, however, an interpersonal conflict may be operating at a more tacit level. Two friends, for instance, may both be avoiding the other and aware that they are engaging in avoidance because both think, "I don't want to see him for a few days because of what he did." The interpersonal struggle is being expressed by the avoidance.

When parties are in an interpersonal conflict, internal conflict usually occurs within each of the parties. However, each could have internal conflicts unrelated to the activities of the other. We are taking a *communication perspective* on conflict because expressed struggles involve communication behavior. It is through communication behavior that conflicts are recognized, expressed, experienced, and managed.

Finally, most expressed struggles have a "triggering event" (Walton 1969). When the worker says, "I don't like this job" to his boss, the wife stays out late, or the teenager says, "Why do you always pick on me?" such events are often triggering events. While a conflict is often over issues that are longer lasting than the triggering event, the event makes it clear to all that an expressed struggle is occurring. However, the triggering event is not, by itself, the conflict.

Perceived Incompatible Goals

What do people fight about? (We use the word "fight" to mean verbal conflict, not physical violence.) The safest statement is that people usually engage in conflict over goals they often deny as being important to them. One company with which we consulted had an extreme morale problem. The head cashier said, "All our problems would be solved if we could just get some carpet, since everyone's feet get tired—we're the ones who have to stand up all day. But management won't spend a penny for us." Her statement of incompatible goals was clear—carpet vs. no carpet. But as the interviews progressed, another goal emerged. She began to talk about how no one noticed when her staff had done good work, and how the "higher-ups" only noticed when lines were long and mistakes were made. There was a silence, then she blurted, "How about some compliments once in a while? No one ever says anything nice. They don't even know we're here." Her stated goals then changed to include not only carpet, but self-esteem and increased notice by management—a significant deepening of the goal statement. Both goals were real, carpets and self-esteem, but the first goal may be incompatible with management's desire, while the second might not; the goal of recognition could be more important than the carpet.

We would not support the overly simple notion that if people just worked together, they would see that their goals are the same. Opposing goals are a fact of life. Many times, however, we have witnessed people who are absolutely convinced that they have opposing goals, and that they cannot agree on anything to pursue together. They then find that if goals are reframed or put in a different context, they can agree. Recently a supervisor of a student teacher outlined her goals for the student. Included in the list was the demand that the student turn in a list of the three most and least positive experiences in the classroom each week. The student asked to be transferred to another supervisor. The dean asked why, saying, "Ms. Barker is one of our best supervisors." The student said, "That's what I've heard, but I can't be open about my failures with someone who's going to give me my ending evaluation. That will go in my permanent files." In discussion with the teacher and the student together, the dean found that both were able to affirm that they valued feedback about positive and negative experiences. Their goals were more similar than they thought; the means for achieving the goals were different. The teacher agreed to use the list as a starting point for discussion but not keep copies; the student agreed to list honestly felt experiences so the teacher would not feel that she was hiding her negative experiences. Trust was built with a discussion of goals. Perception of the incompatibility of their goals changed through clear communication.

Perceived Scarce Rewards

A reward can be defined as "any positively perceived physical, economic or social consequence" (Miller and Steinberg 1975, 65). The rewards, or resources, may be real or perceived as real by the person. Likewise, the perception of scarcity, or limitation, may be apparent or actual. For example, close friends often think that if their best friend likes someone else, too, then the supply of affection available to the original friend will diminish. This may or may not be so, but a perception that affection is scarce may well create genuine conflict between the friends. Sometimes, then, the most appropriate behavior is attempting to change the other person's *perception* of the reward or resource instead of trying to reallocate the resource. Ultimately, one person can never force another to change his or her valuing of a reward or the perception of how much of the reward is available, but the persuasion coupled with supportive responses for the person fearful of losing the reward can help.

Everyone is familiar with money, oil, land, promotions, jobs, and positions seen as scarce rewards. But as we have discussed, intangible "commodities" such as love, esteem, attention, respect, and caring may indeed be scarce or *may be seen as scarce*. A poignant example concerns dropouts in the school system. Videotapes installed in classrooms documented the fact that researchers could predict by the fourth grade which students would later drop out of school. The future dropouts were those students who received, either by their own doing or the teacher's, very limited eye contact from the teacher. They became, nonverbally, nonpersons. The glances, looks, smiles, and eye contact with the important person in the room became a scarce resource on which the students were highly dependent. Often children fight with one another over this perceived scarcity—teacher attention. Or they fight with the teacher, resulting in a gain of that resource—attention. The child would rather get negative attention than none. When rewards are perceived as scarce, an expressed struggle may be initiated.

In interpersonal struggles, two rewards often perceived as scarce are (1) power and (2) self-esteem. Whether the parties are in conflict over a desired romantic partner or a coveted raise, power and self-esteem can be seen as limited. People engaged in conflict often say things that are easily translated as power and self-esteem struggles. In the following scenarios, we have translated the verbal expressions into the rewards seen as scarce.

"She always gets her way."
(She has more power than I do.)
"He is so sarcastic I can't stand him."
(He interferes with my self-esteem when I'm around him.)
"I've got to get an 'A' on that test."
(I failed chemistry. If I don't do well in something, my parents will
     think I'm not trying and quit paying my way to school.)

We maintain that in interpersonal conflicts, regardless of the content issue involved, the parties usually perceive a shortage of power and/or self-esteem. And the key is the perception that power or self-esteem rewards are scarce.

Interference

Individuals who are in relation to one another and perceive incompatible goals and scarce rewards may still not be in conflict. Conflict occurs when these conditions are present and when the parties *interfere* with one another's goal attainment. Your relationship with another can be used to assist or to interfere; conflict is always coupled with interference or blocking activities (Peterson 1983), which can take a variety of forms. If you refuse to cooperate with your roommate, if your parents do not send you the money you were expecting, or if others build coalitions to block your goals, interference has occurred. Or if an employer wants all employees to volunteer extra work time, and the employees want to spend no extra time on the job, when they pursue their goals, each will be interfering with the other. Often interference clarifies for the conflict parties that the conflict is engaged. Interference only exists because we are interdependent with one another; it is part of a larger issue. Our human interdependencies, so necessary for goal attainment and satisfaction, also set the stage for possible interferences and enactment of conflict.

Interdependence

Conflict parties engage in an expressed struggle and interfere with one another because they are *interdependent*. "A person who is not dependent upon another—that is, who has no special interest in what the other does—has no conflict with that other person" (Braiker and Kelley 1979, 137). Each person's choices affect the other because conflict is a mutual activity. People are seldom totally opposed to each other. Even two people who are having an "intellectual conflict" over whether a community should limit its growth are to some extent cooperating with each other. They have, in effect, said, "Look, we are going to have this verbal argument, and we aren't going to hit each other, and both of us will get certain rewards for participating in this flexing of our intellectual muscles. We'll play by the rules, which we both understand." Schelling (1960) calls strategic conflict (that conflict in which parties have choices as opposed to conflict in which the power is so disparate that there are virtually no choices) a "theory of precarious partnership" or "incomplete antagonism." In other words, even these informal debaters concerned with a city's growth cannot formulate their verbal tactics until they know the "moves" made by the other party.

Parties in strategic conflict, therefore, are never totally antagonistic and must have mutual interests, even if the interest is only in keeping the conflict going. Without openly saying so, they often are thinking, "How can we have this conflict in a way that increases the benefit to me?" These decisions are complex, with parties reacting not in a linear, cause-effect manner, but with a series of interdependent decisions. Bateson (1972) calls this ongoing process an "ecological" view of patterns in relationships. As in the natural environment, in which a decision to eliminate coyotes because they are a menace to sheep affects the overall balance of animals and plants, so no one party in a conflict can make a decision that is totally "separate"—each decision affects the other conflict participants. In all conflicts, therefore, interdependence carries elements of cooperation and elements of competition.

Even though conflict parties are always interdependent to some degree, their perceptions of their interdependence affect the choices they make. They will decide whether they are acting as (1) *relatively independent agents* or (2) *relatively interdependent agents*. Is it desirable to say something like "I am making my choices and doing my thing with very little regard for your choices" or "We are in this together—neither of us can decide what we want to do without taking the other into account"?

An example of this struggle to determine the degree of interdependence occurred recently in our lives as a dual-career couple. When we were deciding where to spend a year studying, completing research projects, getting additional training, and taking a break from our regular academic careers, we struggled over how interdependently the decision would be made. One of us (we won't say which) wanted each to rank the possible cities in order of preference, then choose from the top group after consolidating the lists. The other wanted to talk over pros and cons of the cities and placements first, then decide together how to rank the places. The conflict was not only over how to balance the often conflicting preferences and demands, but also how to structure our degree of interdependence. Before we were able to resolve the content question

("Where shall we go, assuming we have several choices?") we had to come to agreement on the relationship question of interdependence, which was, "How much will we share in the initial phases of this decision—how much will we open up to influence from the other early in the process?"

A second example of the struggle over interdependence happened in one of our classes when a student challenged the teacher's choices about the most appropriate way to run the class. This challenge went on for several class periods, with the rest of the large class becoming very restless and annoyed. Finally, a representative of a group of students spoke up to the challenger and said, "Look, you are taking our time to work on this personal conflict, and we are really getting angry. We're not able to do what we came to this class to do. Don't involve us in your personal hassles." The student initiating the challenge said, "But you're involved—you're in the class, and you ought to be concerned about how the sessions are run. You're in this just as much as I am." They proceeded to carry on a short-term conflict based not only on the issues of class goals, but also on the issues of "How interdependent are we?" The most salient issue at that point was how the parties perceived themselves in relationship to each other. The issues of power and class goals had to wait until the first-order issue was settled. The basic question, then, in any conflict is, *"How much are we willing to allow each other to influence our choices?"*

Persons who define themselves as interdependent must enter into the process of determining who they are as a unit after they decide individually how much influence they want the other person to have with them. (Sometimes, as we have stated, these choices are not available.) They must decide, tacitly or overtly, which rules bind them, how they will communicate, where "belt-lines" are (Bach and Wyden 1968), and dozens of other relationship issues that define them as a conflict unit at the same time that they are proceeding toward mutual and individual goals. People who see themselves as relatively independent are primarily concerned with *acting* issues—where will I go, what will I get, or how can I win? But those who view themselves as highly interdependent must, in addition, decide *being* issues—who are we and how will this relationship be defined? For instance, two persons in competition for a job are more interested in maximizing their own gains than the gains of the ephemeral relationship. They want to win—separately. But the same two individuals one year later, after both have been hired by the company, perceive themselves as highly interdependent when asked to come up with a plan for implementing an environmental impact study together. They want to win—together. And in the second relationship, while still in competition with each other for promotions, they also must define for themselves a workable relationship that enhances desired goals for them both.

Sometimes parties are locked into a position of mutual interdependence whether they want to be or not. Not all interdependent units choose to be interdependent, but are so for other compelling reasons. Some colleagues in an office, for instance, got into a conflict over when they were to be in their offices, available to receive calls and speak with customers. One group took the position that "What we do doesn't affect you—it's none of your business." The other group convinced the first group that they could not define themselves as unconnected, since the rest of the group had to be available to fill in for them when they were not available. They were inescapably locked into interdependence. Therefore, the first mutual decision that must be made in any conflict is the mutual influence issue. Then other procedural and goal-oriented decisions can be made as the relationship issue is solved. If a working decision is not made, the parties have almost guaranteed getting themselves into an unproductive conflict, with one party acting and making choices as if they were only tenuously connected.

Most relationships move back and forth between degrees of independence and interdependence. At times there will be an emphasis on "me"—what I want—and on my separateness, while at other times, "we"—our nature as a unit—becomes the focus for attention. These natural rythmic swings in relationships are receiving study and attention (Frentz and Rushing 1980; Wilmot 1979; Galvin and Brommel 1982; Olson, D. H. et al. 1982; Baxter 1982; Bochner 1982; Stewart 1980). Just as we all need both stability and change, conflict parties have to balance their independence/dependence needs.

The previous discussion suggests, for clarity's sake, that relationships and interdependence issues precede other issues in the conflict. Actually, these negotiations over interdependence permeate most conflicts throughout their history, never becoming completely settled. A helpful practice is to address the interdependence issue openly in ongoing, highly important relationships. In more transient and less salient relationships, the interdependence may be primarily tacit or understood.

An expressed struggle, perception of incompatible goals, perception of scarce rewards, and interdependence coupled with interference are the common elements underlying all conflicts. As Wehr notes, "There is more . . . commonality in the origin, dynamics, and regulation of conflict than we have been aware of in the past" (Wehr 1979, xvii). Our purpose in this book is to examine those commonalities across conflicts and provide suggestions for productive management.

Destructive Conflict

Conflicts are destructive if the participants are dissatisfied with the outcomes and think that they have lost as a result of the conflict (Deutsch 1973, 158). Sometimes an outside observer might think a party has "won," but the person involved might think that a loss has taken place. A church in a large city was involved in a bitter dispute carried out in an extremely divisive manner over a three-year period. Two dissident groups fought over the kind of leadership they wanted in the church. Both sides would have thought they had "won" if

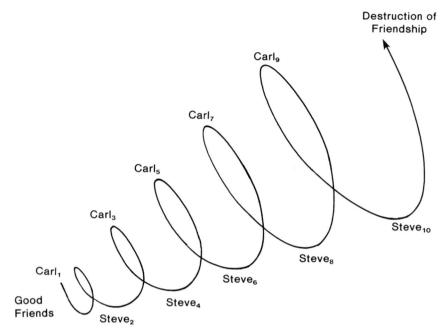

Figure 1.1. Destructive conflict spiral.

they could get the other side angry enough to leave. Although they are still involved in bitter fighting, including shouting and screaming at each other in meetings, both sides now feel hopeless about the situation. Because of financial interdependence, neither side can survive without the other. They are locked into a destructive conflict and have not been able to make the situation a productive one. Everyone is dissatisfied.

Destructive conflicts come in a variety of forms, but the easiest to recognize are *conflict spirals* (North et al., 1964; Wilmot 1979). Conflict spirals have only one direction—upward and onward. They are characterized by a heavy reliance on overt power manipulation, threats, coercion, and deception (Deutsch 1973). In a conflict spiral, the relationship continues to circle around to more and more damaging ends; the interaction becomes self-perpetuating (Folger and Poole 1984). Its characteristics are misunderstanding, discord, and destruction (Wilmot 1979). Figure 1.1 illustrates the dynamics that occur in a typical "runaway" destructive conflict spiral.

In this example, two friends begin with a misunderstanding that accelerates each time they communicate. While it is difficult (if not impossible) to specify the beginning of such destructive conflict spirals, we will examine a conflict already in process. Carl and Steve are roommates; Carl begins complaining about Steve in response to Steve's "messiness." At each crossover point in the spiral, the thinking and actions might proceed as they do in this version of an actual conflict:

1. Carl says to Steve, "Hey, why don't you do your part? The place is a pig pen."

2. Steve says, "Off my case, man!" (He then leaves the apartment.)

3. Carl, still upset about the messy apartment, finds Steve's ex-girl-friend and says, "Has Steve always been such a pig? I can't stand living with him."

4. Steve hearing from his ex-girlfriend that "even Carl knows that you are a rotten roommate," decides that he will get back at Carl for his "meanness." So Steve begins deliberately messing up the bathroom, knowing that it will "bug" Carl.

5. Carl comes home, sees the untidy bathroom, and puts an ad in the campus newspaper that says, "If anyone sees Steve K., tell him to clean up his half of the apartment."

6. Steve, angered at the public announcement, comes home late one night. Carl is already asleep, so Steve lets the air out of Carl's tires.

7. Carl, after accidently running into a mutual friend the next day, hears that Steve is the one who let the air out of his tires. So Carl goes home, moves all of Steve's belongings into the hall, changes the locks on the door, and puts a sign on Steve's belongings that says, "Pig's Pile."

The conflict continues to escalate, with more and more destructiveness occurring. A destructive conflict in an intimate relationship between spouses, for example, will be characterized by the above features, in addition to "hitting below the belt" (Bach and Wyden 1968). Each person seeks ways to harm the other, uses hit and run tactics, and goes out of his or her way to damage the other person. The injunction "don't fight unless you mean it" is ignored in a destructive conflict, and the interlocking, damaging moves occur repeatedly.

In a destructive conflict, one party unilaterally attempts to change the structure, restrict the choices of the other, and gain advantage over the other. While conflict spirals are the easiest form of destructive conflicts to recognize, others do exist. For instance, some personal relationships are characterized by ongoing destructive conflicts that are enacted very subtly. If one person withdraws, knowing that "withholding" will have a negative impact on the other, and gains advantage by refusing to communicate with the other, then destructive conflict is beginning.

Probably the best index of destructive conflict is a situation in which one or both of the parties has a strong desire to "get even" or damage the other party. When you hear a friend say, "Well, she may have gotten me that time, but just wait and see what happens when I tell some things I know about her part in it!" you are overhearing one side of a destructive conflict in action.

Productive Conflict

Conflict can have highly desirable, productive functions in a relationship. As Coser has pointed out, conflict is only threatening to a society when there are no avenues to handle it. Elastic systems, which allow the open and direct expression of conflict and adjust to shifting power balances, are not likely to be highly threatened by explosions in their midst (Coser 1967). In a family in which the father's word is law, since there are no channels to deal with conflict and so no opposition from the children is tolerated. When systems create channels for handling conflict, they further the possibility that the system will continue to exist. A friend of ours has instituted a democratic voting system in his family council. The family is made up of highly individualistic children and parents, who all have strong identities. Since the children are growing up, the possibility for disruptive and highly threatening conflict is present—so the family set up a "council" system of government. Even though all the members are not always happy with the results, thus far it has kept the family functioning well as a unit.

Conflict can play an important part in the development of relationships ranging from nation states to personal friends. The relationship that successfully moves through episodes of conflict will grow, change, and be altered in important ways (Braiker and Kelley 1979, 160). The presence or absence of conflict is not the sole determiner of a relationship. For example, both unhappy and happy marriages have conflict, but the latter are characterized by how they manage it (Braiker and Kelley 1979; Altman and Taylor 1973; Navran 1967; Locke 1951; Birchler, Weiss, and Vincent 1975).

What, then, is a productive conflict as contrasted to a destructive conflict? Productive conflicts are characterized by a *transformation of the elements* of conflict. A productive conflict alters the underlying conflict dimensions in a positive direction. One or more of these elements would change as the result of a productive conflict:

- Mode of expression of struggle
- Perception of incompatible goals
- Perception of scarce rewards

- Degree of interdependence/dependence

- Kind of cooperation and opposition

The two parties will find that their relationship has been altered in some way at the end of the conflict. The residual impact is positive—they are more willing to cooperate, able to have a more productive conflict the next time, and more satisfied with the result.

The transformation of the elements in a conflict does not have to occur at each conflict episode. Most conflict exchanges are embedded within a context of continuing interaction. Relationships move in and out of productive conflict, in and out of degrees of harmony and conflict (Baxter 1976; Altman and Taylor 1973; Wehr 1979). Productive conflict is a dynamic process that occurs within the bounds of already existing patterns. For instance, if the husband says to the wife, "You never pick up your shoes, and I'm getting sick and tired of tripping over them in the dark," one cannot understand the importance of the event without knowing their prior patterns of interaction. If this is the first time he has complained, the episode will proceed to quite a different outcome than it will if he has lodged this complaint unsuccessfully for thirty days in a row. Conflict episodes are bounded by other nonconflict episodes, and productive conflict can emerge anywhere in the ongoing process. Regardless of its location in the ongoing relationship, it serves to transform the elements underlying the relationship and has residual impact on the subsequent episodes.

Once a transformation has occurred in a relationship as the result of productive conflict, the positive functions of productive conflict are easily seen. The business partners discover a new ally, the husband and wife recommit themselves to their joint unit, and the college roommates decide that their "roomies" aren't so bad after all.

Coser(1956), one of the first to write extensively on the positive functions of conflict, documents that conflict can bind groups closer together, can preserve the group by providing a "safety valve" for blowups, can unite a group against a common "outside enemy," can further group cohesiveness by helping them define their structure, and can promote helpful associations and coalitions. Additionally, strong group cohesiveness as a result of conflict, both internal and external, can set up a functional "balance of power" among groups, so that one group finds it harder to totally dominate the other. Everyone is familiar with the feelings "you and me against the world"; "if we survived this, we can survive anything"; "united we stand, divided we fall"; and other expressions of group unity that come from experiencing conflict and surviving it. The same benefits are derived from individuals in dyadic relations and small, informal groups when they learn to experience conflict productively.

The Need for Productive Management

At the beginning of this chapter we said that conflict brings both danger and opportunity. The dangers of tragic and ineffective conflict regulation or management are well known. As humankind becomes more vividly aware of the need for an end to war, as people begin seriously to consider nuclear disarmament, as we begin the search for new forms of family conflict management, and as we confront the scarcity of resources on our planet, conflict management begins to emerge as the central issue of our century. We live in the first era in which humankind has the almost incomprehensible possibility of eliminating itself. Forms of conflict containment developed in the past do not appear to be adequate for the demands of our time. Human beings may need to engage in less conflict altogether; certainly we must create new productive forms of conflict.

Conflict has been with humankind since the beginning and will likely continue to be. We do, however, have some options for handling the differences in goals, power, and aspirations that occur in our relationships with others. When violence is used to control or subdue another person, the need for effective tools of conflict management become apparent to all. For instance, in many families, violence is an "accepted and integral part of the way the family functions" (Strauss et al. 1980, 4). More than one household in six has been the scene of a spouse striking his or her partner in the last year; over two million women and children (and some men) are battered and beaten by family members each year (Strauss et al. 1980, 4). "Americans run the greatest risk of assault, physical injury, and even murder in their own homes by members of their own families" (Strauss 1980, 4). Not only homes are the scenes of destructive conflict management; each year thousands of people are displaced from jobs because of poorly managed conflict in the work place.

Conflict can be creative, bring new growth, and be useful for the human race as well as for individuals in relationships with each other. Clearly, however, this creative conflict can only take place in an environment of relative safety, or the potential for destruction is overwhelming. All of life is a process of life and death, growth and decay, disintegration and integration, construction and destruction. Without some breaking apart, no new growth is possible. Forces propel people away from each other, only to bring them together again into relationship, community, understanding, and harmony. Out of conflict come new patterns of relatedness; out of new patterns comes new conflict. The cycle of birth and death, disintegration and renewal repeats itself in all of life.

For creativity and life, new visions are needed. Almost twenty years ago, Martin Luther King articulated his new dream for racial integration. This dream is beginning to take solid form and continues to guide those who work for racial unity. Who will provide the new dream of how humankind is to continue to live together? Who will knit together the wisdom of the past with the exigencies of today? How will we finally come to understand and act on the process of opposition and accommodation?

Leonard Bernstein, the great composer and conductor, in speaking to a graduating class, called for this vision to come from all of us, rather than from some charismatic leader.

> . . . you are, can be, a new and separate generation, with fresh minds, ready for new thinking—for imaginative thinking—if you allow yourselves to cultivate your fantasy. . . . Far too many people speak of World War III as if it were not only conceivable but a natural inevitability. I tell you it is not conceivable, not natural, not inevitable . . . the mind boggles. . . . .Mind-boggling time is the perfect moment for fantasy to take over; it's the only way to resolve a stalemate. . . . We need desperately to cultivate new fantasies, ones which can be enacted to make this earth of ours a safe, sound, and morally well-functioning world, instead of a disparate collection of societies limping along from crisis to crisis, and ultimately to self-destruction. . . . Only think: If all our imaginative resources currently employed in inventing new power games and bigger and better weaponry were reoriented toward disarmament, what miracles we could achieve, what new truths, what undiscovered realms of beauty!. . . .

Bernstein then explained his own vision for peace.

> . . . At the very least you must admit that nothing I have fantasized, lunatic artist that I may be, is actually inconceivable. After all, we did imagine it together, from beginning to end, which is a hell of a lot better than trying to imagine Armageddon, the extinction of mankind, which, for this artist, at least, is indeed inconceivable. (From an address at Johns Hopkins University, 1981.)

We hope that in your study of conflict management on the interpersonal level, you will use your imagination to guide you to productive conflict possibilities. We must warn you now that we have no set of techniques that will always work, no one best guiding metaphor, or even a list of behaviors to avoid to keep you out of conflict. We do know, however, that people can and do change their orientation toward conflict so they are able to experience creative growth in their relationships even in the midst of conflict. If enough of us are willing to use conflict in this way, we will build creative relationships.

Summary

Conflict is a pervasive human activity. It is often viewed as abnormal, destructive, pathological, or related to personality clashes. A more constructive perspective defines conflict as a normal human event that occurs in all important relationships. Conflict provides the opportunity for both danger and growth.

It is expressed through spontaneous metaphors generated by people in their everyday speech as they discuss their struggles. Metaphors provide compact versions of conflicts and often describe vividly the subtleties of conflicts. Common metaphors of conflict reflect visions of a war, an explosion, an upward struggle, a trial, a mess, a ball game, or a situation requiring that the hero rescue the participants. A productive metaphor, that of the bargaining table, can be used as an alternative to win-lose conceptions of conflict. The table metaphor implies that conflict can be managed through communication.

All conflicts are expressed through communication; the "expression of the struggle" is one element in the definition of conflict. Other elements that define conflict are a perception of incompatible goals, scarce rewards or resources, and interference between the parties who are interdependent on each other. At the heart of all interpersonal conflicts are issues of self-esteem and power; all conflicts are at some level struggles over these two aspects of relationships. Destructive conflicts leave the participants dissatisfied with the outcome, feeling that they have lost. Productive conflicts, on the other hand, leave participants satisfied and feeling that they have gained something. The problem is solved and the relationship is enhanced for future work together. Finally, productive conflict occurs as the elements in a conflict are transformed to be collaborative instead of win-lose. Throughout, constructive communication sets the stage for productive conflict outcome.

2 Conflict Styles

I guess my boss is mad at me. I have left three messages for her to return my phone calls, and she hasn't. I wonder why she is avoiding me.

My boyfriend is really something. Every time I ask him to change something, like the time to go out, he explodes at me.

John is a good manager. He can sit and listen to our disagreements without being defensive or jumping in to argue. He is (as far as managers go) easy to talk to.

I handle conflicts with my wife by not involving her in them. If I tell her that she is doing something I don't like, she pouts for two days. It's just better to avoid the whole thing.

Kevin and Sharon are quite a pair! They fight all the time and don't seem to get anywhere, except ready for the next round.

People develop characteristic *styles* they typically use in conflict situations. The purpose of this chapter is to examine and discuss (1) the styles that individuals use in conflicts and (2) the styles that characterize an overall system of relationships, such as a family or organization. We will examine the advantages and disadvantages of common style choices and point the way toward the use of productive individual and system conflict styles.

Individual Conflict Styles

Several assumptions underlie the discussion of conflict styles that follow. Our first assumption is that people develop patterned responses to conflict. Many times they develop two or even three styles in response to different situations. Avoidance and competition often are used by the same person, for instance, when the individual believes that conflict is an "all or nothing" phenomenon. The woman who leaves the kitchen table when a conflict erupts, the boss who shouts at the employees, and the small group member who says, "Let's get this out on the table so we can generate some creative options," are all expressing their preferred styles for that particular conflict. Sometimes the preferred styles are seen as the only option. One friend says, "I just do what comes naturally; when I'm jealous, I terminate the relationship." Another says, "I usually avoid conflict, even though I know I shouldn't." Whether one sees many options or sees oneself as locked into an "automatic" response, preferred conflict styles do emerge for various situations. In fact, if one consistently maintains that no other style choice is possible, that "no choice" stance serves the function of keeping that person stuck in that style.

Another assumption is that *people develop conflict styles for reasons that make sense to them.* Experiences provide a background for judging what style is best for a certain conflict. If you work in an organization of ten associates who depend upon each other for creative approaches to their work, such as a group of city planners in a medium-sized community, you may well have developed an "office style" of managing conflict by accommodating each other when possible, taking each other's wishes into account most of the time, holding frequent meetings to check your progress, and spending some time over coffee testing out new ideas on each other before "springing" them in more formal planning meetings. This style, which might be labeled "accommodation," was developed for good reasons and may be highly appropriate for your work group. The planners have created a low-key, consensus style as a group.

People learn conflict styles by observing others' behavior and trying out different behaviors with varying degrees of success. You may try hard to use a style different from one that you found to be unproductive. For instance, if you grew up in a family in which overt conflict was expressed in a hostile, destructive manner, you may organize your life, as much as possible, in a manner that allows you to avoid conflict. Or, you may develop a style that is similar to the one with which you grew up if the style worked well for you and your family. If you grew up with family councils, written notes used during stressful conflict, open conversation around the dinner table, or other potentially productive conflict behaviors, you may say, "I want to be sure my family sits around the table and talks," or something similar describing the set of styles that characterized your family. People's conflict styles make sense if you can understand what they have experienced and learned. Certain styles are not moral issues of right and wrong—they developed for good reasons. Walking in the other person's shoes would give us insight into conflict styles that might have previously appeared to be random, surprising, or evil.

We also assume that *no one style is automatically better than another.* Schuetz (1975) discussed bargaining styles in terms of "reasonableness, rationality, and logic," giving different connotations to these words than the usual ones. As discussed, each person's conflict behavior is *reasonable* to that person—the behavior is chosen, consciously or unconsciously, because it makes

reasonable (to the person)
rational (to his ends)
patterns are logical (system of behavior that makes sense to person)

sense to him or her in that situation. Conflict behavior can be judged as *rational,* but not by some outside standard of what constitutes rational behavior, such as reliance on formal logic, use of expert evidence, or a calm, unemotional approach. Rationality is judged by how well a person's choice of behavior moves him or her toward desired goals, given the facts of the people involved in the conflict, their particular relationship to each other, and the requirements of the situation at that time. Therefore, compromise might be appropriate to the office situation involving the planners mentioned above, while if the same people were involved in arguing for a growth-management plan on which they had worked for two years in front of the county commissioners, compromise could be disastrous for their goals. Assertive, strong argumentation aimed at gaining adherence to their point of view would be more appropriate for experts arguing their case in front of policymakers.

Logic, using a person-centered explanation, is a system of reasonable and rational behavior, which may be inferred or observed from watching an individual's patterned interactions. Although we often claim that someone's choices are illogical, the claim usually is derived from one of the following beliefs:

1. I couldn't predict what he/she would do.
2. I don't like the choice that was made.
3. The reasons behind the choice are unclear to me.
4. Emotion and rational behavior cannot co-exist.

Conflict management is largely the art of becoming expert at moving within different logical systems.

A fourth assumption about styles is that although most people have preferred styles, *people's styles undergo change in order to adapt to the demands of new situations.* If rewards are available, people do change. They can make decisions to change their styles, especially when their past preferred styles are no longer working well for them. This notion is detailed in the section entitled "Adapting and Unfreezing" later in this chapter. Thus, we can make reasoned, rational choices to change. These changes, in turn, create the new logic from which we operate.

Identifying Personal Styles

The first step in making effective choices about conflict is to understand your present conflict styles. Conflict styles can be classified several ways; we are choosing one that will help you determine your present styles and how they can be compared to other available styles.

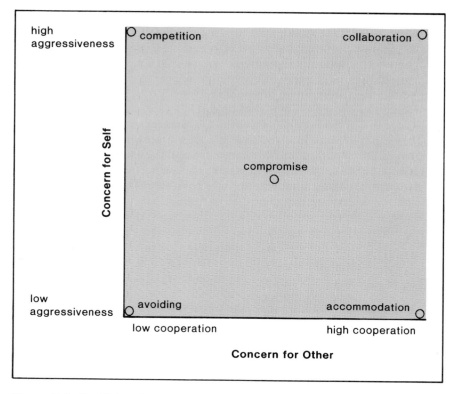

Figure 2.1. Conflict styles.

Kilmann and Thomas (1975) provide the following diagram, which will help you compare your conflict styles with styles of others.[1] The system is based on the notion that each style is composed of two partially competing goals—*concern for self* and *concern for the other.* We noted in chapter 1 that every conflict contains degrees of cooperation and competition and that conflict parties are necessarily interdependent. The chart in figure 2.1 uses those ideas as the basis for classifying the modes of conflict.

1. We have taken the liberty of changing Kilmann and Thomas' original designation of "assertiveness" to "aggressiveness," since we believe that assertiveness has come to connote a highly desirable manner of behavior with the growth of the "assertiveness training" movement. "Aggressiveness" describes the more self-centered behavior better than the term "assertiveness," which has come to mean appropriately insistent behavior that does not deprive others of their rights. The Thomas and Kilmann scheme is very useful for identifying one's personal styles, but it has some limitations that make its use in research problematic. For research purposes, we recommend the Putnam and Wilson (1982) instrument, which found three factors describing conflict styles: nonconfrontation, solution orientation, and control.

If your style is *competitive,* it is characterized by aggressive and uncooperative behavior—pursuing your own concerns at the expense of another. People with competitive styles attempt to gain power by direct confrontation, by trying to "win" the argument without adjusting to the other's goals and desires. A person with a competitive style is one who usually thinks it necessary to engage the other participant in overt disagreement. The conflict is seen as a "battleground," where winning is the goal and concern for the other is of little or no importance. Someone who adopts a competitive style in conflicts would probably agree with statements such as "Once I get wound up in a heated discussion, I find it difficult to stop," and "I like the excitement of engaging in verbal fights."

Since we altered Kilmann and Thomas' "assertive" dimension to be "aggressive," a brief contrast between assertiveness and aggressiveness is in order. If you are trying to win against other parties, destroy them in some way, or actively work against them, such behavior is aggressive rather than assertive.

There are other useful classification for the degrees of assertiveness that are not specified in figure 2.1. While nonassertive people deny themselves and inhibit their expression of feelings and open striving for goals, assertive people enhance the self, work toward achieving desired goals, and are expressive. The aggressive person, however, carries the desire for self-expression to the extreme. Goals are accomplished at the expense of others. The aggressive style results in a "put down" of others while actively working against their goals. The assertive person can be competitive without berating, ridiculing, or damaging the other. The aggressive person is competitive primarily by trying to destroy the opponent's options. The followng quotation from a student's paper exemplifies the aggressive style of conflict:

> When I get into an argument with a person over something I really stand for, then I really like to get involved and have a good battle. If my competitor has a good stand on his issues, then I like to "rip" at him until he breaks or if things go wrong, I break. The excitement of confrontation when I'm battling it out with another person has a tremendous thrill for me if I come out as the victor.

Later in the paper, the student referred to his conflict partner as his "foe," "my adversary," and said that he enjoys "being at each other's throats." Obviously, the student is operating from an aggressive conflict style.

The competitive style of managing conflict is not always unproductive. One can openly compete to accomplish individual goals without destroying the other person. Furthermore, such a style of conflict is often very appropriate. Intimates often report that "we fight hard and really actively work to achieve our own goals. And the process works for us." Such an approach can often be productively used in conflict, especially if the participants are in agreement over the amount of aggressiveness that can legitimately be used in their conflict.

When high assertiveness aimed at reaching one's own goals integrates with a high concern for the other person, a *collaboration* style is the result. Collaboration is characterized by statements such as "When I get in conflict with someone, I try to work creatively with them to find new options," or "I like to assert myself, and I also like to cooperate with others." Collaboration differs from compromise because in compromise, one looks for some intermediate position that partially satisfies both parties. In collaboration, the parties work creatively to find new solutions that will maximize goals for all. An example is a married couple who have a conflict about their priorities. The wife thinks the husband works too much and does not spend enough time with her. The husband believes the wife is not interested enough in his work. A simple shortening of his working hours to spend more time with the wife and an increase of her interest would be one possible way to manage the conflict. But if the two parties were to collaborate, they would work together on the conflict to identify the underlying concerns of both parties. It may be, for example, that both of them want more warmth and affection in the relationship, and the conflict arose because neither one's way of attempting to get affection was working. Through such collaborative effort, they explore the disagreement in order to learn from one another's insights. They may discover, for instance, that the time of day for time being together makes a big difference. They may be able to meet for lunch occasionally; or the husband can work at home late during the evening.

Collaboration as a style means that one person asserts individual goals and just as actively works toward the goals of the other. Collaboration is a highly involving, energetic style of conflict management. Collaboration is not the same as "being cooperative." In cooperation, a viable choice might be to accede to the wishes of another person (accommodation). But when parties collaborate, they replace the "you" and "I" perspectives with a "we" perspective.

Compromise is an intermediate style between assertiveness and cooperativeness. If one uses a compromise style, conflict behavior is characterized by beliefs such as "You have to be satisfied with part of the pie," or "When disagreements occur, you each have to give a little." As you can tell by figure 2.1, in a compromise style you address the issue more directly than in the avoiding style, but you do not explore it in as much depth as would someone using a collaborative style. Some sample conflict management tactics consistent with the compromise style are to get two parties to split the difference, exchange equal concessions, or seek any middle-ground position. For instance, if a person is buying a used car from a dealer and the dealer's asking price is $6,000, the potential buyer may offer $5,600. Since the dealer has to make a profit and the buyer does not want to pay more than the car is worth, they begin to bargain over the price. After many rounds of offers and counteroffers, they finally agree on a price of $5850, an approximate middle ground.

Wage and fringe benefit disputes in industry often are settled in a compromise manner, sometimes by trained third-party arbitrators. When neither party can agree on terms, yet both want to avert a strike, they will sometimes submit to a third party to specify the terms of the binding compromise agreement.

One problem with the compromise style is that people sometimes give in too easily and fail to seek a solution that gives significant gains to either party. "Giving in" can become so habitual that it becomes a goal in itself.

Avoidance is a style often characterized by nonassertive, passive behavior. The person does not openly pursue his own concerns or those of the other person, but effectively "goes weak," refusing to engage openly in the conflict. The avoider may sidestep the issue by changing the topic or simply withdrawing from dealing with the issue. Interestingly enough, just as the competitive style does not mean that you will get what you want (remember, you are interdependent with the other party), avoidance as a style does not mean that the avoider will be ineffective. For instance, if a person is having a conflict with a large organization that overcharged for some goods, the organization can enhance its position by not responding to correspondence on the matter. By pretending that the conflict does not exist, the high-power party is freed from dealing with the low-power party. Avoidance can serve similar functions in interpersonal conflicts as well. If two roommates are both dating the same woman, they may refuse to discuss the subject openly, even if both of them are aware of the problem. Avoidance is a way of dealing with conflict by trying not to overtly recognize its existence or your part in its creation. As a final example, in intimate relationships the style of avoidance is often invoked on sensitive matters. If a couple is having some difficulty in dealing with each other's families, they may not feel free to discuss the problem. Avoiding a conflict, however, does not prevent it. Conflict occurs when parties have the perception of incompatible goals, regardless of the style they choose to use in responding to this perception. The avoidance simply becomes an alternative mode of conflict expression.

Accommodation occurs when one is nonassertive and cooperative. It is the opposite of competing. When adopting the accommodating style, the individual puts aside his or her own concerns in order to satisfy the concerns of the other person. Accommodation can, like the other styles, take many forms. One may obey another's directives when preferring not to do so, or one may gladly yield to another's point of view. Individuals in groups often succumb to pressures to make decisions quickly by not pushing their point of view. Then, when the group reaches "consensus" and agrees on a decision, the individuals will later say that they did not agree but "the group had to reach a decision."

We noted earlier that no one style is automatically superior to another. Each style can have advantages or disadvantages depending on the circumstances of its use (Phillips and Cheston 1979). Here are some examples of appropriate and inappropriate situations for employing the five styles, depending on the goals desired. This list incorporates Thomas's (1977) report of how executives see appropriate situations for each style. It is a distillation of experiences from a variety of people with whom we have worked in training seminars and classes.

COMPETING

Advantages	Disadvantages
Competition can be appropriate and useful when one has to make a quick, decisive action such as in an emergency. Competition can generate creative ideas when others respond well to it or when one is in a situation in which the best performance or ideas are rewarded. It is useful if the external goal is more important than the relationship with the other person, such as in a short-term, nonrepeating relationship.	Competition can harm the relationship between the parties because of the focus on external goals. Rands et al., for example, show that continued escalation in marriages is related to unhappiness with the marriage (1981). Competition can be harmful if one party is unable or unwilling to deal with conflict in a "head on" manner. Conflict waged competitively can encourage one party to go underground and use covert means to make the other pay if he or she is so aggressive as to be a difficult coworker. Competition tends to reduce all conflicts to few options— "either you are against me or with me," which limits one's roles to "winning" or "losing."
Competition also informs the other of one's degree of commitment to the issue and can be used to demonstrate the importance of the issue to the other party. Competition can be useful in situations in which everyone agrees that competitive behavior is a sign of strength and is treated as a natural response, such as in games and sports or a court battle. In these cases, other styles may confuse the resolution of the conflict.	*Example:*
	Greg and Marcie live together and are both aggressive young salespersons for the same company. High sales, naturally, are rewarded by their manager. The couple keeps track of who's ahead of the other by placing a chart on the refrigerator. Marcie becomes ill and misses a lot of work. In the past, the week's loser has had to do the laundry for the week. Marcie angrily proclaims to Greg, "I'm not your slave! Do your own damn laundry!
Example:	
A human service agency competes with others for grant money from United Way. A limited amount is available, so the one best proposal for solving a human services problem will be funded. The director competes with other directors for funding. The larger good of the community is served by the best program's gaining support.	

COLLABORATING

Advantages	Disadvantages
Collaboration works well when one wants to find an integrative solution that will satisfy both parties. It is useful for generating new ideas, showing respect for others, and gaining commitment to the solution from all parties. It is useful for incorporating feelings of the parties so they will feel that the solutions are "reality" based. Collaboration is a high-energy style that fits people in a long-term, committed relationship, whether personal or professional. Collaboration is an active affirmation of the importance of relationship and content goals, thus building a team or partner approach to conflict management. When collaboration works, it prevents one from using destructive means such as violence. It gives the parties a belief that conflict can be productive.

Example:

Five people are interns at a hospital. Anne has been given a "mission impossible" assignment that requires that she diagnose and chart patients under the supervision of four different doctors. Her fellow interns work collaboratively to relieve her of some of the work, knowing that they want to (1) demonstrate the need for more reasonable assignments, (2) support Anne as a friend, and (3) avoid being assigned Anne's work if she gets sick or resigns. | Like any style, if collaboration is your only style choice, you can be imprisoned in it. If investment in the relationship or issue is low, then collaboration is not worth the effort, for it is time and energy consuming. Further, collaboration can be used in very manipulative ways by persons who are more verbally skilled than others, resulting in a continued power discrepancy between the parties. It can be used as a "one up" move. For example, if one party uses collaboration, he or she may accuse the other of being "unreasonable" because of choosing a different style. Often, high-power persons use pseudocollaboration to maintain the power imbalance. These latter cases are not really collaboration. Ultimately, at least two people are required to collaborate. One avoider can frustrate the intentions of four collaborators.

Example:

Members of a small group in a communication class were under time pressure to finish their project, due in one week. They overused collaborative techniques such as consensus building, brainstorming, paraphrasing, and bringing out silent members. The individual and relational goals of the group would have been better served by quickly deciding to break up into subgroups, but the group clung to a time-consuming method of making decisions long after they needed to adapt to the time pressure of the deadline. |

COMPROMISING

Advantages	Disadvantages
Compromise sometimes lets one accomplish important goals with less time expenditure than collaboration requires. It also reinforces an equal power balance that can be used to achieve temporary or expedient settlements in time-pressured situations. It can be used as a backup method for decision making when the other styles fail. Further, it has the advantage of having external moral force, and it appears reasonable to other parties. Compromise works best when other styles have failed or are clearly unsuitable.	Compromise can become an easy way out that provides a "formula" solution not based on the demands of a situation. For some people, compromise always seems to be a "form of loss" rather than a "form of win." It prevents creative new options from arising because it can be easy and handy to use. For some people, "flipping a coin" or "splitting the difference" can be a sophisticated form of avoidance of issues that need to be discussed. These chance measures, such as drawing straws or picking a number, are not really compromise. They are arbitration, with the arbiter being "chance." True compromise requires personal involvement in the proposed solutions and can be creative.
Example:	
Mark and Sheila, aged 10 and 8, both wanted to play with the new video game they received for Christmas. After a noisy argument, their parents told them to work something out that is fair. They decided that if no one else was using the game they could play without asking, but if they both wanted to play at the same time, they had to either play a game together or take turns by hours (every other hour). The compromise of taking turns worked well as a conflict reduction device. The parents could intervene simply by saying, "Whose turn is it?"	*Example:*
	Two friends from home decide to room together at college. Sarah wants to live in Jesse dorm with some other friends she has met. Kyle wants to live in Brantley, an all-female dorm, so she can have more privacy. They decide that it wouldn't be fair for one to get her first choice, so they compromise on Craig, where neither knows anyone. At midyear, they want to change roommates since neither is happy with the choice. Sarah and Kyle might have been able to come up with a better solution if they had worked at it.

AVOIDING

Advantages	Disadvantages
Avoidance can supply time to think of some other response to the conflict; some people cannot "think on their feet." It is useful if the issue is trivial or if other important issues demand your attention. If you think you have no chance of getting anything from the relationship or others can manage the conflict without your involvement, avoidance is a wise choice. Avoidance can keep one from harm, for example, when you are in a relationship in which anything other than avoidance will bring you a negative response. If one's goal is to keep the other party from influencing him or her, then avoidance helps to accomplish that goal.	Avoidance tends to demonstrate to other people that you do not "care enough to confront" them, and gives the impression that you cannot change. It serves to let conflict "simmer" and heat up unnecessarily rather than providing an avenue for improving it. It keeps one from working through a conflict and reinforces the notion that conflict is terrible and best avoided. It allows one to go on one's own course and pretend there is no mutual influence when, in fact, each influences the other. It usually preserves the conflict and sets the stage for a later explosion or backlash.
Example:	*Example:*
Shirley is a twenty-three-year-old recent graduate who has recently broken off a long relationship with a man her parents like very much. They ask her to tell them "what went wrong," and offer to pay for a trip to visit him. Shirley decides not to take them up on the trip offer, and says, "Many things happened to make us want to break up. Thanks for caring about me." She avoided a discussion that she felt would end in conflict.	*Professor Lane has made several sarcastic comments about low class attendance lately. Chuck has missed three classes. Upon receiving his midterm exam grade of "C," Chuck decides to wait for a while before asking for the reasons. Later he decides to forget trying to get a "B" in political science and instead concentrate on geology, in which he has a higher average.*

ACCOMMODATING

Advantages	Disadvantages
When you find you are wrong, it can be best to accommodate to the other to show your reasonableness. If an issue is important to the other and not important to you, you can give a little to gain a lot. In addition, it can keep the other from harming you—you minimize your losses when you will probably lose anyway. If harmony or maintenance of the relationship is the most crucial goal at the moment, then accommodation allows the relationship to continue without overt conflict. Accommodation to a senior or seasoned person can be a way of managing conflict by betting on the most experienced person's judgment. *Example:* *A Forest Service manager asks the newest staff member if he is interested in learning about land trades with other Federal agencies. The new employee knows that the manager must assign someone from his office to help the person in charge of land trades. The employee says "It's not something I know much about, but I wouldn't mind learning." The manager, who could have assigned the new employee anyway, thanks him for his positive attitude about new responsibilities. The new employee's goals would not have been well served by saying, "I have no interest in getting into that area. There is too much red tape, and it moves too slowly."*	Accommodation can foster an undertone of competitiveness if people develop a pattern of showing each other how nice they can be. People can one-up by showing how eminently reasonable they are. Accommodation of this type tends to reduce creative options. Further, if accommodation is overused, the commitment to the relationship is never tested, since one or the other always gives in. This pattern can result in a pseudosolution, especially if the accommodation is resented; it will almost surely boomerang later. Accommodation can further one person's lack of power. It may signal to one person that the other is not invested enough in the conflict to struggle through, thus encouraging the other party to withhold energy and caring. A female student wrote this example of a learned pattern of avoidance and its resulting accommodation. *Example:* *"In our home, conflict was avoided or denied at all costs, so I grew up without seeing conflicts managed in a satisfactory way, and I felt that conflict was somehow 'bad' and would never be resolved. This experience fit well with the rewards of being a 'good' girl (accommodating to others), combining to make a pattern for me in which I was not even sensitive to wishes and desires that might lead to conflict."*

Any conflict style can be cast as negative or positive, depending on one's goals. For instance, if you avoid a conflict with someone who is active and competitive, the other person might say, "He has no push—I wish he would stand and argue like a man" (sexism intended!). If your orientation is more cooperative (accommodating, compromising, collaborating), one might label the competitive style as "hostile, pushy and arrogant." Personality descriptions are mistakenly applied to behavioral actions. Then, of course, if one has developed a stereotype about competitive people (hostile and aggressive) or about accommodating people (spineless and wimpy), the conflict takes on a prejudiced quality.

Limitations of Individual Style Approaches

Assessing one's style to see how it is functioning, and making decisions regarding choices in future conflicts are useful. However, disadvantages of the entire approach of looking at individual conflict styles need to be discussed also.

First, perceptions of style differ according to one's vantage point. Thomas and Pondy (1977) asked sixty-six managers to recall a recent conflict and state which style was used by each party. Overwhelmingly, the managers saw themselves as cooperative or collaborative and the other party as primarily competitive, demanding and refusing. Unfortunately, your perception of what you did will probably not be corroborated by the other person. In conflict, we tend to see ourselves in a positive light and others in a negative light. Human beings tend to value their own individual approaches to life. All too often we assume that our choices about behavior, values, and goals are the *right* ones. Therefore, we are *right* if we are "aggressive," "cooperative," "polite," "fair-minded," or "realistic." Since people evaluate styles depending on whether they are theirs or someones else's, the vantage point makes a crucial difference.

Second, views of styles from questionnaires such as the Thomas-Kilmann Conflict Mode Instrument are not process oriented. Results tend to lead one to assume that his or her choice at one time is the same as it is at another. Some individuals develop preferred *sequences of styles;* for example, one may begin a conflict by avoiding, then move to competing, then finally collaborate as the parties work together. Most measuring instruments or quizzes, however, treat personal styles as if they are a "trait" belonging to the person—something one always does, or something that describes the *person* instead of the behavior. The accurate assessment of one's conflict style should presuppose some change over time to reflect the variability that most of us enact in our lives. Baxter (1982), for example, demonstrated that conflict expressions for small-group participants are altered depending on the phase of group decision-making in which the group is engaged.

Third, conflict-measuring instruments assume situational consistency. For example, looking at one's predispositions for conflict choices (Yelsma 1981, 1984; Brown, Yelsma, and Keller 1981) presumes that one's choices do not vary according to different contexts or relationships or across time within the same conflict. But most available evidence indicates that people change their styles depending on many such factors. It has been demonstrated that people make different choices in business settings, depending on whether their supervisor is male or female. Likewise, Putnam and Wilson (1982) demonstrated that employees prefer nonconfrontation when in a peer-related conflict in an organization, but they choose forceful communication to manage conflict with subordinates. Eric, a college debater who has an analytic approach to problems, serves as an example of this situational variability. In public situations, he competes every chance he has. He loves to match wits with others, push hard for what he wants, and be seen as the winner of an argument. He is a good-humored and driving young man in public situations. Yet in private with his wife, he avoids conflict as if it were a dread disease. When Joan brings up issues that are conflictual, Eric either avoids or completely accommodates—he cannot stand conflict with someone intimate with him, for fear of losing the relationship. Yet if Eric were to fill out a widely-used style instrument, he would be asked to think of how he acts in conflicts, without a specific context designated. Putnam and Wilson (1982) argue that one's decision to use a particular style is largely governed by situational rather than personality constraints. Some of these situational variables might be:

- Nature of the conflict (degree of interdependence, perception of scarce rewards, perception of power).

- One's success with the style in similar situations.

- Situational constraints such as the nature of one's family or organization. Some actions are not appropriate in some settings, although they may be preferred by the conflict participant.

It is easy to watch someone in conflict and assume that the chosen style reflects some underlying personality dimension. But since most people adapt to different situations, with a preferred choice in one context and another preferred style in another, to give them a single label, such as a "compromiser," is a gross oversimplification.

Fourth, the focus is on the individual and not in the pattern of communication in the relationship (Folger and Poole 1984). Focusing on individual styles gives the impression that a certain style has a predetermined impact regardless of the relationship in which the style is used. For instance, avoidance may or may not be positive—you have to know what the other parties are doing. If they are also avoiding, you may be buying valuable time; if they are secretly competing, engagement would be a better choice to protect your interests. The style combinations below give a different view of the usefulness of avoidance, depending on the other party's choices:

- Person A avoids—person B competes.

- Person A avoids—person B tries to collaborate.

- Person A avoids—person B accommodates.

If you role-play these and other style pairings, you will discover that one cannot play the role of a "pure style," since the impact of style choice is dependent on the other party's choices. To treat style in isolation from the other party's choices leads to a partial understanding of conflict dynamics.

Fifth, we often assume that one's style of conflict is a clear reflection of an underlying motivation. Competers, however, may not want to "run over you," and avoiders may actually care about the relationship. Ellen and Mick provide an example. In Ellen's first marriage, she developed the pattern of occasionally throwing dishes when she was really angry. Her first husband would then leave the house. A few years later, after she had married Mick, they got into a screaming argument. Ellen threw a dish at Mick, who promptly went to the kitchen and threw some back at her, smashing them on the wall and shouting that she wasn't going to throw dishes at him! In response to this competitive, or at least aggressive, interaction, Ellen realized that what she wanted was someone who would stay and fight out the problem instead of leaving the scene. Neither has thrown a dish since. At first glance, one could say that Ellen's aggressive style was an attempt to get her own way, stifle all opposition, and dominate Mick. The "true" motivation emerged in the interaction—which was a desire for intimacy.

Sixth, the conceptual classification of styles is subject to alteration. Take a look at figure 2.2, which classifies styles according to the enactors' *concern for others* and *concern for self*. Is avoidance always connected with low concern for the self? If you are married and you are afraid that open conflict means that the marriage is "on the rocks," then to avoid a conflict demonstrates a high concern for the self—you want to protect yourself from perceived harm.

Further, the styles can be ordered according to other conceptual schemes. Milt Thomas (1982) has suggested an adaptation of the Thomas and Kilmann scheme that allows for "concern for the relationship." In many instances, increasing one's use of compromising and collaborating conflict choices signals to the other a commitment to the relationship. Notice that collaboration combines high concern for the self, the other, and the relationship. As is shown in the diagram, one can tend toward competition or accommodation while still

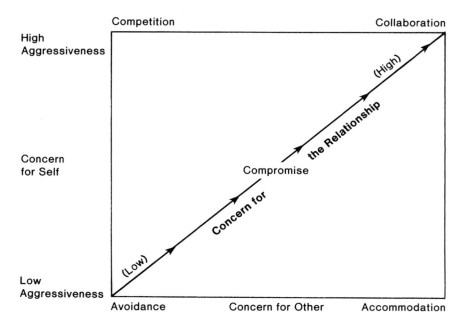

Figure 2.2. The relationship dimension underlying styles.

concerned for the relationship. No one can be perfectly collaborative—collaboration is best thought of as a conglomeration of conflict moves which, taken together, add up to a collaborative approach. It is a mixed style, far more complex and difficult than the other styles.

Few alternative schemes for classifying styles have been offered, but one is especially worthy of note. Putnam and Wilson (1982) have provided evidence that in organizational conflicts, there are three main dimensions or underlying properties of style choices. They found that all style choices clustered around these three dimensions:

1. *Nonconfrontation*—indirect strategies for handling a conflict; choices to avoid or withdraw from a disagreement; such communicative behaviors as silence, glossing over differences, and concealing ill-feelings.

2. *Solution-orientation*—direct communication about the conflict; behaviors that aim to find a solution, to integrate the needs of both parties, and to give in or compromise on issues.

3. *Control*—direct communication about the disagreement; arguing persistently for one's position, taking control of the interaction, and advocating one's position. Putnam and Wilson (1982).

It has yet to be demonstrated which dimensions for understanding styles have the most utility. For example, the work of Brown, Yelsma, and Keller (1981) on "predispositions" to conflict may help us understand general life orientations that predispose one to use a particular style. As more research focuses on individual style choice in conflict settings, we will be able to have more confidence in whatever scheme appears most useful.

As discussed, your own style in a conflict directly affects the direction and productivity of the conflict. If you are convinced that your choices are only "natural," this belief may be a warning sign that you are not examining your choices closely. Each party to a conflict contributes to the relational dynamics; becoming clear about your own contribution can be one large step in preparing for more creative management approaches.

System Styles

If individualized stylistic approaches are not the best ways to characterize conflict styles, then what other approaches are available? A fruitful body of literature has developed in the last twenty years. It describes how "people-in-interaction" may be analyzed as more than the sum of individual actions. This approach describes the *interactive group* rather than Sally (who's aggressive) plus Tom (who's accommodating) plus Linda (who avoids), and leads us to a system-wide view of conflict styles. Examine these comments:

> The research and development department runs like scared rabbits whenever the bottom line is mentioned.
>
> They fight like cats and dogs, but they always make up.
>
> That whole group is plastic. They look so sweet, but I would't trust them farther than I could throw them.

Such statements illustrate that relationships or entire groups develop styles for conducting conflict.

Identifying System Styles

Many system descriptions have emerged from researchers of family interaction (Fisher 1982). Lederer and Jackson's seminal book on *The Mirages of Marriage* (1968) focused attention on how marital partners act as a unit rather than as individuals. In their work, such phrases as the "gruesome twosome" and the "heavenly twins" were used to describe marriages rather than individuals. One often-cited description comes from Cuber and Haroff (1965), who described marriages as:

1. *Conflict-habituated* relationships, in which conflict recurs constantly but has little productive effect. The fighters "don't get anywhere."

2. *Devitalized* marriages, in which the relationship is a hollow shell of what originally was vibrant and living.

3. *Passive-Congenial* relationships, in which the partners have always had a conventional acceptance of a calm, ordered marriage that maintains little conflict.

4. *Vital* relationships, which involve intense mutual sharing of important life events.

5. *Total* marriages, characterized by the sharing of virtually every aspect of life, fulfilling each other almost completely.

The impact of conflict, itself, as well as the way it is enacted, differs, depending on the relational type. In a conflict-habituated couple, for example, conflict is so common that it may go almost unnoticed, but it slowly drains the energy of the couple away from important growth or conflict. Devitalized partners might experience conflict as so devastating that it tears apart the fragile fabric of their shared life. Conflict, after all, is energy producing *and* energy draining, which may not be acceptable to a devitalized couple. Likewise, avoidance in a total relationship would be a distress signal, whereas anything but avoidance in a passive-congenial relationship might break its implicit rules.

Another relational-level description comes from Rands et al., (1981), who provided an alternate view of conflict resolution types. They found that couples could be seen as belonging to one of four types:

1. Type I: *Nonintimate-Aggressive* relationships foster escalation without corresponding intimacy. Couples are aggressive toward each other without enjoying the benefit of growing emotional closeness. Conflict for couples who maintain this pattern is usually not satisfying, since more energy is drained than is gained.

2. Type II: *Nonintimate-Nonaggressive* couples lack vitality, intimacy, or escalation. Thus they are more satisfied than Type I people, since they do not have to contend with runaway escalating conflict.

3. Type III: *Intimate-Aggressive* couples combine intimate behavior with aggressive acts. Their conflict usually results in intimacy, even though they use aggressive or attacking conflict modes. Their satisfaction depends on whether their conflicts lead to intimacy or not.

4. Type IV: *Intimate-Nonaggressive* partners use small amounts of attacking or blaming behavior, retaining their intimacy in other ways. These couples are satisfied, whether they are "congenial" (i.e., they avoid full discussion of issues) or they are "expressive" (i.e., they confront important issues).

Rands et al. (1981) help us see that multiple paths may be taken toward the goal of satisfied relationships. Conflict, using their typology, cannot be assessed outside its relational context. In an intimate relationship, for example, conflict avoidance reduces feelings of satisfaction for the couple, but in a nonintimate relationship, avoidance tends to increase satisfaction. The nature of the relationship, its definition, and its underlying patterns determine the existence and impact of conflict.

Other categorizations of system styles are available. For example, Fitzpatrick (1977) labels couples as *independents, traditionals* or *separates,* with corresponding different views and uses of conflict. This and other typologies, however, are not easily generalized to nonmarital systems (see Filsinger, McAvoy, and Lewis 1982; Moos and Moos 1976). One system-style description that we do find applicable to a large variety of contexts and systems is the extensive systems description of Olson, Sprenkle, and Russell (1979), overviewed in Galvin and Brommel (1982). The *circumplex model* is a productive starting point for describing systems on wholistic levels.

Olson et al. suggest that families (and, we would argue, any system of interrelated individuals) differ in regard to two primary dimensions:

1. the degree of *cohesion*

2. the degree of *adaptability*

Families and other systems differ according to their cohesion, or the degree of connectedness to each other.

Low	**Cohesion**		**High**
Disengaged	Separated	Connected	Enmeshed

Minuchin (1967) writes about "disengaged" families, those low in cohesion. Similarly, any system such as a work organization could have high or low amounts of cohesion. If the factory or office workers are "disengaged," they are not tightly organized; their relationships with one another are weak. As Weick (1982) describes, they are "loosely coupled." Many academic departments are disengaged because they manifest few "bonding" behaviors, do not prize community, and are unconnected as a system. Disengaged systems can be described as "the right hand not knowing what the left hand is doing," or as a system maintaining a low degree of information about its members, few coalitions, lots of separate space and relying primarily on individual decisions (Olson, Sprenkle, and Russell 1979).

The opposite end of the disengagement extreme is enmeshment. A system is enmeshed when there is a "disproportionate focus on minor issues or when no issue seems to stay settled" (Gaughan 1982). People who are in enmeshed systems often feel that the system of people is "sticky"; so much relational glue binds the people that they cannot exercise independent actions. The enmeshed system keeps everyone bound to the other in such a fashion that it seems impossible to alter the grip of the relationship. People remain "unfree in the system, there is little or no private space, all decisions are made jointly, they are closed to outsiders, and most activities are shared by all" (Olson, Sprenkle, and Russell 1979).

The other dimension underlying system dynamics is *adaptation,* which ranges from rigid to chaotic.

Low	**Adaptation**		**High**
Rigid	Structured	Flexible	Chaotic

Adaptability is the ability of a system to adapt to changing conditions by altering roles and relationship rules (Olson et al. 1979). Systems that undergo continual change are chaotic; no order is apparent, therefore, they are unpredictable. At the other extreme, if a system does not respond to alterations in the environment, it becomes rigid because of repressing growth and change. An organization that gives the workers the message "It is done this way because it always has been" would be described as being toward the rigid end of the spectrum.

The two dimensions, cohesion and adaptation, are considered jointly in order to assess their operation in a system. Figure 2.3 illustrates the combination of the dimensions.

By examining Figure 2.3, you can chart the system, based on its properties of cohesion and adaptability. For instance, if a marital couple is moderately high on cohesion (connected) and extremely low on adaptability (rigid), they are characterized as "rigidly connected." A system that has high disorder while being low on cohesion is "chaotically disengaged." A system is characterized by its joint properties of cohesion and adaptability. The FACES instrument by Olson and his colleagues is devised to provide a point on the graph reflecting how different family members view their system (see appendix). The questionnaire may be useful for other groups as well, since it provides a way to compare different perceptions of the same system.

The forms and functions of conflict within these system styles obviously differ. Gaughan (1982) has adapted the Olson et al. model to use in divorce

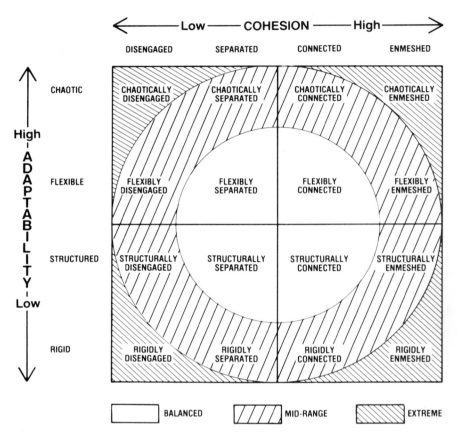

Figure 2.3. Sixteen types of marital and family systems derived by Olson, Sprenkle, and Russell (1979). From David H. Olson and Hamilton McCubbin, *Families: What Makes Them Work.* Copyright © 1983 by Sage Publications, Inc. Reprinted by permission of Sage Publications, Inc.

mediation, specifying the role of conflict within each system type. Figure 2.4 lists some of the communication events that correspond to the placement on the Olson et al. two dimensions.

Note that possibilities for conflict actions are bounded by the system definition. Negotiation, for instance, is a functional conflict management choice in a system that is relatively balanced on the two dimensions. However, if a system is enmeshed, negotiation would not be very successful as a management tactic because of the confusion over self and other goals. Negotiation presumes that the parties are identifiable and can work together to reach harmony. An enmeshed system would preclude any party's taking an identifiable position apart from the group. Further, if a system is disorganized, negotiation

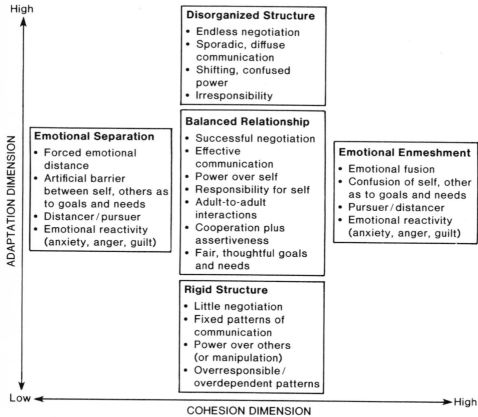

High

ADAPTATION DIMENSION

Disorganized Structure
- Endless negotiation
- Sporadic, diffuse communication
- Shifting, confused power
- Irresponsibility

Emotional Separation
- Forced emotional distance
- Artificial barrier between self, others as to goals and needs
- Distancer/pursuer
- Emotional reactivity (anxiety, anger, guilt)

Balanced Relationship
- Successful negotiation
- Effective communication
- Power over self
- Responsibility for self
- Adult-to-adult interactions
- Cooperation plus assertiveness
- Fair, thoughtful goals and needs

Emotional Enmeshment
- Emotional fusion
- Confusion of self, other as to goals and needs
- Pursuer/distancer
- Emotional reactivity (anxiety, anger, guilt)

Rigid Structure
- Little negotiation
- Fixed patterns of communication
- Power over others (or manipulation)
- Overresponsible/ overdependent patterns

Low ◄———————————————————————————► High
COHESION DIMENSION

Figure 2.4. Communication behavior according to system dimensions. From Gaughan, Lawrence, "Toward a Structural Theory of Family Mediation", in *Therapy with Remarriage Families,* Lillian Messinger, Ed. Copyright © 1982 Aspen Systems Corporation. Reprinted with permission of Aspen Systems Corporation.[1]

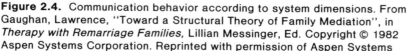

turns into endless rounds of frustrating individual moves that do not alter the system. Agreements are not binding, the parties continually change their priorities, and clear communication toward agreement is subverted by the disorganization inherent in the system.

Extremely disengaged individuals feel too little involvement in the relationship for negotiation to be successful. Kressel et al. (1981) have suggested that the type of marital system determines the success of attempts at mediation in divorcing couples. Couples who are most likely to manage their divorce

1. We have altered Gaughan's presentation so that the coordinates conform to the Olson et al. original formulation.

successfully in mediation appear to be neither enmeshed nor disengaged. They maintain enough connection to solve problems together. Whatever the particular focus, it is abundantly clear that the nature of the system, itself, has tremendous influence on the operation of conflict and on the use of approaches for effective management.

We have examined a variety of "system styles" for behavior related to conflict management. Entire systems, not unlike individuals, develop preferred ways of relating, and these styles of communication can be as enduring as can individual traits. While systemwide descriptions usually do not focus exclusively on conflict management, we remain convinced that once you understand a system's usual style, you can alter the system if it is dysfunctional for you or for the group goals.

Limitations of System Styles

Just as with individual approaches to styles, a systemwide view has some limitations. First, conflict can be occurring in the system because the participants disagree about the type of system they want. One partner may want to be enmeshed, involving the other in all decisions, while the other may be moving toward more disengagement. As a result, individual behaviors indicate a struggle with the definition of the system as a whole. The nature of the conflict may be over what the system will be, or what the pattern of relations is that structures the system. Rather than categorizing a system as "nonintimate—aggressive," the system may reflect a struggle-in-process. When people work toward who they are together, the rules that shape their interaction may be in flux. Some of the typologies discussed in the previous section give the impression that conflict patterns are fixed, whereas they may change rapidly. Sharon and Don, for example, are the parents of three children who are growing into their teens. In the past, the family could be described as "structurally separated." Now that the children are growing up, the parents are rediscovering their intimacy with each other, which results in confusion in the family interactions, since the children are used to being the center of attention. No system description adequately reflects the complexity the family experiences in the time of transition.

Second, just as with individual styles, various system styles can be functional or not, depending on the needs of the situation. Not all groups are automatically better off with a "flexibly connected" or "intimate nonaggressive" style all the time. Relationships go through cycles of change on various dimensions. Enmeshment may be appropriate, for instance, if a remarried couple is determined to avoid the disengaged, laissez-faire behavior of their first marriage. Enmeshment may not continue to work for this couple for ten years, but it may serve their goals well at first.

Recently one of us participated in a group in which persons discussed their families of origin. Having filled out the FACES scale and given considerable thought to their families, group members began to rather sheepishly describe their families as disconnected, or enmeshed, or chaotically connected, assuming that their families had somehow missed the golden ideal. As the discussion progressed, we were able to hear how useful different system styles had been for each individual. For example, Linda, a successful social worker, grew up in a disconnected and structured family. Her adolescent rebellion included "every form of acting out known to woman." Yet Linda performs as a skilled and wise counselor, who leads a positive life. Another work group of eleven people with whom we consulted was very enmeshed—each decision was exhaustingly checked with all others. Yet this group was enmeshed at a crucial point and it helped them through a transition when they were getting rid of a dictatorial supervisor. Whether one's system is disconnected, enmeshed, or any of the other styles, it can be functional or dysfunctional, depending on the total circumstances.

Third, descriptions of system styles are relatively recent in communication and the other social sciences. The precise role of conflict in each system is yet to be charted, and other systemwide conceptualizations will undoubtedly be created.

Adapting and Unfreezing

Individual Styles

On the individual level, people often get "frozen" into a conflict style. Each time they are in a conflict, they make the same choices. The work associate who always avoids any conflict, smoothes over everyone's feelings, and habitually refuses to talk about the difficulties between herself and others is frozen in a particular style. Individual lack of adaptation can occur in many forms. For example, a person might always avoid conflict until it heats up, at which point violent behavior occurs. The pattern is self-sealing and difficult to alter. The person who competes on the job and is unable to relax off the job is just as stuck as the person who is unable to openly admit that conflict exists. People who are inflexible in their style selection are often unaware that their choice of style is an important contributor to the conflict.

People often get stuck in behaviors that fit what we call their "Golden Age." The golden age is that period in which you felt best about yourself and from which you possibly still draw many positive feelings. The person who still looks back to high school athletics, even though he may be a forty-five-year-old history teacher, might operate from the rule that, "The way to handle conflict is to get out there and give it everything you've got, fight to win, pull with the team, and never let anything move you from your goal." This rule probably worked beautifully in a football game, but it may cause real havoc when the man is faced with a principal who does not want to work with aggressive teachers and recommends his transfer to another school.

We know a man who is "stuck" in the style of the 1960s protester. Everything is an antiestablishment fight for Carl. He identifies with the underdog (without thinking clearly about whether the underdog is right) and plots ways to make the people at the top take notice of the less powerful people. This style became dysfunctional when Carl was suddenly elected chairperson of his department. He looked for enemies at the top, while having to work in a problem-solving, cooperative manner with them. Others may have learned a conflict style appropriate for a scared child. We recall with amusement and understanding the young man who mistakenly set fire to a neighbor's garage, ran madly into his room and hid under his bed, only to be pulled out by the inevitable strong arm of his father. When this young man "hides" from situations and assumes there is no way to save himself except escape, he uses behavior appropriate for a scared child but not for a competent professional.

Often people are stuck in a personal style because of their gender identity. For example, women are often taught to avoid conflict (Bardwick 1971). Young girls learn specific styles of conflict activity; they may have been taught to smooth others' feelings and not "make waves." If you were raised with such prescriptions and bring them to a conflict situation, you will accommodate the other and fail to assert your own desires. In the following excerpt, a woman details some of the disadvantages of this particular lack of flexibility:

> As a child, I was forbidden to "talk back." As a result, I stifled all my replies until I was of sufficient age to walk out and did so. That was fifteen years ago—I have never been back. . . . Thus, my strategy has been one of avoidance of a conflict to which I can see no resolution. Because I was raised by my father and stepmother, I scarcely knew my mother. When I was seventeen, I went to live with her. She wanted a mother-daughter relationship to which I could not respond. Legally bound to her, my attempts at confrontation ended in failure. Once again I walked out—this time into marriage. After seven years of marriage and abortive attempts at communication, I again walked out—this time with two children.

Likewise, many men are taught to compete regardless of the situation, learning that accommodation, compromise, or collaboration are all signs of weakness. While the competitive style might be appropriate for certain business situations, in which everyone understands the tacit rules making competition functional, carrying competition as one's only response into an intimate relationship can often result in its destruction. Gender conditioning, whatever its particular form, is just one kind of learning that helps keep people stuck in their choices of style for conflict that may not work in the next situation.

How do you tell if you are stuck in a conflict style? Here are some guidelines for your consideration as a diagnostic aid to see if you are "stuck" in patterns that do not work well for you.

1. Does your conflict response feel like the only natural one? For example, if your friends or family suggest that you "might try talking it through," but you repetitively escalate, such new options seem alien and almost impossible for you to enact.

2. Does your conflict style remain constant across a number of conflicts that have similar characteristics? For example, in every public conflict, do you accommodate others regardless of the issues at hand or your relationship with them?

3. Do you have a set of responses that follow a preset pattern? For instance, do you "go for the jugular," then back off and accommodate the other because of feeling uncomfortable for having made a "scene"? If you follow regular cycles of behavior, whatever the particulars, you may be in a process that could be altered.

4. Do others seem to do the same thing with you? If different people engage in similar behavior with you, you may be doing something that triggers their response. For instance, has it been your experience that in public conflicts, others are *always* competitive? If so, their behavior may be a reaction to a competitive posture that you take toward public conflict. It might be that if you were conciliatory, others would not find the need to respond competitively to you.

5. Do you carry a label that is affectionately or not so affectionately used to describe you? If you grew up as "our little fireball," you may not have learned how to collaborate. If you are referred to as a "powerhouse," a "mover and shaker," or "a bulldog," your conflict style might be overly inflexible. If you're known as "the judge," or "chicken," you may need to take notice of an overly rigid style. Labels, while they often hurt and are overgeneralizations, may carry an embedded grain of truth.

Individuals who can change and adapt are more likely to be effective conflict participants, gaining private and group goals better than people who avoid change. Hart and Burks (1972) discuss the concept of *rhetorical sensitivity,* the idea that people change their communication style based on the demands of different situations. The following five communication characteristics describe people who are rhetorically sensitive:

1. They are able to alter their roles in response to the behaviors of others and accept their alteration of roles in response to someone else.

2. They avoid stylizing their communication behavior, so they are able to adapt.

3. They are able to withstand the pressure and ambiguity of constant adaptation and will develop skills of dealing with different audiences.

4. They are able to monitor talk with others to make it purposive rather than expressive. They speak not so much to "spill their guts" as to solve problems.

5. They alter behaviors and carry on adaptation in a rational and orderly way.

In other words, effective interpersonal communicators expect change and adapt to change in their communication with others. They avoid getting "stuck" in certain conflict styles.

Why should you try to change your conflict style so you will not get "stuck?" As we have discussed, people present themselves in conflicts according to what they take to be a suitable manner (Harré and Secord 1973). But if this presentation of self seldom changes, problems occur. For instance, some people are committed to solving conflicts by searching for "objective" solutions that are best for everyone. Such an approach often ignores the uncomfortable reality that objectivity is in the eye of the beholder. Majority voting, for instance, is usually seen as an objective way to solve a conflict in a group. After all, the American way of life is based upon majority voting—who could object? But if the people in the losing faction think that the majority block forced their own way and that the people in the majority were "overbearing" and inconsiderate, then the minority's judgment about the style employed by the majority will affect the outcome of the decision. Other people in the majority could show more consideration of the feelings of the minority. In the former case, the minority group often wages a campaign against the majority decision by halfheartedly working for the decision, postponing the implementation of the decision, or even actively (although subversively) working against the decision. Then the majority members accuse the minority members of not playing fair, of backstabbing, and of similar offenses. Clearly, the style of the parties in conflict has an impact on the subsequent development of the conflict. Overreliance on a tried and true conflict style, whether that style is majority vote or accommodation, has built-in problems.

One clear reward for developing a repertoire of conflict styles is that we are then able to see the behavior of others in a different, more rational light. When we have a wide repertoire of conflict behaviors, we assume that other people do, too. We are far less likely to judge the behavior of others as automatically having evil intent, being "childish," or being "improper." If you can remember your own use of many styles, you will probably be able to judge others as reasonable when they switch styles. After all, if *we* are reasonable and justified in our choices, so are others.

A final reason for actively working to widen one's repertoire of conflict styles is that many styles were developed from rules of etiquette (Harré 1974) that may also be outdated. These rules often help us make sense out of social situations—without some expectations of what constitutes appropriate behavior, we would be confused much of the time. However, while it may well be appropriate to "respect your elders" when you are eight years old, over-generalizing that rule to include not bringing up situations that might cause conflict with respected elders when you are an adult can be much less appropriate. Learning to seek permission to speak might be fine for behavior in the third grade, but waiting for permission to speak in a bargaining session, whether formal or informal, may well assure that you will never be heard. Using polite forms may foster accommodation; overusing parliamentary procedure sometimes stifles debate. Rules of etiquette must be tempered with the exigencies of conflict behavior. Raising one's voice may not be as great a sin as stifling it.

Your choices of individual styles of doing conflict are vitally important. By unfreezing your style options, you can adapt to conflict situations, depending on the goals you have for yourself and the relationship with the other person. Most of us learn that our styles are dysfunctional only by a retrospective view. We examine our past conflicts and see that we have been stuck in a particular individual style, or in a style sequence. Developing a repertoire of style choices opens the way to productive management of our conflicts from personal relations to work, group, or public relationships.

System Styles

Systems can get into repetitive patterns of conflict management that need to be challenged. On the system level, repetitive patterns become *rituals*.

If a mother and daughter develop a relationship style of shouting at one another, and you ask them to describe their conflicts, they will probably detail how the yelling match goes. Conflicts are composed of the issues, styles, power, goals, strategies, and tactics used by the participants, but often the persons involved only see the individual styles as characterizing the conflicts. While regularity in relational styles is useful, it can be carried too far. If the pattern becomes a ritual—a preset pattern of interlocking behaviors—then the rigidity can work against successful management of the conflict. For instance, a father and his daughter have a ritual that goes like this: She comes home and is upset with his limitations on her freedom (she is fifteen, going on twenty). He tends to be inflexible about the hours he has set for her to be home from social occasions (he is forty-four, going on eighty). About every three weeks, the girl comes home, starts talking about not having any friends, and starts crying. The father, each time this occurs, responds by saying, "Oh, let her cry, it will blow over the way it always does." He characterizes the conflict as the emotional outbursts of a teenager, and she characterizes the conflict as the inflexible position of her father. This conflict, in fact, can be seen from many directions (such as analyzing the power moves that each participant makes), but the ritual gets acted out in a similar fashion each time. And the father and daughter continue to build up hostility over time.

Rituals for conflict develop most strongly in ongoing relationships in which the participants want some sense of order, even if it is chaotic. If the qarties perceive themselves as very interdependent—two coworkers who share in the profits or two intimates each of whom invests emotionally in the other person—then rituals will develop as guides for their ongoing interaction. As a result of the typical relationship styles that develop over time, people tend to develop beliefs about who they are. For instance, new couples like to focus on the lack of overt hostility as a sign of relational health. The "Heavenly Twins" (Lederer and Jackson 1968) when asked, "How is the relationship going?" respond with, "Great! We haven't even had a fight yet." The Heavenly Twins settle on the ritual of avoidance and convince themselves that since there are no open disagreements, everything is fine. They undoubtedly have other ways of managing their conflicts, but they cling to the "no conflict" ritual as evidence that things are fine.

Another common ritual, especially for intimates, is the game of "Uproar." In "Uproar," the parties get into frequent battles. The fighting may serve the function of avoiding intimacy (Berne 1964) so that every time intimacy is appropriate, like before bed, someone picks a fight over a trivial matter. Or if the intimates have been successful in building intimacy by fighting productively (Bach and Wyden 1968), then the battle continues for positive outcomes. In either event, participants can characterize the nature of their relationship based on how they, as a unit, conduct conflict. Fighters are often heard to say such things as, "We fight a lot, and we really love each other," or "It may seem that we are unkind to each other, but we both understand that underneath all this acrimony is a real commitment to work things out. We find that by sharing our disagreements openly, we are then free to love openly, too." Metcoff and Whitaker (1982) refer to these repetitive patterns in interaction as *microevents,* or a "repetitive pattern of family interaction leading over and over to the same behavioral outcome for . . . members, thereby functioning to define, sustain, or provide a springboard for modification of interpersonal relationships." Rather than viewing redundant patterns as negative only, they point out that a group may find the key to change in these patterned events. While their work refers to families, the ideas apply to other groups as well. The microevent may be understood as the way the group has learned to solve a problem *so far.* Since life is full of unpredictable stress, the microevent serves as a way to handle events that are potentially devastating or unsettling. Thus, the group "puts on its most comfortable and characteristic problem-solving pattern as an individual would put on his or her most comfortable shoes for a walk" (Metcoff and Whitaker 1982, 263).

Dan and Betsy's microevent developed as a way for them to work as a team—Betsy felt positive about Dan's future career goals, while Dan was not so sure about his desires and abilities. Through time, however, the problem-solving focus, "I'll push a bit so you'll feel more confident" (Betsy) and "I'll

> Dan and Betsy are two college seniors who have been dating for several years. Betsy has taken the role of "encourager" of Dan and is supportive of his future plans. Dan appreciates Betsy's help but sometimes wants to be left to figure things out for himself. The following conversation ensues:
>
> **Dan:**   "I worked five hours at the recreation program booth at the fair today."
>
> **Betsy:**   "With all that homework? How do you expect to get any school-work done? Don't you care if you get anywhere? You have got to take more responsibility!"
>
> **Dan:**   "I don't know."

let you know this is hard for me, but I want to move ahead so I'll use your help with thanks" (Dan), became an overused communication structure, ineffectively applied to too many events in the life of the couple. As Metcoff and Whitaker (1982) further note, "The healthy (family) uses Mendelssohn for weddings, *Dies Irae* for death, and "Happy Birthday to You" for birthdays; the communicationally depleted (family) uses one song for all occasions." Since microevents originally functioned to solve a problem for your friendship or your group, a careful analysis of the original purpose or function of the solution will give you keys for unfreezing the pattern to provide the best music for the current dance.

Summary

People often react to conflicts with a particular style. They enact those styles that, to them, are reasonable choices. There are many possible styles one can use in a conflict; they are categorized by Kilmann & Thomas as competition, compromise, avoidance, collaboration, and accommodation. The advantages and disadvantages of each style type are examined in detail.

After discussing the limitation of focusing on individual styles, system-wide styles are identified. System styles are the ways entire systems, such as a small group or a family, respond to conflict. Both the uses and limitations of assessing system styles are set forth.

Finally, both individuals and systems can become frozen into particular styles. Sometimes one is limited in choice of styles because of social gender conditioning or observations of other's conflicts. Guidelines are presented to assess whether styles for conflict are frozen or flexible. Systems also get into repetitive patterns of style use. Both individuals and systems can engage in more productive conflict management by embracing a flexible approach to the use of styles.

3 Power in Interpersonal Conflict

Just as a fundamental concept in physics is energy, one of the fundamental concepts in conflict theory is power. In interpersonal conflict situations especially, the power structures in the conflict are at the heart of any analysis. In fact, Duke (1976) says that "the central core of what we call conflict theory is not conflict at all, but rather *power*." This chapter examines the role that interpersonal power plays in conflict situations by noting assumptions about power, examining the existence of power in conflict, discussing the bases of power that individuals have, analyzing power imbalances, and specifying how conflict parties move to balance power.

Orientations toward Power

Power as a concept provokes disparate reactions. Seldom are responses bland—people have opinions about power and its use. As Kipnis notes, "Like love, we know that power exists, but we cannot agree on a description of it" (1976, 8). Respond quickly to the word "power," as we asked you to do with the word "conflict" in chapter 1. What comes to mind? Common associations are—

power play	high powered	bull-headed
power politics	low powered	bulldozed
power source	power behind the throne	run over
powerhouse	sneaky	powerful
power corrupts	devious	authority
overpower	strong-arm	influence

As reflected in this list, people have differing views of power, some positive and some negative. One group of researchers (Cavanaugh et al. 1981a, 1981b; Goldberg et al., 1983) classified differing views of power. Using samples of sales people, government employees, corporate executives, and law enforcement personnel, they concluded that the prime orientations toward power were varied. Some people viewed power as good—that the responsibility and challenge of power is exciting and they would like to be powerful. Others saw power as instinctive—something we all possess innately. Still others saw power as consisting of valued resources, such as political skill, as a charismatic thing that people "have" within themselves, or as reflected in control over others and autonomy of the self. This research is still in its embryonic stage, but the major point is clear: people have vastly different orientations toward power.

Examine the list of words associated with power once more. You will notice that many of the associations with "power" are negative, similar to the negative associations many people have for "conflict." For some, "explicit references to power are considered in bad taste" (Kipnis 1976, 2). Cahill, conducting research on married couples, discovered this when he interviewed them about their relationships. When he asked them about decision making, persuasion of each other, disagreements between them, or how they influenced one another, the discussion flowed smoothly. But when he asked about their relative amounts of power, he encountered long silences, halting answers, obvious embarrassment, and reluctance to speak of the topic (Cahill 1982). McClelland (1969) noted that if people were told they had high drives to achieve or affiliate, they derived great satisfaction in the feedback; but if they were told they had a high drive for power, they experienced guilt.

Some people are so "antagonized by any discussion of power" (Madanes 1981, 217), they may deny that power and influence are appropriate topics for discussion. Attempts abound to convince ourselves and others that control is not part of our interpersonal patterns. One student wrote that in her relationship with her boyfriend, "No one has to have power—we just listen to each other, try to respond with love, and always put the relationship and each other first." She seemed to feel that power use would destroy their perfect relationship. Haley (1959) has listed four common attempts people use to deny that they exercise power. They can (1) deny that *they are responsible* for communicating something; (2) deny that something *was* communicated; (3) deny that it was communicated *to the other person;* or (4) deny the *context* in which it was communicated. The speaker can deny that he or she is doing the communicating by a number of common ploys, such as saying "I'm not myself when I drink," or "It's just the pressure I'm under that's making me act like such a grouch." You may hear the claim, "I couldn't help it—it's *your* fault because I told you I was jealous." To say that you are not responsible for your communication (if others accept your claim) lets you exercise control while denying that you are.

Denying that a message was communicated is another way not to recognize the existence of power. The simplest way to deny communication is to say, "I did not say that." Since this kind of denial usually gets you in trouble after a while, another form develops, such as "I forgot I said that. Did I really say that? I didn't mean to." One supervisor we know consistently forgets to include the new members of a staff in the lines of communication in an agency. As a result, the newer, less powerful members are often late for meetings or miss them totally, having to reschedule other meetings to make last minute changes. When confronted by the worker about being left out of the message flow, the supervisor says, "I thought that was taken care of. I'm sorry."

Denying that a message was communicated to a particular other person is another form of showing discomfort with the exercise of power. An example of this is shown in an episode in which a salesperson rings the doorbell of an apartment complex.

Salesperson: Hello, I'd like to take this opportunity . . .

Apartment Dweller: People are bothering me too much! Oh, I'm not talking about you. It's just that everyone bugs me day in and day out. I get no peace of mind. I wish the world would calm down and leave me alone.

Salesperson: Maybe I can see you another time. I'm sorry I bothered you. . . .

The person who was bothered is exercising considerable control in the communication transaction and also denying it by pretending that the remarks are not meant for that particular salesperson. Another common way of denying that the comments were addressed to the other person is to claim that you were "just thinking out loud" and did not mean to imply anything toward the other person. For instance, a boss might say, muttering under his breath, "If I could count on people. . . ." Then when a subordinate asks what is wrong, the boss could say, "What? Oh nothing—just a hard day."

The last way to deny communication power attempts is to deny that what has been said has been said in this situation. Saying, "I'm used to being treated unfairly by others; I probably always will be," denies the clear implication that the person now present is acting in a demeaning manner.

All of the above examples are ways that people can deny exercising power in a relationship when, in fact, they really are. Whenever you communicate with another, what you say and do does exercise some communicative control by either going along with someone else's definition, struggling over the definition, or supplying it yourself. Even when you would rather be seen as a person who does not exert power, you are *exercising influence on how the conflict relationship is going to be defined.*

Often, underlying assumptions about power are not so easily observed as they are during denial of its use. However, many assumptions about power are embedded in a person's language use. For example, if one says, "It's a dog eat dog world," a clear impression is given that one person loses and the other wins. Or if you say, "He was trying to undermine my power with the director so he could get the position," similar win-lose assumptions are reflected. One

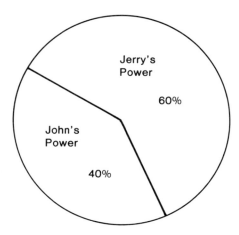

Figure 3.1. Power pie—a finite view of power.

prevalent assumption about power is the treatment of *power as a finite resource*. Phrases such as "when the chips are down" or "in the game of life" clearly have their underpinnings in a finite view of power based on game rules. Figure 3.1 illustrates this view of power, which we call the "power pie."

John and Jerry are two employees at the same level of the organization, each vying for a promotion to vice-president. If they see their personal resources as opposing—what one wins the other loses, then their task in their conflict is to get a "bigger slice of the pie." Further, they may try to widen their own slice by taking part of the other person's slice—to tip the balance in their own favor. Such finite views may predispose the actors to engage in destructive moves in a conflict and not seek productive mutual power by expanding options.

We have sketched many approaches to power without clearly delineating our own orientation. We develop our view throughout this chapter, but for now, here are our philosophical assumptions:

1. Power is present in all social interactions.

2. Power is neither inherently positive nor negative.

3. Power is a product of the interpersonal relationship, not of the individual.

4. Acts of power balancing are at the heart of conflict interactions, resulting in destructive or productive power use.

5. Productive power balancing can occur by an expansion of individual and relational power rather than by a struggle over winning a bigger part of finite power.

6. Individuals can have either too much or too little power to be able to manage conflict effectively. A relative balance is necessary for productive conflict management.

The Prevalence of Power

We all try to exert some form of communicative influence—to influence others in order to accomplish our goals. This influence can, have as its primary goal either independent, individuals goals or goals that are interdependent and relationally oriented. Influence and attempts at gaining more power in a conflict do not have to be seen as negative; power is necessary to move a conflict along to some kind of productive management. If people have no influence over each other, they cannot participate in conflict together, since their communication would have no impact. With no influence, persons are not in a conflict but are simply in a mutual monologue. Influence, therefore, is necessary. We will discuss attempts to gain power that enhance either individual goals or relationship goals. Further, we will discuss cases in which power attempts are made that directly harm the relationship or hinder individual goals. Power is central to the study of conflict and can be used for productive or destructive ends; as we noted earlier, it is always present.

The centrality of power in conflict can be seen in the following example. A college student is trying to add a course after the normal registration period has closed. The professor is letting the student know that the course is full of students and, therefore, "closed."

Student: Hey, are you the teacher of that introductory class that meets at 9:00 every day?

Professor: Yes. Are you trying to add it?

Student: Yes. You see, I have to graduate at the end of the next semester and this is the only elective that fits my schedule. If I don't get to add this course, then I won't graduate. This registration system is really archaic—it messes up seniors like me. Can I add your course? I really need it!

Professor: I just don't see how I can help you. The class is full and there are no empty chairs in the room.

Student: Well, I would be willing to stand in the back of the room or just sit on the floor. I promise that I won't disturb your lecture. If you will let me add the class, I'll be like a little mouse who never causes any trouble.

Professor: Well, maybe you could come to class tomorrow, and we can see if anyone is going to drop the course, and then you could take that space.

Each of the participants in this conflict is attempting to exercise communicative influence (Miller and Steinberg 1975). In fact, such attempts to exercise influence or control are seen as one of the basic human needs. Schutz

(1966) postulates that all people need a sense of inclusion, affection, and control to be satisfied and growing in their relationships. The ability to meaningfully influence important events around you is necessary for a sense of well-being and personal effectiveness. When we speak of power as being central to the study of conflict, we do not mean that people are always sneaky and try to get power illegitimately. As we have discussed, the productive exercise of your personal power is crucial to your self-concept. Without some exercise of power in your interpersonal relationships, you would soon feel worthless as a person. As you read this chapter, we suggest that you use your sources of feedback (friends, memories, personal writing, family members) to gain understanding about your own uses of power. Try to gain a "power profile" of your own behavior—the way you really communicate, not just the way you might want to be seen. Sometimes there is a difference! Remember that just as one cannot not communicate (Watzlawick, Beavin, and Jackson 1967), *one does not have the option of not using power.* We only have options about whether our use of power will be destructive or productive for ourselves and our relationships.

Power Currencies

You may have had the experience of traveling in a foreign country and trying to adapt to different currencies. Drachmas in Greece suddenly are worthless in Italy, where huge numbers of lira buy items of value. A pocketful of pounds is worthless in France unless you exchange them for the local currency. Just as money depends on the context in which it is to be spent (the country), your power currencies depend on how much your particular resources are valued by other persons in your relationships. You may have a vast amount of expertise in the rules of basketball, but because your fraternity needs an intramural football coach, you are not valued. Power depends on controlling currencies that other people need. In the same manner, if other people possess currencies you value, such as the ability to edit a term theme or the possession of a car, they potentially maintain some degree of power over you in your relationship. Conflict is often confusing because people try to spend currency that is not valued in the particular relationship.

Power currencies are classified many different ways by researchers.[1] The central issue is that everyone has potential currencies that may be used to

1. Raven and French (1960) list the bases of power as reward, coercive, legitimate, referent, and expert. Kipnis (1976) maintains that influence tactics are best classified as threats and promises, persuasion, reinforcement control, and information control. And, to further complicate the issue, Rollo May says there are five types of power: exploitative, manipulative, competitive, nutrient, and integrative. Folger and Poole (1984) supply this list: special skills and abilities, expertise about the task, personal attractiveness, control over rewards and/or punishments, formal position, loyal allies, persuasive skills, and control over critical group possessions.

balance or gain power in a relationship. Even when you are used to devaluing your own currency, a careful analysis can show you areas of wealth. The following list presents power currencies.

1. *Expertise:* Special knowledge, skills, and talents that are useful for the task at hand. Being an expert in a content area such as budget analysis, a process area such as decision-making methods, or a relational area such as decoding nonverbal cues may given you expertise power when others need your expertise.

2. *Resource control:* Often comes with one's formal position in an organization or group. An example is the controlling of rewards or punishments such as salary, number of hours worked, or firing. Parents control resources such as money, freedom, cars, and privacy for teenagers.

3. *Interpersonal linkages:* Your position in the larger system, such as being central to communication exchange. If you are a liaison person between two factions, serve as a bridge between two groups that would otherwise not have information about each other, or have a network of friends who like each other, you have linkage currencies.

4. *Personal qualities:* Attractiveness, warmth, conversational skills, or social status. Some people gain interpersonal power because others like to be around them, trust them, and gravitate to them.

5. *Intimacy:* Love, sex, caring, nurturing, and the ability to form close bonds with others. All people need to be seen as specially related to persons in their lives. If you provide intimacy for a few important people, they will grant you interpersonal power.

Expertise currencies arise when the person has some special skill or knowledge that someone else values. The worker who is the only one who can operate the boiler at a large lumber mill has power because the expertise is badly needed. The medical doctor who has learned about a specialty area has expertise power because the information and skill are needed by others. Almost all professions develop specialized expertise valued by others which serves as a basis of power for people in the profession. Family members develop expertise in certain areas that others come to depend on, such as cooking, repairing the car, or babysitting.

Resource control often results from attaining a formal position that brings resources to you. The President of the United States, regardless of personal qualities, will always have some resources that will go along with the job. Leadership and position, by their very nature, place one in a situation in which others are dependent upon him or her, thus bringing ready-made power. Whatever your position—secretary, boss, chairperson, teacher, manager or volunteer—you will be in a position to control resources that others desire.

Many resources are economic in nature, bringing control of money, gifts and material possessions. We know one man who tries hard to be close and supportive with those around him; unfortunately, he manifests his closeness needs in one main way—buying gifts for his friends. He is trading on economic currencies in order to obtain intimacy currencies from others. His gifts are not always valued enough to bring him what he wants, however. Not surprisingly, people who give gifts to each other often try to work out an agreement, probably implicitly, about the amount of money that can be spent to keep the dependence (and power) equal. If an inordinate amount of money is spent by one person, then typically the other person feels overly indebted. As Blau (1967, 108) writes, "A person who gives others valuable gifts or renders them important services makes a claim for superior status by obligating them to himself." Persons without enough money usually have little access to the other forms of power mentioned above. College graduates who cannot find jobs must remain financially dependent on parents, thus limiting independence on both sides. Elderly people whose savings shrink due to inflation lose power; mothers with children and no other means of support lose most of their choices about independence, thus losing most of their potential power. Economic currencies are not the only important type of power currency, but they operate in interpersonal conflicts as well as in social conflicts.

Another cluster of power currencies comes from one's *interpersonal linkages,* a set of currencies that depend on your interpersonal contacts and networks of friends and supporters. People often obtain power based on whom they know and with whom they associate. For instance, if you have a good friend who has a mountain cabin you can share with others, then you have attained some power (if your family wants to go to the cabin) because of your ability to obtain things through other people. Young children try to trade on their linkage currencies when they say such things as, "My Uncle Ben is a park ranger, and he will give us a tour of the park."

Interpersonal linkages help one attain power through coalition formation. Whenever you band together with another (such as a good friend) to gain some sense of strength, this coalition can be a form of power (Van de Vliert 1981). The small boy who says, "You better not hit me, because if you do, my big sister will beat you up," understands the potential value of coalitions. When others will come to our aid, our interpersonal power is usually strengthened. Jason, a four-year-old boy, invented a friendly ghost, Karsha, who would come and help him in times of difficulty. After one particularly trying day with his younger sister (who was two years old), Jason recited to his father the virtues of Karsha. Karsha was "bigger than a mountain, a giant, who comes in the mornings and kills spiders with his hands. Karsha also makes electricity and has long hair. And Karsha is mean to babies that bite little boys." In the Senoi culture, the value of fantasy coalitions is so commonly recognized that children are taught to call upon friends in their dreams to help them overcome any threatening dream monsters (Garfield 1974).

One's *personal qualities* such as attractiveness, warmth, and conversational skills serve as currencies for power. Considerable research demonstrates that physically attractive people are treated differently from people seen as unattractive (Berscheid and Walster 1978). Further, if you can facilitate the social process of a group, serve as the fun-loving jokster in the family, or be the catalyst for meaningful conversation in the workplace, others will typically value you. When one becomes the informal leader of a group or works to keep group members working well with one another, functions are served that can yield power. It is not the qualities, per se, that bring you power, it is that these currencies are valued by others. As a result you attain power.

Finally, the cluster of *intimacy* currencies incorporates the abilities to form intimate bonds with others through love, sex, caring, nurturing or understanding. For example, if a father provides warmth and understanding to his teenage daughter who is going through a difficult time at school, his support is a currency for him in that relationship. Often, we develop currencies at the expense of others. For instance, women are seen as providing more warmth and affection than are men (Johnson 1976). If the mother in a family takes on the role of soothing hurt feelings, providing empathy and understanding to the children when they are buffeted by the world, and generally being the one who handles the relational needs of others, then her specialization at the task will sometimes make it difficult for others such as the father to trade on the same currency. Intimacy currencies exist in both formal and informal relationships. Even in highly structured situations such as a very impersonal work environment, when the boss says, "I like your work," the phrase is a form of intimacy. The distance between the people is lessened with the phrase. When a person who uses intimacy currencies chooses to "trade" on them during a difficult conflict, he or she can either activate the currency by providing more warmth or by withdrawing it from others. Both offering and withdrawing warmth activate it as a currency in the relationship. The "silent treatment" is a common form of intimacy currency withdrawal.

Clarifying the currencies available to you and the other parties in a conflict helps in the conflict analysis. People are often unaware of their own sources of potentially productive power, just as they do not understand their own dependence on others. Desperation and low-power tactics often arise from the feeling that one has no choice, that no power is available. Analyze your potential power currencies when you find yourself saying, "I have no choice." In the following section, the relational view of power analysis is presented so you can compare your own power to the power of others in the conflict.

A Relational View of Power

A common view of power characterizes it as an attribute that people possess. For example, if you say, "Lynn is a powerful person," you attribute power to Lynn as a person. But *all power in interpersonal relations is a property of the social relationship rather than a quality of the individual outside of the relationship.* Lynn, for example, has power over her friends because she has currencies they value; when she asks people to do tasks for her, they usually do. But if they did not value Lynn's currencies (such as friendship, warmth, prestige), she would not have power over them. The concept of the powerful *person* often leads others to act in manipulative or covert ways because they do not acknowledge their own part in helping to make that person powerful.

Our orientation, then, is that power is not some individualistic "thing" that people have but is a product of the social relationship (Rogers 1974; Harsanyi 1962, Deutsch 1958; Dahl 1957; Solomon 1960). Deutsch (1973, 15) states the case well:

> Power is a relational concept; it does not reside in the individual but rather in the relationship of the person to his environment. Thus, the power of an agent in a given situation is determined by the characteristics of the situation.

Rather than residing in people, "power is always interpersonal" (May 1972, 23). It is a product of the relationship between the parties involved. In the strictest sense, power is *given* from one party to another in a conflict. Each person in a conflict has some degree of power, though one party may have more *compared to* the other, and the power bases can shift during a conflict.

A way to analyze one's degree of power has been explored by Emerson (1962). He specified that a person's power is directly tied to the nature of the relationship. In terms of two people, A and B, person A has power over person B to the extent that B is dependent on A for goal attainment. Likewise, person B has power over person A to the extent that A is dependent on B. A simple formula expresses it this way:

$$P_{AB} = D_{BA}$$
(the power of A over B is equal to the dependence that B has on A), and

$$P_{BA} = D_{AB}$$
(the power of B over A is equal to the dependence that A has on B).

To illustrate this point, return to the example of the college student who is trying to add the course. To determine the professor's power over the student, we need to know these things: (1) What is the student's goal? (to add the class) and (2) How dependent is he on the professor to get the class? (very). To determine the power that the student has over the professor, we ask the same questions: (1) What is the professor's goal? (to have a full but not over-loaded class and to appear to be "reasonable") and (2) How dependent is the professor on the student to accomplish goals? (slightly). In this case, the pro-fessor has more power than the student because the student is more dependent on the professor than the professor is on the student. Note, however, that both the professor and the student have some power, and the professor is more pow-erful only because she can mediate the goals that the student wants to achieve. If power is the ability to influence the other persons' goal achievements, then both have power, although the professor has more *in that situation.*

One further refinement is necessary. You are dependent upon the other person to the degree of (1) the *importance* of the goals the other person can influence and (2) the *availability of other avenues* for you to accomplish your goals. As Emerson states, "The dependence of Actor B upon Actor A is di-rectly proportional to B's motivational investment in goals mediated by A, and inversely proportional to the availability of those goals to B outside of the A-B relation" (Emerson 1962, 31). In the case of the college student and the professor, the professor is less dependent on the student because there are other students available to fill the seats in her class and provide feedback to her.

One way to reduce power others have over you is to change your goals. If after a few years in a new job a person is not valued by an organization and thus is not rewarded, a change of goals is likely. The disenchanted employee might remark, "It is not important to me what they pay me for this job. I'll just do the minimal amount of work and spend all my creative energy at my hobbies." By altering the importance of the goal, you reduce the power the other has over you. And the often-heard remark, "There are other fish in the sea," when a person has been dropped in a love affair is just another way of saying that you have alternative sources for accomplishing your goals. (Or at least you hope you do, and you want other people to think you do!)

We have power over people and they over us because our social relation-ship means that we are interdependent—we influence one another's ability to attain goals. Furthermore, the degree of power is a function of the comparison of the dependence the two parties have on one another. And the degree of dependence is a product of one's investment in the goals the other can mediate and the number of other avenues available for the attainment of those goals. The example on p. 78 illustrates various degrees of dependence.

While at first glance the power may appear to be organized such that Tom has more because he is the boss and Helen has less because she works at a lower grade in the organization, a closer look reveals that the parties are ac-tually fairly well balanced in their power. The balancing act is, however, tak-ing a toll on their relationship, and the work could be managed more creatively. Tom is dependent on Helen for getting his work out error free, quickly, and with the benefit of Helen's experience. He depends on Helen to respond to him, since he is carrying more of the work in the office than the other three

---

Conflict Parties: Tom, junior boss in an office
                  Helen, secretary for four people

Repetitive Conflict: Often when Helen is too busy to get the work done immediately, she will set priorities and plan her schedule based on known deadlines. Tom's work comprises the largest share of Helen's work. Tom and the other three supervisors are equal on the organizational scale. Tom, when busy and pressed, rushes to Helen's desk with work to be done.

> **Tom:**   Helen, I have just this one little thing that has to go out today.
>
> **Helen** (sighing noticeably):   Yes, Tom, I know—just one little thing. But I have to get this out for Joe today, and it MUST be done first.

Tom puts more pressure on Helen to do his job by saying that it won't take long and that just this once she needs to respond to the emergency pressures. Helen gets angry and tries to persuade him that it can wait one more day. Then she pouts a bit.

> **Helen:**   I am only one person, you know. Just put it there and I'll *try* to get it done.
>
> **Tom:**   Helen, you're a sweetheart. When this madhouse calms down, I'll take you out to lunch. I knew I could count on you.

Helen then stays late to finish the work, but she asks her office manager to speak to Tom again about interfering with her ability to manage her work. Tom comes in a few days later.

> **Tom:**   I didn't mean to make you mad. I didn't think that one report was going to tick you off so much.
>
> **Helen:**   It's OK; it's just that I can't please everybody.

---

at his level are. He sees himself as a pleasant and noncontrol-oriented person whose employees work because they want to. He depends on Helen to see him as a reasonable and professional person because this is how he views himself. Helen depends on Tom for some of her self-esteem. She prizes her ability to use her skills to organize her work so that it gets done on time. She wants to be treated as a valuable, decision-making employee. She knows, too, that if Tom becomes dissatisfied with her work, he will complain to her immediate supervisor in the office, and she might not be promoted next time, or might even lose her job. So Helen depends on Tom for positive ratings, a good work climate, and self-esteem. Restructuring their conflict could allow each to gain more of their independent and interdependent goals. Helen could ask Tom to help her solve her problem of how to respond to the disparate pressures; Tom could ask Helen how to set up a way to take care of emergencies. A problem-solving approach to conflict management would allow both to balance the power more collaboratively.

Assessing Power

"Power, like heat, has many sources:
(McCall 1979)

Since power is a dynamic product of shifting relationships, precise measurement of the amount of power parties have is a difficult process. Several approaches are useful. The most common way to measure power is to compare the relative resources of the parties in a conflict (Berger 1980; Galvin and Brommel 1982; McCall 1979). For instance, in organizational work, it is generally agreed that power accrues to "those departments that are most instrumental in bringing in or providing resources which are highly valued by the total organization" (McCall 1979). People have power in the organization when they—

- are in a position to deal with important problems;

- have control over significant resources valued by others;

- are lucky or skilled enough to bring problems and resources together at the same time;

- are centrally connected in the work flow of the organization;

- are not easily replaced; and

- have successfully used their power in the past (McCall 1979).

This listing of power resources places high reliance on the resources controlled by a person or group on whom the organization is dependent. Such resource views, while providing a useful starting point, serve to perpetuate two limitations of an adequate view of power:

1. They define resources too narrowly (Berger 1980).

2. They put too much emphasis on the source of the power influence. Such an over-emphasis on the source is a characteristic of most studies of power, such as the "bases of power" work of Raven and French (1960) and the research of Kipnis (1979). Most assessments of power view the relationship as one-way. Person A is seen as exerting influence *on* person B. In diagram form, the relationship looks like this:

The relational perspective we have presented characterizes the communication as two-way; each participant has power over the other. The relationship would look like this:

Most research presents power as a static property and disregards the dynamic elements of power (Bochner 1976). Resources are treated as possessions rather than as a changing part of the relationship process. One would assess power, using this perspective, by examining the resources that the one party possesses. Many popular books on power take this individualistic approach.

Most research on power has focused on (1) decision making or (2)conversational control within the family unit. Decision-making approaches began with the classic Blood and Wolfe (1960) study of Detroit housewives. They asked wives questions such as "Who decides where the family will take a vacation?" and "Who decides what job to take?" Researchers in subsequent years tried to analyze power similarly by asking "Who has the last say about spending money?" (Safilios-Rothschild 1970), "Who is the real boss in the family?" (Heer 1962) and "Who would decide how you would spend $300?" (Kenkel 1975). It seemed reasonable that the most powerful member of a family would be the one who decided most of the important decisions; unfortunately, there were difficulties with this popular method of measuring power. First, the researchers did not ask both spouses the questions. They might have received different answers if they had asked each partner separately. Second, the questions asked for "perceived authority"—who they thought made most of the decisions rather than who actually did (Bochner 1976; McDonald 1980). As a result, the participants may well have answered according to who they think *should* have been making decisions. Given the sex-role stereotypes of that period in American culture, a woman may not have wanted to tell a researcher that she was "the real boss." As a result, they usually reported that the husband made more decisions than did the wife (Turk and Bell 1972).

Another way researchers have tried to measure power by looking at decision making was done in the laboratory through decision-making tasks such as responding to conflict stories or trying to match subtly different colors (Olson and Strauss 1972; Olson and Rabunsky 1972). The problem with this approach is that many times the people completing the decision-making task were strangers to each other. Obviously, people act differently with strangers than they do with intimates.

In an extensive review of the decision-making assessments of power, McDonald says, "After twenty years of studying marital decision making, we actually may know little more than the authority expectations of couples" (1980). He then argues that more research should focus on the "powering processes" or the interaction between the parties (Sprey 1972; Scanzoni 1979).

Conversational control is the other main way researchers have attempted to study power. You have probably made the judgment that someone was powerful because he or she tried to control the conversation. The research by Mishler and Waxler (1968) and others studied conversational control in couples. Assuming that conversational control and power were the same thing, they studied who talked the most, who interrupted the most, who changed topics the most, and who engaged in "one-up" moves (Rogers and Farace 1975; Rogers-Millar and Millar 1977; Ellis 1979).

These two measures of power (decision making and conversational control) do not measure the same concept. If you look at different measures of power, you will reach different conclusions about who is most powerful (Olson and Rabunsky 1972; Turk and Bell 1972; Bochner 1976; Berger 1980; and McDonald 1980). Try this experiment for yourself: watch a movie, role-play, or video presentation of two people in conflict, with the audience making notes on who appears to be more powerful. You will probably find, as we have, that almost everyone in the audience has a different way of deciding who *really* is the more powerful. For some it may be nonverbal dominance, for others, vocal quality, for still others, amount of time spent in overt argument, and on and on. In essence, no single validating criterion for assessing power has been discovered by researchers; possibly such a sure-fire technique does not exist (Gray-Little 1982; Berger 1980).

A final problem with measuring who has the most power is that often power is exercised covertly or in hidden ways. This is manifested in two ways: (1) reacting to another person's potential power and (2) exercising power in supposedly weak ways. Social power can be "potential, that is, an available capacity of a social actor" (Himes 1980, 77). Most of us have trouble deciphering covert power or choices made based on another person's potential influence. For example, Will is an outdoorsman who would like to take a weeklong hunting trip, but he "knows" that his wife will not like being left alone for such an extended period of time since she works and would have to assume all the care of the children. Will proposes a two-day trip and in the process, talks more and controls the discussion. An observer might guess that Will was in control of both process and outcome, since they agree that he will go on the two-day trip. Yet all Will's conversation was structured around his estimate of his wife's reaction. Her power was important to his decision, yet an outside observer could not have known that without asking.

Power is exercised in supposedly weak ways, also. Sometimes the most powerful behavior is to submit, go weak, or act in a nonresistant way. An example of this form of power was Martin Luther King's civil rights tactics, based on Gandhian principles, in which civil rights workers were trained to sit down when confronted by powerful persons, to protect their bodies if attacked but not to attack in response, and to use nonaggressive verbal responses. As happened in India, weakness in the face of strength made stronger persons question their use of force and coercion. A less productive "weak" way of exercising power is the apocryphal case of the army private who, ordered to do KP duty, does as sloppy a job as possible while asking constantly, "Is this the way?" "Am I doing it right?" This "reluctant soldier" example can be seen in offices, in families, and on work crews where one person is "trying" (but failing) to get it right. The supervisor, parent, or crew boss then gets disgusted and does the job himself or herself.

People who look the most powerful to outsiders often are less powerful than they appear. In fact, without knowing the structure of a relationship, you cannot guess who has the most power, since people balance their power currencies in complex ways. For instance, if one person "lets" the other do the talking for the group, the person who gives tacit permission for the other to talk is actually controlling the situation.

Another supposedly weak way to gain power is to refuse to cooperate when other people are depending on you. When this tactic is used in conjunction with unexpressed anger, it is labelled *passive aggressive behavior.* In passive aggression, the person is acting aggressively (in one's own self-interest, without much regard for the other) by being passive or unconcerned when the other person needs a response. Especially when people feel they have low power, whether they do or not, passive aggression may be used since it appears to be a safer way of expressing anger, resentment or hostility than stating such feelings directly. Additionally, "nice" people (Bach and Goldberg 1974) may use passive aggression instead of direct conflict statements because they have been taught that it is not nice to engage in conflict. Bach and Goldberg (1974) provide a discussion of common passive aggressive behaviors; we have added items to their list, which appears below. You may be acting in a passive aggressive manner if the following behavior is continually present:

- Forgetting appointments, promises, and agreements
- Slipping and saying unkind things, then apologizing
- Acting out nonverbally, such as slamming doors, banging objects, but denying that anything is wrong
- Getting confused, tearful, sarcastic, or helpless when certain topics come up
- Getting sick when you've promised to do something
- Scheduling two things at once
- Evading so others are inconvenienced

Two college roommates have a practice of borrowing each other's possessions. When Jan and Charla first moved in together, they decided it would be inconvenient to ask each time they wanted to use a record or borrow an article of clothing. Charla has been keeping Jan's things longer than Jan wants her to, however, often causing Jan to have to look for her records, textbooks, car keys, sweaters, skis and gloves. Recently, Jan has lost several of Charla's possessions and has scratched a record she took to a party. She feels justified since Charla has been misusing the privilege, too. They are avoiding the issue and spending time away from each other.

The "cure" for passive aggression is to confront the angry feelings directly instead of indirectly. The college professor who double-schedules may feel overloaded and underappreciated, communicating that fact by mixing up schedules. A better practice would be to tell people directly that too many appointments are interfering with the rest of the work, so people know why the professor is less available.

Power, in summary, is a complex and elusive concept. Conflict parties inevitably have different views of the power dynamics in their relationships; these discrepant perceptions keep the conflicts going. Power, as we have seen, remains a difficult concept to assess accurately. One kernel of wisdom to remember is this: assume that you and your conflict partners all measure each others' power differently, disagree on who has the most, and disagree on who should have the most.

Power Imbalances

In most relationships, there are times when the participants become aware of discrepancies in their relative power with one another. Conflict behaviors highlight differential levels of power and allow participants to see the discrepancy (Rummel 1976; Dahl 1963; Rollins and Bahr 1976). If one party has more power than the other, the conflict is unbalanced; many of the choices the parties then make are attempts to alter these imbalances. Keep in mind that power is always a relative judgment—each party has sources of power even during times of imbalance. Such power asymmetries have predictable effects on both the higher- and lower-portion parties, and the imbalance produces systemwide effects on the relationship.

The exercise of social power for most people in Western cultures is satisfying and even produces joy (Bowers and Ochs 1971; May 1972). High power is often a goal that people strive for, and those with less power often feel, "If I were just the boss, things would be a lot better around here." The major difficulty with having higher power than someone else is that it may corrupt. Corruption is more than a word that describes a crooked politician. Corruption means moral decay, rottenness, and inability to maintain the integrity of the self. Constant high power may "eat into" one's view of self and other, forming a perceptual distortion that may take on monstrous proportions indeed. Higher-power persons, organizations, or nation states may alter their view of themselves and the other party. Constant feelings of power can bring with them these consequences:

1. The person acquires a "taste for power" and restlessly pursues more power as an end in itself.

2. Access to power tempts the individual to illegally use institutional resources as a means of self-enrichment.

3. With high power, persons are provided with false feedback concerning their own worth and develop new values designed to protect their power;

4. At the same time, they devalue the worth of the less powerful and prefer to avoid close social contacts with them (Kipnis 1976, 178).

These undesirable consequences of higher power can take many forms. For instance, two studies show that if a teacher uses strong power over a student, the relationship disintegrates into the exclusive use of coercive strategies (Jamieson and Thomas 1974; Raven and Kruglanski 1968). Or the person highest in power may claim benevolence, that "harmful" actions are actually "for the good of the other person," thereby dismissing the negative consequences to the lower-power person. When someone is fired in an organization, it is common to hear, "It was for her/his own good—he/she will be better off spending time doing X." According to Guggenbuhl-Craig (1978), persons in helping professions, such as ministers, teachers, health workers, and others, can get out of touch with their need to exercise power in order to feel valued and needed. While helpers undoubtedly are in their professions in order to help, they also must have "helpees," or they have no function. How can a physician be a physician without people who need skill in healing? How can teachers teach if no one values learning? And so on. If helpers do not understand that helping also contributes to one's own sense of self-worth and personal fulfillment, the act of helping can become a high-power move. Just as during the Inquisition, when the learned scholars were sure that they were helping the persons accused of heresy, unrestrained high power may make you blind to the havoc wreaked on others. You may have had times in your personal history when power became unbalanced; if so, you know the harm that unrestrained power can bring, whether you were the one with too much power or the one without enough power.

Striving for higher power can destroy even the best of relationships. For example, in intimate relationships, the person who is least invested in the relationship has the most power (the "Principle of Least Interest," Waller 1937). Paradoxically, decreasing the investment for the purpose of gaining higher power is ultimately self-defeating, since you have to continue your decreasingly fragile investment in order to remain more powerful. And the lessened dependence can lead to the demise of the relationship. If you convince yourself that "I don't have to put up with this," then you don't usually stay in the relationship.

Finally, persons or nations with higher power can deny that power is exercised; they may deny that there is a conflict (it is a "minor disagreement") or use any of the other forms of denial mentioned earlier. Basically, unrestrained higher power can corrupt the powerholder's view of self and view of the other, and it can set the stage for continued unproductive interaction.

Just as higher power can corrupt, powerlessness can also corrupt (May 1972). If lower-power persons are continually subjected to harsh treatment or no goal attainment, they will likely produce some organized resistance to the higher-power people. In fact, as Bach and Wyden (1968) and May (1972) have noted, it is the powerless who become the most violent. When one reaches the stage where "nothing matters" (you cannot attain your goals through accepted means), violence or despair is spawned. It is the person who feels powerless who turns to the last resort—giving up, aggression, or violence. Too much losing does not build character, it builds frustration, aggression, or apathy. A typical example of how perceived unequal power builds aggression is the case of students and teachers. In one study, when students were asked what options they considered using to resolve conflicts they had with more powerful teachers, they replied on paper "Use a .357 magnum," "Blow up his mailbox," "Sabotage him," and "Beat him up" (Wilmot 1976). At the very least, asymmetry in perceived power can lead to coercion in an attempt to "get even" (Jamieson and Thomas 1974; Raven and Kruglanski 1968).

Often, even if the lower-power person wants to act aggressively, there are restraints against doing so. The powerless will try to restore equity, and if that fails, then they have few options; one of those is to use passive-aggressive behavior, as discussed previously. In addition, Madànes (1982) notes that developing severely dysfunctional behavior is an exercise of power—you affect all your close associates. Lower-power parties will sometimes destroy a relationship as the ultimate move to bring about a balance of power.

The combination of denigration from the higher-power person, and destructive power-balancing moves from the lower-power person contributes to a system of interactions that is not productive for either party. A cyclical, degenerative, destructive conflict spiral is produced in the ongoing interactions. The power disparity promotes struggles over power (Brown 1983), increases the underlying bases of the conflict (Raven and Kruglanski 1970), and leads to a lesser involvement in the relationship for both parties. Here is one concrete example:

> Craig is a supervisor in a community agency, and Marilyn is a staff member who works part time. Craig coerces Marilyn to take on a program of working with community volunteers—a job she neither wanted nor had time to develop at a competent level. Marilyn resists working on the program, and deadlines are looming. Craig, seeing her subversion, escalates and forces her in a public meeting to agree to work hard on the program. Marilyn accedes (on the surface) and talks to her friends about how poorly she is treated. After two months of Craig's being unhappy with her progress and with her seeking social support elsewhere, she resigns.

Craig did not accomplish his original goal, the community program, and Marilyn lost her job. They achieved a power balance in an unproductive manner, much like a game of leapfrog. When one person is behind, he or she then jumps into the lead, and the other person, sensing that he or she is "losing," adds more of the same. Pretty soon the relationship has suffered, and neither person achieves any of the original goals.

In cases of power disparity such as this, agreements are "basically unstable since they are grounded on unilateral threats rather than on mutually established norms" (Apfelbaum, 1974, 151). The continued ever-accelerating unproductive moves are the result of attempts at power balancing through counterproductive means. The alternative is to balance the power through productive avenues and recognize that with extreme power asymmetry, effective long-term management is not likely.

Power Balancing

Balancing interpersonal power is an effective avenue for the management of ongoing relationships (Walton 1969). Conflict participants have an opportunity to make a long-range relationship work when they move toward equity in the power relationship. Equity doesn't necessarily mean equality. It simply means that one's rewards are proportionate to one's costs. You get back what you invest in the relationship (Hatfield et al. 1979). Models for productive power balancing, while scarce, do exist. Repeatedly we find in research and everyday life that individuals *can* learn to cooperate and to find agreements if power is distributed equitably (Apfelbaum 1974, 138). For relationships to work over time, people continually realign the power balance as the situation warrants (Rummel 1976).

Outside observers are notoriously poor at determining the balance of power in a relationship. Many times, powerful-looking persons are not perceived the same way by "those who know best." People may separate on "orchestration" and "implementation" kinds of power (Safilios-Rothschild 1970). One person decides what will be done, and the other activates the movement. Again, to outsiders, the active person may appear to be the most powerful, yet all the activity may be done within the confines of the other person's direction (Herbst 1952). If James says to Alexis, "I think I should make the decision about what kind of car to buy because I read *Consumer Reports,*" Alexis maintains a certain amount of power if she can say, "No, we'll make the decision together as we always do," and make that statement stick. Deciding who gets to decide is one of the best indicators of the current balance of power in any relationship.

What do friends, coworkers, family members of intimates do when they discover a power asymmetry in their relationships? Basically, one can (1) work to make the relationship more equitable, (2) try to convince oneself and one's partner that the relationship is more equitable than it might seem (by restoring psychological equity), or (3) eventually abandon the inequitable relationship (Hatfield, Utne, and Traupmann 1979). For instance, we hear family members negotiating household tasks by saying, "I should get more credit for taking out the garbage than you do for cleaning the counters because I *hate* to take out the garbage and you don't mind doing the counters." The person who hates garbage is trying to balance power (by reducing the number of times the garbage has to be carried out by her) through attempting to restore psychological equity. We are all too familiar with ruined or deteriorated friendships that fail because of inadequate power balancing. We will now examine productive balancing options.

Interpersonal relations with a power disparity between participants can be moved to a more productive focus by moves toward balance. Just as the destructive attempts by lower-power parties to balance power are a move toward reciprocity, a move toward some equitable arrangement of power can lead the way to effective management (Wehr 1979). Parties can (1) limit the power use of the higher-power party, (2) empower the lower-power party, or (3) transcend the win-lose aspect of many conflicts and create a collaborative structure.

Higher-power parties can limit their power by refusing to use the currencies they have at their disposal. A militarily powerful nation that refuses to invade a neighboring country and a spouse who refuses to inflict damage on the other spouse are examples of a higher-power party's limiting power usage. If the high-power person refuses to engage in "natural" responses, this restraint can alter the automatic nature of a destructive cycle. We know one college teacher who does not use punitive power when students present last-minute pleadings for more time to write final papers. Instead, Art simply says, "Why don't you set a deadline for the final paper that you can meet, and it will be fine with me. What day and time do you want to hand it in?" A married couple we know found a way to lower one member's economic power, thereby providing more balance in their relationship. They valued monetary equality and were used to having separate accounts and almost the same spendable income. He got an unexpected raise, however, and suddenly had more money to spend. They started arguing frequently because he would propose expensive weekends for recreation—and she had difficulty paying for her half. In response to increasingly destructive arguments, he had more withheld from his monthly paycheck, to be put in a joint long-term savings plan. Then they would use this money occasionally for a "lost weekend." Even though he still had more money than his partner, the effect on them as a couple was lessened, while he gained the long-term advantages of saving more money. He limited his use of his higher monetary power, with positive effects on their balance of power.

Since power is always relational in nature, a higher-power person can also move toward equity in the relationship by increasing dependence on the other. Rather than limiting use of already existing currencies, the higher-power person unilaterally decides to increase the investment in the other's currencies— all for the sake of relational harmony. For example, the higher-power person can "allow" influence by increasing dependence on the other, which will move the power toward equity (Koile 1977). Since power asymmetry pushes the weaker party to raise the level of violence, building a true collaborative structure sets a different course for the relationship (Wehr 1979). Take the case of the employer who is dissatisfied with the employee's job performance. Instead of reducing dependence and complaining about the employee to others, the employer can invest in the employee and become more dependent. This creates the chance of *not* automatically firing the person, then working jointly for more productive solutions.

The second major route to balancing the power is the *empowerment* of the lower-power party (Laue and Cormick 1974; Wehr 1979). In a community setting, empowerment is created by altering political structures so lower-power groups can influence the political process. In interpersonal relations, one form of empowerment is to increase the currencies of the lower-power person. One way to increase the currencies of the lower-power party is to divide work or responsibilities into different spheres of interest (McDonald 1980). Then, increasing the areas of expertise or work for the lower-power person may bring more equity. One example of reaching equity is in an organization in which one person may be an excellent fund raiser while another is an organizer who keeps track of activities. Each sphere of expertise is valuable for the organization. The same principle is operative in personal relations as well. For example, our brother-in-law thinks nothing of washing multitudes of pots and pans, while the other family members shop, plan meals, and set the table. Some couples try "rigid egalitarianism," with each performing exactly equal tasks to stay in balance.

A related form of empowerment occurs when you alter your actions so the other party becomes more dependent upon your currencies, thereby building your power. For instance, on the job you can secure new expertise, build interpersonal linkages, or get in a position to control more resources, making you more valuable to the organization. Empowerment also occurs when third parties are invested with the power to intervene on the behalf of less powerful persons. For instance, children who have been abused by their parents or caretakers, if their plight is reported to the proper agency, can be empowered by society. The legal system will provide an attorney, a caseworker to monitor the situation, counselors to work with the parents, judges to arbitrate decisions involving the children, and free services to help the children recover from the effects of the abuse. Our society has decided, by passing certain laws, that extreme forms of power imbalance, such as abuse, will not be allowed to continue when they are discovered. The children are empowered by laws giving rights and responsibilities to others.

A third way to balance power is to transcend a win-lose structure by jointly working to preserve the relationship during conflict. By metacommunicating during or before conflicts (talking about their relationship or about how they will handle their conflicts), the parties can make agreements about behaviors that will not be allowed (such as leaving during a fight). True, they are not forced to keep their agreements, but the moral force behind such agreements propels many people into more productive struggles. They can make agreements about bringing in outside mediators or counselors when any one person begins to feel like leaving. They can agree ahead of time that whenever a serious imbalance occurs, the high-power party will work actively with the low-power party to alter the balance in a meaningful way. Usually committed partners, friends, family members, and work partners can accomplish such joint moves if they agree that the maximization of individual power, left unrestrained, will destroy any relationship. They see that individual power is based relationally, that dependence begets power, and that successful relationships necessitate a balancing of dependencies and therefore of power. The lack of a balanced arrangement is viewed as a signal to *reinvest* in the relationship, rather than as a clue that the relationship is over. The person temporarily weaker in the relationship can draw on the relationship currencies, almost as if the relationship were a savings bank of currencies. The weaker party can claim extra time, space, money, training, empathy or other special considerations until the power is brought back into an approximation of balance. Here is an example of an interpersonal peacemaking agreement:

Cheryl and Melissa are two teenage girls who share a room in a foster home. Cheryl is more outgoing and friendly than Melissa, who is shy in groups but demanding of Cheryl's time and attention. Recently, Melissa escalated small demands for Cheryl to shut the door, turn down the radio, bring her a drink of water, include her in phone gossip, and lend her clothes, records, and other items. Cheryl, after discussing the situation with several helpers, decided she did not want to continue to respond to Melissa in anger and disdain. ("Get your own water—I'm not your slave!") She then took the following steps to restore the balance of power:

1. She reminded Melissa that they had agreements about chores in the room, made at a family meeting, that Cheryl wanted to follow.

2. She voluntarily began to fill Melissa in on happenings at school that involved people whom Melissa admired.

3. She complied with the first request only, getting a drink of water, but then said, "I'm glad to get it this once, but remember we agreed to be equal in who does what in the room. So you're on your own now."

4. She asked Melissa to go to basketball games with Cheryl's friends. Melissa became sociable, made new friends of her own, and needed Cheryl's assistance less.

Granted, Cheryl was a remarkably compassionate teenager. But she reported that her life was better, too, since she got along so much better with her roommate.

Most of us are caught in a paradox of power. To be effective people, we need to maximize our abilities, take advantage of opportunities, and use resources at our disposal so we can lead the kinds of lives we desire. Yet within the confines of an ongoing relationship, maximization of individual power is counterproductive for both the higher-power and lower-power parties. The unrestrained maximization of individual power leads to damaged relations, destructive moves, more destructive countermoves, and an eventual ending of a relationship. Since people are going to take steps to balance power—destructively if no other means are available—we can more productively manage conflict by working to balance power in productive and creative ways. Equity in power reduces violence and enables all participants to continue working for the good of all parties, even in conflict.

Summary

Power is a central concept in all conflict mangement theory. While most people dislike discussions of their own power, one cannot avoid using power. Power is a necessary part of conflict management, since interdependence presupposes mutual influence. Power currencies of expertise, resource control, interpersonal linkages, personal qualities, and intimacy provide ways for this mutual influence to be enacted.

Power is a product of the social relationship, not of the individual, stemming from people's mutual dependencies. Accurate assessment of power remains difficult, even though researchers have tried to measure decision making and conversational control as indicators of power. The difficulty is compounded by the common use of covert or supposedly weak power moves such as passive aggression. Power imbalances over time harm relationships, since negative results occur from both too much and too little power. Power balancing can restore options for productive conflict management; such techniques as limiting the power of the high-power party, empowering the low-power party, and restructuring the conflict from win-lose to collaborative structures are desirable. People balance power either productively or destructively; far better is the exercise of productive power balancing for ongoing relationships.

4 Clarifying Goals

In 1964 an American father and his twelve-year old son were enjoying a beautiful Saturday in Hyde Park, London, playing catch with a Frisbee. Few in England had seen a Frisbee at that time and a small group of strollers gathered to watch this strange sport. Finally, one Homburg-clad Britisher came over to the father: "Sorry to bother you. Been watching you a quarter of an hour. Who's winning? (Fisher and Ury 1981, 154)

Incompatible goals are part of every interpersonal conflict. Goals are the results conflict parties want to obtain, such as winning a game, being selected for a position, making an A in a course, or gaining more in a bargaining session than the other party. Goals range from simple to complex. In this chapter we will discuss the advantages of goal clarity, how goals change over the course of a conflict, and how you might negotiate productive goals. Conflict builds as people gradually perceive that they want different things; often the dawning awareness of conflict's existence comes when people say to each other, "That is *not* what I want." Learning to intervene early in the process of clarifying and communicating one's goals emerges as a central skill of productive conflict management. Goals are frequently incompatible; one must face the hard reality that "I can't get all of what I want if you get all of what you want" much of the time. For the experienced conflict manager, this statement of incompatible goals alerts one to begin the process of productive conflict management. The other option is to assume that you are enemies—a choice full of consequences. The following story by Fisher and Ury (1981, p. 41) illustrates this choice point:

> Consider the story of two men quarreling in a library. One wants the window open and the other wants it closed. They bicker back and forth about how much to leave it open; a crack, halfway, three quarters of the way. No solution satisfies them both.
> Enter the librarian. She asks one why he wants the window open: "to get some fresh air." She asks the other why he wants it closed: "to avoid the draft." After thinking for a moment, she opens wide the window in the next room, bringing in fresh air without a draft.

Advantages of Goal Clarity

People direct a persistently large amount of energy toward creating relationships that fit their individual and shared relational goals. Yet a discussion of goals in interpersonal conflict often elicits the same avoidance reaction we have mentioned in earlier chapters. "I don't want to be manipulative. If I figure out what I want ahead of time, I'm being pushy and presumptuous—I'll let the chips fall where they may." However, all effective communication is *rhetorical,* or goal directed (Phillips and Metzger 1976). What this means is that communication is purposive, not that it is manipulative, and that people communicate for reasons and to reach goals. Since no one can avoid being goal directed, especially in conflict communication, conflict management, to be productive, depends on parties taking open responsibility for their goals. This occurs when you know what your goals are, can state them clearly to yourself, and can communicate them in a flexible manner with your conflict partners. Advantages of clarifying your goals follow:

Solutions go unrecognized if you do not know what you want. If the parents are not clear about whether they want their eighteen-year-old to live at home or to board in the dorm at a local college, they will not know how to manage the conflict with the son who wants to live in the dorm but does not have a job. If the goal of saving money is the primary goal, the possible solution of the son's living in the dorm and getting a job may be considered. If the parents have decided that they do not want him to live in the dorm under any circumstances, the son's offer to get a job may trigger a covert conflict that is unclear and unproductive for all the parties.

Only clear goals can be shared. Since people cannot read your mind, you must communicate your goals by clarifying what you want, both separately and together. An example of this kind of goal sharing occurred in an academic department. The chairperson complained that the faculty was not paying enough attention to university politics. He made several statements over a period of a week or so, urging more attendance at meetings, more discussion of long-term budget and curriculum plans, and voluntary participation in activities around campus. Since all this happened at the beginning of a quarter, when the rest of the faculty were feeling busy, hassled by bureaucratic demands, and underappreciated, the response from the faculty was negative. A genuine conflict began to brew. Finally, the chairperson said, "Since keeping us involved in the university is my job, I feel really down when nobody supports what I'm doing. I need some feedback on what you think so I'm not just floundering around." Because he changed his goal statement from "Why don't you people work more?" to "I need support for what I'm doing," the conflict was reduced and productively managed.

Clear goals can be altered more easily than fuzzy goals. One group with which we consulted was embroiled in conflict over whether a certain program should receive the funding and staff support of their agency. The three staff members who had been charged with the responsibility for setting up a new program to aid recently unemployed families did not know whether the agency director wanted to support that particular new program or whether he wanted to demonstrate to the funding sources that the agency was committed to be responsive to families in general. When the director clarified that the specific program should serve an underserved population, the staff members altered their previous goals so that the new program would assist with community problems of child abuse. The change in staff goals was possible because the larger goals were clarified for them, along with their important role in reaching the goals.

Clear goals are reached more often than unclear goals. Having a map helps travelers reach a destination. Similarly, Raush et al. (1974) found that 66 percent of the conflicts in which the issue was clearly stated were successfully resolved, whereas only 18 percent of the conflicts in which the issue remained vague and nonspecific were resolved. A couple we know is considering where to move after college. If they decide on one option, "We will stay in the same city no matter what," they will have made a significantly different choice than if they choose the second option, "We will both get the best jobs we can." Those with shared individual and relational destinations are more likely to arrive at some desired point together. Clarifying goals has one risky outcome: it may make seriously incompatible goals apparent. They become apparent sooner or later, however. Additionally, when goals are "stated explicitly and directly there is control on escalation" (Rausch et al. 1974, 99). Unclear goals often promote overreaction from the other party, who misjudges the nature of the conflict. We are remarkably poor at second guessing the goals of our conflict partners.

Often people will have extra difficulty just because they assume that their goals cannot be attained—that the other will stand in their way. How many times have you planned and schemed for days, only to find that the other person was perfectly willing to give you what you wanted? A friend we know was miserable because her children would not give her any free time on the weekends. She began to believe they did not respect her needs. Finally she said in tears one Thursday night, "If I don't have some time alone, I'll go crazy." The teenagers were glad to make plans to give her time with no responsibilities. She simply never had asked. Clear goals are attained more often than unclear ones; as Isaiah writes, "Without vision, the people perish."

In conclusion, clarifying goals is a key step in conflict management. People assess the conflicts in which they participate by making decisions about which goals are worth pursuing. In common language, they get a "grasp" on the situation to decide how to proceed (Liska and Conkhite 1982). Clarifying goals helps in making decisions about how the conflict will proceed.

Goals Change over Time

We have discussed the importance of mutual involvement in setting goals and the advantages of identifying goals clearly. Now we turn to the dynamic nature of goal development as important for collaborative conflict. Goals, once "set," don't stay put, but shift and change over time, even after a conflict episode is supposedly finished. Additionally, multiple goals for interactions usually exist. People may hold different content and relationship goals, they may hold different short- and long-term goals, and they may disagree about which shared goals are most important and deserve the most energy. Take the following example:

How Much Is Too Much

Mr. Quentin, the program director at a hospital, is conducting the biannual review of employees. Ms. West, who has been public relations director at Metro Hospital for one year, is reading her review letter prior to the conversation.

Ms. West (to herself):   He wants me to show more initiative! I'd like to know how I can do that when he's made it clear that I need to check everything out with him first. I'll ask him about that.

In Mr. Quentin's Office:

Mr. Quentin: Ms. West, the one area I'd like you to give some attention to is showing more initiative. You see I've checked you the lowest in that regard.

Ms. West: I'm glad you are giving me the opportunity to change in that area. I have some ideas I'd like to try.

Mr. Quentin: That's great. Your job is to come up with some new ideas for keeping us first in the community.

At the next biannual review, Mr. Quentin placed Ms. West on probation for acting without the authority of the program director and the hospital administrator. Ms. West was appalled, thinking she was supposed to act with less "checking." Mr. Quentin, however, wanted her to initiate more new ideas so that he could take them to his boss, the administrator, and the administrator could decide which way to go in the public relations effort. No one clarified goals and now the conflict is structured overwhelmingly against Ms. West. The hospital may lose a talented employee if the parties cannot untangle the conflict over multiple, unshared, unclear goals.

Prospective Goals

Goals are often understood to be statements that people make publicly or privately ahead of a conflict. This prior view of goals is labeled as a *prospective* view by Hawes and Smith (1973). Most attention given to goal development in organization consultation, for example, as well as by teachers setting learning goals for students, takes this approach. Mager and Pipe (1972), in his popular manual on goal setting, gives the following useful suggestions:

1. Write down the goal using whatever words best describe the intent.

2. Write down the performances that would cause you to agree the goal has been achieved. . . .

3. Sort out the list, deleting duplications and unwanted entries on the list.

4. Then write a complete statement for each performance, describing the nature, quality, or amount you will consider acceptable.

5. Test the statements with the question, "If someone achieved or demonstrated each of these performances, would I be willing to say he has achieved the goal?" When you can answer yes, the analysis is finished.

All of the above procedures work well for figuring out what you want. For instance, a woman might say before an important personnel meeting, "I want that promotion more than Kathy does, so I'm going to do everything I can, including direct competition with her, to get it." This is a clear prospective goal. But we disagree with Mager that a statement of prospective goals ends the analysis.

Most couples in love do a fine job of setting out prospective goals for their relationship during the early stages of development. They make plans about careers, life style, children, family ties, and leisure. The process of making these goals together, working through conflicts over life style ("I want to live in a big city and he wants to live in a small town") set the patterns for the shape of the relationship. Couples often feel elated that they are able to work through conflicts so well, feeling that the really big decisions are made—their goals are clear. But couples, as well as business groups, families, departments, and housemates, get into trouble if they see prospective goal setting as the end of the process. Transactive goals are just as important.

Transactive Goals

Transactive goal development takes place during conflict episodes, rather than before or after. Even though you may have been absolutely certain that you were going to demand an assistant to carry out the new project your boss assigned to you, during a staff meeting in which the goals of the whole team are expressed, you may change your demand for an assistant. You may now say that you can do the work without an assistant for at least six months. What happened? Did you "back down?" Did the boss "win?" Did you have "no guts?" More likely, you became aware of the interdependent nature of your work team and decided to change your demand, given the needs of the entire group. You may have been given recognition for the difficulty of your job. Maybe your boss said in front of the group, "I'd like to give you an assistant, but I don't have the money in the budget and don't know where I can get it." Your conflict goals changed because of the communication transaction. Transactive goal development occurs in response to the specific issues of the conflict. Adaptability makes continuing interdependence possible:

> Adaptability is probably the most distinctive characteristic of life. In maintaining the independence and individuality of natural units, none of the great forces . . . are as successful as that alertness and adaptability to change which we designate as life—and the loss of which is death. . . . There are two roads to survival: fight and adaptation. And most often—adaptation is the more successful (Selye 1974, 57).

Recently, a school board member was trying to decide how to handle her strong opposition to closed, or "executive," sessions of the board while her colleagues on the board were in favor of them. She discussed the incipient conflict with friends ahead of time, rehearsing what she was going to do (prospective goals). When the next board meeting arrived, she found herself not giving her prearranged speech. She compromised and agreed with her colleagues that some closed meetings, in limited circumstances, were acceptable. This change is an example of transactive goal development.

The concept of transactive goals developed from our conviction that communication is *transactional*. To describe communication accurately, we must look at what happens when people are together, instead of adding together each separate person's experiences (Wilmot 1979; Laing, Phillipson, and Lee 1966). Relationships are interpenetrative, with each person influencing and being influenced by the other (Wilmot 1979). Saying that the board member in our example "was persuaded by" the other board members is simplistic. Neither did she "persuade" them to adopt her point of view. They all influenced each other, creating new, transactive goals as a function of the process of a democratically led board meeting.

You may have noticed that your goals change in conflicts as you get a chance to express your feelings, be heard, and talk through your opinions and wishes (while the other party does the same). If you are a person who says, "I don't know what I want until we get a chance to discuss it," you understand transactive goals. The following dialogue exemplifies the way new goals are advanced as a conflict progresses. Note that the two friends see themselves as interdependent and that they value their relationship as well as their solving the immediate problem of finding the lost object. In the dialogue, one woman calls another to request the return of some jewelry she has lent to her friend.

Verbal Communication	Goal Analysis
First phone call:	Amy's #1 prospective goal is to *get the pendant back from Janice.*
Amy: You know that silver star pendant I loaned you? I guess you didn't return it with the rest of the jewelry, because I can't find it.	
Janice: I don't have it. I remember that I didn't borrow it because I knew it was valuable to you. You must have misplaced it somewhere. But I'll look.	Janice's #1 prospective goal is to *convince Amy that she is not responsible for the disappearance of the necklace.* Incompatible with Amy's prospective goal.
Second phone call:	Amy maintains prospective goal #1. Escalates previous goal statement. Still an incompatible goal.
Amy: I still can't find it—I'm getting panicky. I'll hold while you go look. Please check everywhere it might be.	
Janice: You're upset about the necklace, and I don't know what I can do since I honestly don't think I have it. But what really concerns me is that you are upset at me. You mean a lot to me, and this hurts.	Transactive goal #2: *affirm the relationship in spite of the loss of the necklace.*
Amy: I know. I really don't want to put it all on you. I'm glad you understand, though. You know, John gave me that necklace.	Amy reaffirms transactive goal #2, making it mutual. She agrees to discuss, affirming the relationship as a new, additional goal.
Janice: Well, what can we do to get this solved? I feel awful.	Janice restates transactive goal #2. Offers transactive goal #3, *find the necklace together without damaging the relationship.*
Amy: I'll hang up and we'll both go look everywhere and then report back.	Amy advances transactive goal #4: *share the responsibility with a new plan of action.*
Janice: OK. And then we'll come up with something if we don't find it right away. Cross your fingers.	Janice accepts transactive goal #4, advances transactive goal #5: *we will keep working until we solve this problem.*

Retrospective Goals

Goals continue to change and grow even after the conflict episode has sub-sided. The retrospective explanation of goals means that people continue to make sense of their transactions long after they are "over." Toulmin (1958), writing on decision making, suggests that most people spend a large part of their time and energy justifying past decisions they have made. Argument assumes a retrospective quality, with people needing to explain to themselves and others why they made the choices they did. This process often happens with intimates who, for example, have an intense conflict over discipline of the children. Before they discuss the issue further, after the first triggering com-ment, they may say, "Let's decide what's best for the children, not just what fits our own upbringing" (prospective goal). During subsequent conflicts over specific instances of discipline, they discuss everything from how the individ-ual children react to whether Mom and Dad should support each other's choices, even if they don't agree. After they make a choice about how disci-pline is to be handled differently from the way it was in past episodes, Mom might say retrospectively, "I mainly wanted to see whether you would begin to share the discipline with me." Dad might say, "All along I was really trying to get you to see that you need to loosen up on the kids." Assuming that the couple came up with a wise agreement they can follow in future episodes, the retrospective sense making helps them to add to the definition of who they are and to make meaningful statements about the place of the conflict in their lives. Monday morning quarterbacking is important in ongoing relationships as well as in sports.

Since we do not know the size and implications of a conflict until we look back on it, goals serve an *explanatory* as well as a predictive function. Weick (1979) explains this sense-making process as the reverse from the usual way of looking at goals. He explains organizational behavior as "goal interpreted." People act in an orderly fashion, coordinating their behavior with each other, but with little notion of how this is accomplished until after the fact. Then they engage in retrospective meetings, conversations, paper writing, and speeches to explain why they did make what they did. "The organism or group enacts equivocal raw talk, the talk is viewed equivocally, sense is made of it, and this sense is then stored as knowledge. . . . The aim of each process has been to reduce equivocality and to get some idea of what has occurred" (Weick 1979, 134). Talking about "what happened" after an involving conflict is as important as talking about "what will happen" before a conflict episode. In these retrospective accountings, prospective goals for the next episode are for-mulated. Thus we learn from experience.

Retrospective sense making also serves the function of *face saving*. Visi-tors to the United States often comment on our lack of face-saving social rit-uals compared to those in Japan, China, and other countries. Brown and Levinson (1978) argue, on the basis of cross-cultural data, that helping one's fellow communicator to validate a positive social identity in interaction is recognized universally as socially necessary. Even if you have been involved in a competitive conflict and have "won," rubbing it in or gloating over the loser will only serve to alienate and enrage the person, perhaps driving him or her to devious actions in retaliation. If you can provide accurate and empathic ways to give respect to the *person,* even if you did not agree with the *position,* the person's "face" will be saved, and you lay the groundwork for collaboration in the future. This kind of retrospective analysis is equally important in compromise, accommodation, avoidance, and collaboration. Following are some comments that give the flavor of face-saving conversation:

> We looked very highly on you and your application. Our offer to Ms. Shepherd was based on her experience in our particular kind of operation. Even though you and I have been at odds for some time, now, over organization of the new program, I want you to know that your ideas are always sound and well organized. I just have different priorities.
>
> Mother to teenage daughter: I know you didn't want to cause us worry. You couldn't have known how upset we'd be that you were four hours late. But since you did not follow our agreement, we are grounding you for a week, as we said we would if the rule were not followed. I'm sure you understand that we have to know that such an important rule will be followed.

Content and Relationship Goals

All conflicts encapsulate both content and relational goals. Indeed, "every negotiator has two kinds of interests: in the substance and in the relationship" (Fisher and Ury 1981, 20). This is not to say that relationship goals are not "substantive." In fact, with long-term clients, spouses, partners, family members, and coworkers, the ongoing relationship is more important than any particular outcome (Fisher and Ury 1981). *Content* goals are those that participants or outside parties can separate from the particular relationship the parties have developed with each other. They are often treated as "objective" items, such as salary figures, where to have dinner, and other such matters. *Relationship* goals refer to goals that make sense in the context of the unique relationship the parties have developed. Relationship goals have to do with who the parties are to each other, how they are supposed to interpret communication from each other, the emotional tone of their exchanges, and the issue of how interdependent they are to be with one another.

Content and relationship goals reciprocally influence each other. People figure out what they want as a result of and during recurring episodes. When, for example, you are unable to achieve your goals because of interference from the other party, your goals may well change from content to relational. When content goals are blocked, one wants to injure the other party. The desire to strike back at the other sometimes happens when one is deflected from the original content goal. We may begin conflicts with content goals, and when those are blocked, we substitute a desire to harm the other conflict party (Thomas 1976). Goal substitutions such as these reinforce the notion that relationship definitions continually change during our transactions (Wilmot 1980).

One of the difficult tasks of conflict management is the separation of content and relationship goals to the point that they may be negotiated. One truism we have learned from experience and from reading such family therapists as Haley (1963), Minuchin (1972), and Satir (1967) is that *a repetitive conflict that goes over and over the same content issues is a relational conflict masquerading as a content conflict.* If the relationship issues are not addressed, parties have no choice except to use content to say what they want. In fact, the content conflict may become symbolic of the whole relationship, since the relationship is not being overtly addressed. The following example will give an idea of how this interaction occurs:

I'm Right/Are Not/Am Too!

Duane and Kathy are going to a movie. Duane is driving, and they both notice a red car passing them.

Duane: That's a Datsun, like the kind I was telling you about.

Kathy: No, I think it was a Toyota. But it's pretty.

Duane: No, it was a DATSUN!

They argue back and forth about the rightness of their claims. Neither is a car expert, but both are adamant, using sarcasm and biting humor.

Kathy: Well, you may be right, but I still think it was a Toyota.

Duane: Look, I know I'm right!

Kathy: You never think I know anything!

Duane: You don't know anything about cars. Blow it off . . . it's not important.

Kathy sits silently for ten minutes

The couple will continue to argue about identifying cars, but both have stated the relationship concern. Kathy feels she is not given credit as a knowledgeable person. Duane states that he needs to be right on things he knows more about. The couple appears to be negotiating about who has pre-eminence in certain areas of expertise. They haven't worked out how to "call off the conflict," or how to ask for more respect from each other. They are likely to find yet another content issue to fight over unless the relationship is addressed directly. Two openings that might start them off more productively are—

> **Duane:**   I get bothered when you challenge me about something I know a lot about. I start thinking you don't think I'm very smart.
>
> Or
>
> **Kathy:**   Duane, I'm not that interested in Toyotas or Datsuns, either. But I've been thinking that you get the last word on most topics we discuss. It makes me not want to ever give in—even if I know I'm wrong.

To further complicate conflict, people not only confuse content and relationship issues, they *translate* the same event into their own meaning (Wilmot 1979). A conflict is interpreted differently by each participant. Just as Russians have no success in translating English unless they speak the language and vice versa, conflict parties must learn the language of their conflict partners. For example, a father and daughter fight many evenings when the daughter comes home from school and he arrives from work. Mother gets pulled into playing peacemaker, trying to get the daughter to provoke the father less, and convincing father to be more understanding of daughter's needs. The trigger event is usually something like this:

> Daughter scatters books, shoes and lunchbox in the living room while she gets a snack. Father comes home an hour later, sees the mess and explodes. Daughter says, "I forgot," and Father says "You ALWAYS forget."
>
> A simple translation is:
>
> *Content Messages:* "I forgot/You always forget."
>
> *Daughter's Translation*   *Father's Translation*
> It's not important. I wish he'd pay attention to something important to me.   She doesn't listen. She is getting too independent to care what I think.

A revealing exercise in conflict management is to have conflict parties share their relational translations of the content issues. Many times, such clarification of meanings changes the prospective goals the parties have been defending, and they are able to move in a more collaborative direction.

All too often, high-power parties tend to focus on content only. Failure to give attention to both content and relationship goals may be due to a lack of skill or can show hostility, lack of caring, or even desire to compete by ignoring the relational implications of a conflict by focusing exclusively on the content. This devalues the other person and his or her concerns. The most powerful group member usually wins by structuring the conflict and ignoring troubling relational issues from lower-power people. Content discussion is simpler and requires less investment in the other person. Low-power members may wish to bring in relational goals as a power-balancing mechanism. If they can get the higher-power person to agree that relational goals are important, they enlarge the conflict, which is to their advantage. If high-power persons can restrict the issues to content only, they have an advantageous structure, assuming that the object is to win instead of to collaborate.

Building Collaborative Goals

Thus far, we have suggested that mutual participation in goal setting, open goal clarification, and attention to content and relationship analyses are crucial aspects of managing the incompatible goals that define interpersonal conflict. Now we will present four principles for building collaborative goals, which aid in the productive management of conflict. These four principles of collaboration, developed by Fisher and Ury (1981), can be remembered by the key words, *People, Interests, Options,* and *Criteria.* Fisher and Ury term this process "negotiation on the merits" or "principled negotiation."

People: Separate the People from the Problem

The participants should come to see themselves as working side by side on a problem, attacking the problem instead of each other. The overarching process goal is "We, working together, can solve this problem that is confronting us." Part of the self-interest of conflict parties is preserving a workable relationship; focusing on the problem instead of the other people assists in relational maintenance. The problem is faced as one would face an enemy, working cooperatively with one's conflict partner to solve the problem. An example would be a divorcing couple who, instead of asking, "What is wrong with my former spouse?" would ask, "What can we, working together, create that will be in the best interests of the children?"

Relational preservation becomes a superordinate goal, as the classic Sherif and Sherif (1956) study demonstrated. In that case, groups of boys were placed in situations with conflict of interests. The researchers introduced a common enemy, thus stimulating the two groups to work together, which reduced their intergroup hostility. For persons in interpersonal conflicts, long-term relational or content goals can become superordinate goals that reduce conflict over short-term goals but only if you separate the people from the problem.

Interests: Focus on Interests, Not Positions

At the Harvard Negotiation Project, researchers found that when people stated their goals in terms of positions that had to be defended, they were less able to produce wise agreements. The more you clarify your position and defend yourself, the more committed you become to the position. Arguing over positions endangers ongoing relationships, since the conflict often becomes a contest of wills. They found that "whether a negotiation concerns a contract, a family quarrel, or a peace settlement among nations, people routinely engage in positional bargaining. Each side takes a position, argues for it, and makes concessions to reach a compromise (Fisher & Ury 1981, p. 3).

Focusing on interests, not positions, was what the librarian did in the earlier example cited in this chapter. Rather than starting with "Do you want the window closed or open?" (a position), the librarian searched for each party's underlying interest. Interests underly the positions, and many possible positions can be derived from one's interests. But a position is a specific solution to an interest; if you start with the position, you will overlook many creative options for meeting the interests. Interests are more diffuse than positions and sometimes are difficult to identify, but they keep the process of collaboration in motion when you focus on them.

Options: Generate a Variety of Possibilities before Deciding What to Do

Trying to resolve a conflict in the face of an adversary narrows one's vision. Pressure reduces creative thinking at the very time when creativity is most needed. Searching for the one right solution may be futile. You can get around this problem by setting up time to focus on new solutions instead of defending your prospective goals endlessly. Goal setting continues throughout the period of active conflict management, and afterward as well. A good decision is one that springs from the many options generated from concerned conflict parties.

Criteria: Insist That the Result Be Based on Some Objective Standard

One person's will is not enough to justify a conflict solution. Some principle of fairness or judgment should be used. One can develop objective criteria by using fair procedures and/or fair standards. Fair procedures can be used in many cases. In the classic situation of two people dividing a piece of cherry pie, one gets to cut the piece and then the other gets first choice; the procedures guarantee fairness. Or in the case of a marital couple in divorce mediation, they can decide on the specifics of custody, visitation, and child support before they decide which party will have custody.

Fair standards can be based on the following:

market value	costs
precedent	what a court would decide
scientific judgment	moral standards
professional standards	equal treatment
efficiency	reciprocity

(Fisher and Ury 1981, 89)

You may wonder how a private individual may use the four principles of collaboration. They may be informally adopted and used even in one-on-one conflicts that arise. More formal ways of using these principles as a third party will be discussed in chapter 8. The following are some statements that you might use when you are in conflict and are talking about your perceptions of incompatible goals.

Collaborative Principle	Sample Statement
People	"This is a problem you and I haven't had to face before. I'm sure we can work it out."
Interests	"What is it that you are most hoping for?"
	or
	"Let's figure out where we agree, and that will give us a base to work from."
Options	"I'd like to postpone making a decision about filing a grievance until our next meeting. Today I want to explore all the options that are available to us in addition to filing a grievance. Is that all right with you?"
Criteria	"Darling, I can't be satisfied with getting my way if you're miserable. We agreed that neither of us would have to be miserable. Let's keep talking about it—we've got to think of something better."

Action Planning

Action planning provides the mechanism for changing behavior based on problem-solving sessions in which people reach agreements. All too often, conflict parties discover to their relief that they are not totally opposed to each other; they feel closer as a result of collaboration, but they fail to plan for how to make the agreements reached in the conflict management session happen. For instance, a group of roommates held a session in which they agreed that Laura's boyfriend would stay over "less" than he had been, since the other two roommates felt they did not have enough privacy. At the end of the year, the three women were no longer on speaking terms. Laura felt misunderstood and the other two roommates felt betrayed. They failed to set up a plan for how to act on their agreement of "less staying over." The following guidelines for planning may help you avoid such problems.

Short-term goals can be separated from long-term goals. Setting up a timeline of *who* is to do *what* by *when* with *what effect* on others and with what *evaluation* clarifies exactly what short-term goals lead to completing the long-term goal. In a weekend retreat of city council members who met to resolve some of their ongoing conflicts, the need for action planning emerged.

Throughout the course of the weekend, they made over a hundred decisions, which they wrote on charts. A year later, in reviewing the accomplishment of the long-term goals, only a few of the hundred goals had been accomplished. They were the ones that were subdivided into short-term goals and translated into action plans. Short-term goals are series of steps that lead a group to the desired end state. They provide a "how to" blueprint for reaching long-term goals.

Do-able goals are specific. When goals are do-able (Phillips and Metzger 1976), they are in the realm of the possible and can be checked. "I want to improve" might become a do-able goal, but it is not now specific enough to count as a helpful solution to a conflict. Terms used in intimate relations are often more ephemeral than terms used in business and public settings. A corporate vice-president could not get away with telling the president, "I'll try the best I can to remember to turn the reports in on time," but intimates make vague promises to each other frequently. Specificity helps the parties to the agreement feel satisifed that the agreement has been accomplished. Stuart (1980) presents a highly specific way for intimate couples to begin changing by focusing on behavior they are willing to carry out in a series of "caring days" rather than amorphous promises such as "I'll try to show more love."

Constructive goal statements are oriented toward the present and future, not toward the past. The language of change—desired change in the future—is used instead of the language of blame for past misdeeds. A department head might say, "I want our program group to increase services to clients without increasing hours worked by our counselor" instead of "We have got to be more efficient than we were last year." Goals that begin with "we should" or, worse yet, "you should" are not specific and are oriented toward the past. They often serve as a dodge of real change. Mager and Pipe's (1970) book *You Really Oughta Wanta* illustrates the futility of managers', parents', teachers', and administrators' thinking that subordinates "oughta wanta" achieve goals that the higher-ups set without collaboration. Statements designed to produce guilt in others usually lead to avoidance instead of positive action. Take as your motto, "If they have to be reminded of agreed-upon goals, they probably haven't really agreed."

Out of date goals need revising. Couples often give halfhearted energy to early goals developed when they first fell in love instead of developing changing goals. They try to find new ways to make these old goals work instead of revising the goals. For instance, one couple moved around a lot when they were first married, and they developed a "you and me against the world" philosophy, which was quite appropriate for the constant situation of being new in town. Later, as their careers matured and they became more settled, they felt that something was wrong with their relationship since they did not have "goals" anymore.

Goals should be developed in collaboration with the other party. An overriding goal of the productive conflict management process is to remain committed to the process of doing conflict constructively. The particular content can be transcended by adhering to a collaborative process. Fisher and Ury (1981) in their excellent book *Getting to Yes* remind conflict managers that goal setting begins with the participation of all conflict parties. "Give them a stake in the outcome by making sure they participate in the process" (p. 27). For collaborators, "the process *is* the product" (Fisher and Ury 1981, 29).

We discussed earlier that the goal of any conflict is to (1) reach agreement and (2) enhance the relationship for future conflict management. The outcome of constructive conflict should be wise agreements if such agreements are possible. Wise agreements are fair and durable and take the interests of all parties into account (Fisher and Ury 1981, 4). An example of the struggle for wise agreements occurs when a couple with children goes to court for a divorce. The agreement should be representative of both sides, should be fair to all parties including the children, should keep the couple out of court in the future, and should set up care for the children if they are too young to care for themselves. The process should be efficient, involve all parties' interests, and improve or at least not damage the relationship between the parties (Fisher and Ury 1981, 4).

When parties to conflicts are given the opportunity to work together by giving careful attention to clarifying goals, sharing power, trying alternate styles, and specifying what the conflict is and is not about, destructive conflicts subside. Collaboration is a high-energy alternative to avoidance, violence, coercion, frustration, despair, and other forms of destructiveness. You may feel that the view of collaboration presented thus far is overly altruistic. We agree with Selye (1974), however, who views altruism as a kind of collective selfishness that helps the community ". . . by making another person wish that we prosper because of what we have done—and hence, are likely to do for (him) again—then we elicit goodwill" (p. 53). Collaboration is not always possible, but when it is, destructive conflict is transformed into constructive problem solving.

Summary

In this chapter we have presented a comprehensive explanation of the nature of goals in conflict management and offered some practical ways to clarify goals. Clarifying goals is much more than a preliminary step in conflict management since goals are not only prospective, but also transactive, due to the process of conflict. They are, additionally, retrospective, serving the function of making sense out of episodes after the fact. Goals may be further subdivided into content and relationship goals embedded in all conflicts. General principles of collaboration were offered, along with suggestions for action planning so conflict participants may be assured that their hard-won decisions can be carried forward.

5   Conflict Tactics

The Process of Strategizing

Terry: Well, I just got passed over for promotion. My argument with Jack really came back to haunt me.

Lance: Why don't you just lie low for awhile and quit tangling with the boss in public and they'll forget the whole episode—next time you'll get the promotion.

Terry: Yeh—I'll just let it blow over. But next year if a promotion comes up, I won't make the same mistake. A little fence mending with the boss will go a long way.

Lance and Terry are both strategizing in response to Terry's lack of promotion. A strategic choice in a conflict is a "planned method of conducting operations" (Phillips and Metzger 1976, 134). In a conflict, people make strategic plans in order to accomplish their goals.

Most everyday social interactions are conducted without strategizing over each choice that is made. For example, when you see someone you know on the street, you automatically say "Hi" and move on past. Most of us do not preplan all our words and actions; we act spontaneously and then reflect retrospectively on the event. In fact, "*Most* behavior may be enacted without paying attention to it . . . (Langer 1978, 38). However, when we are faced with a novel situation, we cannot go on "automatic pilot" or proceed to operate in a state of mindlessness. Baxter and Philpott (1983) have identified three distinct types of strategizing: (1) preplanned strategizing in which you plan your messages in advance of the situation, (2) emergent strategizing in which you are consciously aware during interaction of what you are doing and its effect, and (3) retrospective strategizing, or reflecting back on an exchange, examining what was said and its effects. Baxter and Philpott (1983) then studied the conditions that promote preplanned strategizing and emergent strategizing. Basically, people strategize more when they expect or experience more interaction difficulty in an important conversation. For instance, Brent is a student in an introductory college course. He received a "D" instead of the "C" he expected in a large mass lecture section. He has never talked personally with the professor and wants to try to get the grade altered. Brent will probably spend some time strategizing and deciding whether to (1) call the professor at home, (2) see the professor during office hours, or (3) see the professor at the beginning of next quarter. Brent decides to see the professor during his office hours to argue that the cutoff point for a "C" was too stringent and that his hard work should be rewarded with a C. Upon meeting the professor, just as Brent is getting ready to state his case, the professor interrupts him saying, "I hope you realize that the cutoff for grades is not changeable in a large class like this." Brent, realizing that his preplanned strategizing will not be helpful, decides to ask if there has been an arithmetic error in computing his final score. Happily, Brent's emergent strategy works to his favor and his grade is changed from a D to a C.

Brent's strategizing, both preplanned and emergent, illustrates that important and difficult communication events promote strategizing. In these types of situations, strategizing is a natural response. While not all conflict participants engage in strategic thought when facing problematic encounters with the other party, most people do strategize over courses of action they might take.

As discussed in the preceding chapter, people's *goals* in conflict are prospective, transactive, and retrospective. Goal development occurs whether or not the conflict is particularly difficult. *Strategizing,* whether preplanned, emergent, or retrospective, appears to be connected to a party's perception of how difficult the conflict is.

The word "strategy" carries negative meanings for many people. One way to damage someone's credibility is to call him or her "strategic" (Gibb 1961). People who are given that label are seen as manipulative, aloof, uncaring, and illegitimately powerful. "Strategies," however, can be described as simply a case of planning. Conflict participants strategize in order to accomplish their goals. Planning a course of action is a natural and necessary human activity, central to most conflict situations. People often strategize for positive ends and for mutual gains, as well as to "gain an edge" on the other party in the conflict. For instance, you can preplan to de-escalate or reduce a conflict and open yourself up to influence from the other party. The process of strategizing can be used for mutual gain as well as for competitive advantage. Conflicts tend to prompt the players to "figure out" what might work to accomplish their goals, and their goals might well be helpful to the other party as well.

The Choice to Avoid or Engage

In each conflict, the basic choice for each party is whether to avoid the conflict or engage one another in the emerging conflict issues. You face this choice repeatedly throughout a conflict; it is so fundamental that parties often get stuck in cycles of *metaconflict*—conflicting over whether they will engage one another in the conflict. The following romantic couple is struggling over diverse levels of recognition of the emerging conflict.

He: There is something bothering me.

She: I'm busy.

He: I'm upset about what you said about me at the party.

She: All you do is pick on me. Leave me alone!

He: Well, you do things that bug me!!

She: I'm going for a walk. See you later.

This couple will probably replay these exchanges at other times, too. He wants to engage the conflict and she wants to avoid it. Each time an issue surfaces, they will have to reach agreement on avoidance/engagement, or else this metaconflict will subsume and exacerbate any other emerging issues. Until they manage their metaconflict on avoidance/engagement, they will be unable to manage their other conflicts. Their fundamental issue is "How much conflict am I willing to risk to get what I want?" (Stuart 1980, 295). Of course, on the next conflict about a different topic, she may be pushing for engagement and he may avoid.

If avoidance or engagement is the fundamental issue, which is the best for use in conflict? Read the four statements below and put a check mark by the one that is the most accurate:

1. Avoidance of conflict leads to unhappy marriages and work relationships—it just keeps important issues buried.

2. Avoidance of unnecessary conflict helps promote harmony and keeps people from getting involved in unnecessary upsets.

3. The only way to really manage conflict is to work through it by engaging the other person.

4. Engagement of conflict leads to escalatory spirals and hurt for all parties.

If you are able to agree more with one of these statements than with the other, you have a clear preference for engaging or avoiding conflicts. While it would be easy to exhort about our own personal preferences, the presence of conflict per se does not signal relationship distress, nor does the absence of conflict indicate a lack of stress (Stuart 1980). Similarly, avoidance can mean that there is a lot of unexpressed discord, or that it is a functional relationship (Raush et al 1974).

Both avoidance and engagement can be workable options in different circumstances. In the case cited above, her avoidance may prompt him to examine his reaction, decide that he was too sensitive, and back off to reduce the conflict. Or her avoidance may signal him that she does not care for his feelings, so he should start exiting from the relationship. Avoidance and lack of overt conflict may foretell that the participants are unable to reach accommodation, that they cannot work through problem areas, and that they will gradually drift apart.

Avoidance can lead to a stressful relationship with considerable unexpressed discord; it can preclude needed change in a relationship (Raush et al. 1974), leading to less understanding and agreement (Knudson, Sommers, and Golding 1980). Avoidance is paradoxical. It is designed to protect the self and other from discord, yet the avoidance may lead to lack of clarity and set the stage for later uncontrollable conflict (Bullis 1983).

Avoidance can also be productive for a relationship. If the issue or relationship is not important to you, avoidance can conserve energy that would be expended needlessly. For example, we cannot invest equally in all relationships. Someone may attempt to engage in a conflict that is of trivial importance to you, so your best choice is avoidance (Thomas 1976). Avoidance serves as a defense against engagement or confrontation with the partner (Raush et al. 1976, 65). When avoidance occurs within a bond of mutual affection, the spouses will describe their marriage as happy (Raush et al. 1974). Therefore, avoidance of a conflict is not necessarily counterproductive. . . . It can be used positively.

Engagement is not always a panacea for a conflict either. The following coworkers are past the metaconflict stage, and both are fully engaged in the conflict.

Steve: Hey Stuart, get the lead out!

Stuart: Get off my back!

Steve: You are always slow. You hold up the entire crew.

Stuart: It's your fault. You keep shoving more at me than any sane man could handle.

Steve: The last worker in your job didn't have any problems.

Stuart: Yeh, and he isn't here is he? If you think it is so easy, do it yourself!

The escalatory engagement could go on and on, with each complaint provoking a counter complaint. Gottman (1982) notes that an endless recycling of cross-complaining characterizes unhappy marriages; the partners engage endlessly without reconciliation.

Engagement can begin the process of constructive management, depending on how it is enacted. It can bring with it an increased understanding of the other party (Knudson, Sommers, and Goldberg 1980), and promote creative solutions to previous stalemates (Fisher and Ury 1981). As Augsburger says, "It is not the conflicts that need to concern us, but how the conflicts are handled" (1981, 6). In the next section, we examine specific moves that conflict participants use to handle their conflicts.

Tactical Options

Endless possibilities exist for organizing different conflict tactics—the specific choices that the parties make in a conflict. For example, Bowers (1974) lists the conflict moves that occur between institutions and their clients. Karrass (1974) provides a lengthy list of tactics, as did the first edition of this book. Brown and Levinson (1978) organize tactics according to whether they support or attack the other person's presentation of "face" or self. Kipnis (1976) divides tactics into accommodation, authoritarianism, dependency, last-resort, and give-up. Marwell and Schmidt (1967) examined dimensions of compliance-gaining behavior. Their list of sixteen persuasive attempts has received considerable research attention (Miller et al. 1977; Sillars 1980; Cody and McLaughlin 1980; Roloff and Barnicott 1978; Cody, McLaughlin and Schneider 1981; Lustig and King 1980). Unfortunately, the research and theorizing is limited to situations in which a "source" tries to persuade a "target." Such one-way, nonprocess views fail to examine the mutual influence that conflict parties have on one another. As Bullis (1983) concludes, this research does not apply directly to conflict because of (1) the relationship between the parties and (2) the nature of the goals involved. In a conflict, *both* parties have goals that face interference, and the parties are mutually dependent on one another.

Recent work has clarified the basic dimensions underlying types of conflict tactics. Recall for a moment the conflict styles treated in chapter two. The work of Putnam and Wilson (1982) concludes that tactical choices (or styles if they are used repeatedly) are clustered into (1) *nonconfrontation* (avoiding, withdrawing, and indirectness); (2) *solution-oriented* choices (behaviors aimed at finding a solution, integrating needs of both parties); and (3) *control* (arguing, taking control of interaction). Similar dimensions have emerged from the work of Falbo (1977), Raush et al. (1974), Walton and McKersie (1965), Ross and DeWine (1982); Cupach (1980), Roloff (1976), and Sillars, Coletti, Parry, and Rogers (1982). The list of tactics that follows is from the work of Sillars et al. (1982) that coded behavior arising during conflicts between roommates. As we mentioned above, the basic choice faced in each conflict is between avoidance and engagement. The tactical types are (1) *avoidance* and two types of engagement: (2) *competitive* (distributive) and (3) *collaborative* (integrative).

Avoidance Tactics

Avoidance acts are those that "minimize explicit discussion of conflicts" (Sillars et al. 1982, 85). They are one of the most common ways to cope with conflict. Table 5.1 lists some sample tactics that are used to avoid conflicts.

Table 5.1.   Avoidance Tactics

Simple denial	Unelaborated statements that deny that a conflict is present
Extended denial	Denial statements that elaborate on the basis of the denial
Underresponsiveness	Failure to acknowledge or deny the presence of a conflict following a statement or inquiry about the conflict by the partner
Topic shifting	Statements that terminate discussion of a conflict issue before the discussion has reached a natural culmination
Topic avoidance	Statements that terminate discussion of a conflict issue before an opinion has been expressed
Abstractness	Abstract principles, generalizations, and hypothetical statements that supplant discussion of concrete individuals and events related to conflict.
Semantic focus:	Statements about the meaning of words or the appropriateness of labels that supplant discussion of conflict
Process focus:	Procedural statements that supplant discussion of conflict
Joking	Nonhostile joking that supplants serious discussion of conflict
Ambivalence	Shifting or contradictory statements about the presence of conflict
Pessimism	Pessimistic statements about conflict that minimize the discussion of conflict issues

Published by permission of Transaction, Inc. from HUMAN COMMUNICATION RESEARCH Vol. 9, No. 1 pp 85–86. Copyright © 1982.

We have all probably experienced the utter frustration of having another person with whom we have a conflict deny that conflict might be occurring. This sensation is much like trying to fight a cloud—nothing we can say makes any difference. Refusal to recognize the existence of a conflict is sometimes a productive, power-shifting ploy for persons in high-power positions who would have to give up some of their autonomy to make decisions if they entered the negotiation process. Often, however, the nonrecognition of conflict is a painful, disconfirming experience. When one person is unsure of his or her ability to handle conflict in touchy, important areas, the chosen tactic may be nonrecognition, which may be better than having to face the issue and use skills of communication with which the threatened party does not feel comfortable. One of us witnessed a couple at dinner who were caught in this regressive communication spiral. (Wilmot 1979). The wife was upset and tense. She appeared to be near tears, answering in monosyllables and looking down at her plate. The husband was seemingly unaware of her distress as he joked and talked to other guests. He made a slightly cutting remark about the wife, and she burst into tears and became embarrassed since company was present. The husband shrugged and said, "I didn't know she was in a bad mood." The wife had been trying to cue the husband that something was wrong, but because of their particular relational pattern, he needed *not to see* what was happening. In his desire to avoid a conflict, a larger one was created.

Avoidance can also be used by people who perceive themselves to be in a low-power position. Sometimes this takes the form of the person's merely refusing to engage the other or leaving the scene for fear of losing even more power. But often avoidance by a low-power person takes the form of what Brockriede (1972) calls "seduction." The low-power person using seduction tries to charm or trick the other conflict party into going along with what he or she desires. Argument tactics from classical reasoning that support this avoidance strategy are such tactics as "ignoring the question, begging the question, the red-herring appeal, and appeals to ignorance or to prejudice" (Brockriede 1972, 4). The clash between issues is not direct; the issues are circumvented in what sometimes turns out·to be a deceptive, charming, or even "cutesy" way. It is not important to the seducer to appeal to the other party's sense of free choice. She or he wants what is wanted, no matter what, but is not willing (or perhaps able) to ask for it directly.

For instance, Liz recently asked friends of hers to help her find a job for the summer. She appeared very weak, took little initiative, and became stuck in a low-energy period in her life. She dropped in on her friends often, politely asking for "any suggestions" they might have for finding a job but was evasive and confused when friends suggested that she needed help from an employment service. It appeared that she was trying to "seduce" her friends into taking responsibility for her but needed, for her own self-concept's sake, to avoid any direct clash over the issues her friends found important. Finally, her choice of the avoidance strategy gained her great disservice because her friends got tired of trying to help her. So they started avoiding her.

You will note that all of the avoidance tactics serve the function of refusing to engage the conflict. We should note, however, that *postponement* of a conflict may not be avoidance, but rather temporary avoidance with a promise to engage in the future. For example, Bach and Wyden, in *The Intimate Enemy* (1968), suggest that setting a time for a later conflict is a productive tactic. They suggest "fighting by appointment." We will give two examples of a conflict—the first using avoidance and the second using postponement.

Gloria is upset. She wants to talk to her husband Sam late at night. Sam has an appointment at eight o'clock in the morning.

Gloria: I am so upset that I can't sleep. What ever possessed you to talk about our summer plans to the Carters at the party? You know we've been trying to get free of doing things with them. You said last week. . . .

Sam: Can't we talk about this in the morning?

Gloria: It's fine for you to say that. You don't have to deal with Sandra when she calls tomorrow to decide where we'll take our families for a joint vacation. *I* have to talk to her and tell her we changed our minds.

Sam: I'm sorry I brought it up. But I'm sleepy, and I don't want to talk about it.

At this point, the avoidance tactic Sam is using—"Maybe if I close my eyes all this hassle will go away"—is certainly not productive. His twin goals—(1) to get some sleep and (2) to avoid further antagonizing his wife—are not likely to be met. By this time Gloria is probably angry not only about his lack of discretion at the party but, also about his refusal to talk to her about it. An example of a productive postponement tactic follows.

Sam: Gloria, I know you're upset. I also feel foolish. But I am exhausted, and I really don't want to deal with all the issues now. When Sandra calls tomorrow, tell her we haven't had a chance to talk yet and you'll call her back. Then when I come home from work tomorrow, we'll discuss the whole thing.

Gloria: You always say that, and it never gets talked about.

Sam: This time it will. We'll sit down before dinner, banish the kids, and the two of us will talk. I know you're upset.

Gloria: OK, if we really will. I know it's hard to know what to say in public like that. They presume so much. . . .

Postponement as a tactic works best when several conditions are present. First of all, emotional content of the conflict needs to be acknowledged while referring other issues to a later time. Sam said, "I know you're upset," acknowledging the depth of Gloria's feelings. She would not have been likely to go along with the postponement if he had said, "It's stupid for you to be upset. We'll work it out later." After the emotional content is acknowledged, all parties have to agree on a time that is soon and realistic. If Sam had said, "We'll talk about it sometime soon," that would not have been precise enough. The other party has to believe that the postponer really means to bring up the issue later. Postponement does not work well as a tactic if the other people involved think they are being put off, never to return to the issue. Statements such as a vague "we'll have to work on that sometime" or "let's all try harder to get along" are often giveaways that the person wants avoidance rather than genuine postponement.

Besides postponement, many other avoidance tactics are common. Following are some further descriptions and dialogue examples of avoidance tactics from table 5.1:

Underresponsiveness: You approach your supervisor and say, "Joan, we have a problem with the new secretary." Joan replies, "Nothing you can't handle, I'm sure."

Abstractness: "I don't think people would go for that," or "Don't you find it annoying when people don't follow through?" or "Things always work out eventually."

Semantic Focus: A small group in a college class worked on a project outside of class. One member volunteered to find a committee for the class group to observe. Dolores confronted Randy after he gave repeated excuses for not having done so:

"You said you'd find us a group to observe. What's going on?"

Randy replied; "*A* group—I said I'd find *a* group. I did. It's not my fault it didn't work out."

Pessimism: "Oh no. Are we going around this issue again? We've been over it a dozen times, and we never come up with anything."

Engagement Tactics

Two clusters of tactics help people engage rather than avoid. One group of tactics is often labeled "distributive" (Walton and McKersie 1965; Sillars et al. 1982). These are competitive, individually oriented tactics that are forms of coercion and control. We will discuss these tactics under the label of "competitive" tactics.

The second form of engagement tactics are "integrative" tactics (Walton and McKersie 1965). These are collaborative tactics that involve cooperative attempts to mutually manage the conflict. We will label them as "collaborative."

Competitive Tactics

Competitive tactics are "verbally competitive or individualistic behavior" (Sillars et al. 1982, 83). These tactics focus on a win-lose orientation and often reflect a belief that what one person gets, the other loses (Thomas 1976). As a result, the party using competitive tactics will try to "one-up" the other party to gain an advantage (Rogers and Farace 1975). Table 5.2 displays the competitive acts identified by Sillars and coauthors.

With these tactics the competer pushes for self-interest, often at the expense of the other. These competitive tactics are so commonplace that many people see them as synonymous with conflict. If you saw two business partners calling one another names, finding fault with each other, and acting in forcing or controlling ways, you would conclude that a conflict is present. At their core, all these tactics involve pressuring the *other* person to change; all the competitive tactics are reflective of that assumption.

Table 5.2.   Competitive Tactics

Faulting	Statements that directly criticize the personal characteristics of the partner
Rejection	Statements in response to the partner's previous statement that indicate personal antagonism toward the partner as well as disagreement
Hostile questioning	Directive or leading questions that fault the partner
Hostile joking	Joking or teasing that faults the partner
Presumptive attribution	Statements that attribute thoughts, feelings, intentions, or motivations to the partner that the partner does not acknowledge
Avoiding responsibility	Statements that minimize or deny personal responsibility for conflict
Prescription	Requests, demands, arguments, threats, or other prescriptive statements that seek a specified change in the partner's behavior in order to resolve a conflict
* Violence	Use of force to ensure one's will against the other

*Violence does not appear in the original list and is discussed below.

Since the tactics in table 5.2 were gathered from roommates discussing their conflicts, it is not surprising that physical violence did not appear. But physical violence does happen in some conflicts and should be added to this list of tactics. Physical violence is the most extreme form of a one-sided competitive tactic. When violence is used in a conflict, it is clear that the stronger party is neither avoiding nor cooperating—he or she is simply forcing his or her will on the other.

Another form of extreme competition is provided by Brockriede's (1972) characterization of a certain kind of arguer as a "rapist." In the "rapist" style (this metaphor is not meant to imply just sexual behavior but all kinds of communication behavior), participants "function through power, through an ability to apply psychic and physical sanctions, through rewards and especially punishments, and through commands and threats" (Brockriede 1972, 2). The conflict or argument is often escalated, since participants are interested in coercion instead of gaining assent as a result of a carefully reasoned argument. The intent of those using the rapist style is to manipulate and violate the personhood of the "victims" or parties in the conflict.

In some situations, the structure of the conflict is set up for the participants to encourage the escalation/rapist strategy. In the courtroom, legislative hearings, political debates, and forensic tournaments (Brockriede 1972, 3), the structure of the conflict encourages the coercion, or rapist, strategy.

When one person has chosen, however tacitly, the rapist definition of a conflict strategy, one of the parties functions as a victim, even though most people would say they most certainly do not want to be victimized. Often, the person who feels out of power and victimized escalates to a point, then gives up, thinking, "There's nothing I can do to win anyway." In effect, the participants have cooperated in the escalation direction. Once we saw a very angry person try to take over the microphone and the floor in a church convention. He shouted loudly, disrupted the proceedings, and was finally given five minutes to state his case. He did so, supporting with vehemence the pullout of his church group from a large national group, which he perceived as being too liberal. He chose the rapist style to escalate the direction of the conflict—soon he and the chairman were yelling back and forth at each other, and tensions were rising. Finally, the man threw the microphone down and stormed out, yelling, "I couldn't even get a hearing." Then he held a news conference out in the foyer, denouncing the leadership of the group. Although the man chose to become an "innocent victim" of the power group, he also strategically escalated so he would have a hearing in the local press. It was to his advantage to be perceived as the victim after escalating.

"Prescription" tactics include demands, arguments, and threats—all attempts to change the other party. Threats are one of the most basic devices used in conflict (Hocker, 1974) and are worthy of more extended discussion.

	Source Controls The Outcome	Source Does Not Control The Outcome
Negative Sanction	Threat	Warning
Positive Sanction	Promise	Recommendation[1]

Figure 5.1. Tactical devices related to threats.

Tedeschi (1970, 1972) has outlined the distinctions between threats, promises, warnings, and mendations. Figure 5.1 shows how the devices are related to one another.

If the source (the other party) is in a position to control the outcome you will experience, the application of a negative sanction is a threat. For instance, the parent who says, "Clean up your plate or I'll spank you," the employer who cajoles, "Get with the program and work harder or you will be laid off," and the lover who shouts, "If you do that once more, I'll leave and never come back," are all in the position to invoke the negative sanction they control. Warnings, however, are used by a source who is not personally in control of the sanctions that he or she is warning you about. The friend who says, "If you don't stop treating your father so badly, he will cut you out of his will" is issuing you a warning—a negative sanction that he does not control. Similarly, the person who promises you reward when someone else controls the goodies can make a "recommendation" to you but not a promise.

A threat in the middle of an argument and brute force can be used productively in conflict situations. Threats are not necessarily unproductive or harmful to either the conflict participants or their relationship. For instance, one of the most productive uses of threats is to give a clear message to the other conflict participant that you feel strongly about the conflict and that you are committed to your goals. Being willing to risk relational harmony for the sake of goal attainment helps the other party assess your seriousness (Walton 1969).

Threats cannot be used productively (or even destructively) unless the person being threatened believes that the threat is credible. A threat is credible only if (1) the other party is in a position to administer the punishment,

1. Tedeschi calls these "mendations," but we prefer "recommendations" because the word makes more intuitive sense.

(2) the other party appears willing to invoke the punishment, and (3) the punishment is something to be avoided. When the other party is not in a position to administer the threat, then an attempted threat becomes a warning. If your work associates (who do not control your salary) say to you, "If you continue coming to work at odd hours, you'll never get a raise," they are not using a threat, but a warning. Similarly, if your friends say, "You had better quit trying to get your dad to buy you expensive gifts, or he will get mad and not give you anything," then it is not a credible threat. The threat is credible only if the person making the threat is capable of invoking the negative sanction. The opposite side of the coin, the person issuing what he or she calls a "warning" has control over sanctions. In hierarchical relations, such as supervisory and parent-child relations, when the higher-power party issues a "warning," a threat exist. If you displease the higher-power person, a sanction that is controlled by him or her may be forthcoming.

Often the other party is *able* to administer a threat, but not *willing* to use it. A coworker who threatens to tell the boss that someone's work is not up to par cannot issue a credible threat if the boss dislikes "squealers." Similarly, in intimate relationships, one intimate will often say, "If you want to make your summer plans alone, go ahead. But if you do, then don't expect to find me here when you come back." Such a threat (relational suicide) is effective only if the person who makes the threat is willing to lose the other person over this one issue. It is the *perception* that the other party is willing to use the threat that makes it effective. As a result, intimates and others often never test out the willingness of the party to invoke the threat and live under the control of the other person for years. Poker players all know that a "bluff" is being able to maneuver the other party into thinking that you are willing to bet all your winnings on this single draw of cards. The only successful bluff is one that the other party believes is true.

A special case of threat is a blackmail attempt used as a tactic to accomplish preset goals. In blackmail, the victim is relatively powerless and passive. Furthermore, it is assumed that the victim is rational, that one can weigh the risks associated with not going along with the blackmailer's demands (Hocker 1974). Just as in other kinds of threats, the blackmailer must assure the victim that he *will* invoke the sanctions, not just that he *might* (Schelling 1960). The effectiveness of the blackmail attempt rests on an assumption that the victim wants to avoid the punishment and that the blackmailer can convince the victim of the unfavorable power structure. Blackmailers' seizures of hostages often demonstrate that while the hostages and their friends fear for their lives (thus giving the blackmailer power), outside forces such as the police can also track down a blackmailer. So even if the blackmailer gets his or her wishes, superior force may be called during the commission of the blackmail or later. Harsanyi (1962) labels the one-sided thinking of the blackmailer as the "Blackmailer's

Fallacy." If the blackmailer reasons that he can cause $1,000 worth of damage to a victim, then he should be able to extract a ransom worth any amount up to $1,000 because the victim will still be better off paying. But, as Harsanyi notes, similar reasoning could also apply from the other point of view. The victim (or the victim's friends) could argue that the blackmailer should accept any ransom greater than zero since the blackmailer would be better off than if no agreement were reached. The key, however, is that the blackmailer has control of all the significant power, and often the power balance shifts once the threat is carried out or the ransom received. The blackmailer's power is derived from holding destructive forces in check while threatening to use them.

Finally, threats are effective only if the threatened negative sanction is something the party wants to avoid. In the case of attempted relational suicide in which the intimate threatened to leave if the other made summer plans alone, that action may be precisely what the person planning the separate summer wants. It is not uncommon for intimates to set the other up to destroy the relationship by continually engaging in conflicting behaviors. So before you issue your next threat to a close friend or family member, keep in mind that your threat is effective only if he or she does not want the "undesirable" end result. Similar scenarios happen in all levels of relationships. One faculty member we know was offered a job at a competing university; when he went to his chairman and threatened to leave unless his salary was raised, the chairman replied, "Gee, I hope you enjoy the climate down South."

We have discussed the conditions necessary for the use of threats. As you have seen, threats can be either destructive or constructive. They can be used constructively to highlight the importance of the conflict topic to you, to get the attention of the other party, and to clarify one's perceptions of the power balance. On the other hand, threats can start escalatory conflict spirals, block collaborative agreements, and undermine trust in the relationship. If two dormitory roommates have been getting along well except for the issue of sweeping the floor, then a threat of "If you don't sweep more often, I'll process a room change!" will likely damage the trust in the relationship. The recipient of the threat will likely respond with a feeling of "OK, then go ahead. Who needs you anyway?" Once the trust is shattered, unless it can be regained, forging agreements will be extremely difficult. If a threat has damaged the trust in the relationship, in a very real sense one cannot withdraw.

Threats are just one of the many types of engagement tactics. The other major category of engagement tactics is collaboration.

Collaborative Tactics

Collaborative tactics bring about a search for mutually favorable resolution by inducing or persuading the other party to cooperate. Collaboration involves all parties working together for solutions that are more than simply agreements that stop the conflict; the agreements also maximize the gains for all

Table 5.3.   Collaborative Tactics

Description	Nonevaluative statements about observable events related to conflict
Qualification	Statements that explicitly qualify the nature and extent of conflict
Disclosure	Nonevaluative statements about events related to conflict that the partner cannot observe, such as thoughts, feelings, intentions, motivations, and past history
Soliciting disclosure	Soliciting information from the partner about events related to conflict that one cannot observe
Negative inquiry	Soliciting complaints about oneself
Empathy or support	Statements that express understanding, acceptance, or positive regard for the partner (despite acknowledgement of a conflict)
Emphasizing commonalities	Statements that comment on shared interests, goals, or compatibilities with the partner (despite acknowledgement of a conflict)
Accepting responsibility	Statements that attribute responsibility for conflicts to self or both parties
Initiating problem solving	Statements that initiate mutual consideration of solutions to conflict

Published by permission of Transaction, Inc. from *Human Communication Research* Vol. 9, No. 1 pp. 85–86. Copyright © 1982.

the parties in the conflict. The term "integrative" can be used to describe collaborative tactics, since the tactics help people recognize their interdependence (Walton and McKersie 1965). The goals of the individuals and the relationship as a whole are paramount. The list of collaborative tactics in table 5.3 is adapted from Sillars *et al.* (1982).

Collaborative tactics involve a stance toward conflict management very different from competitive tactics. A competitive tactic assumes that the size of the pie is finite; therefore one's tactics are designed to maximize gains for oneself and losses for the other. Collaborative tactics, however, assume that the size of a pie can be increased by working with the other party. All can leave the conflict with something they value. For example, Filley (1975) maintains that integrative decision making paves the way to effective management; similarly, Fisher and Ury (1981) emphasize joint problem solving.

Some people only experience competitive attitudes toward conflict and have a difficult time visualizing a collaborative approach. If you immediately say "You are wrong" each time you have conflict, you will likely receive a competitive response in return. Collaboration comes from a willingness to move *with* the other rather than against.

Collaborative tactics call for a willingness to explore and struggle precisely when you may not feel like it. You do not give up your self-interest, you *integrate* it with the other's self-interest to reach agreement. Usually, a collaborative approach to conflict management involves the multiple use of the tactics listed in table 5.3. Both the chapter on self-regulation in conflict and the chapter on third-party intervention develop a collaborative approach to conflict management dependent on a wide range of collaborative tactics.

Brockriede (1972) offers a final metaphor that adds to our description of collaboration. In the "lover" approach to argument, conflict relationships are bilateral and equal. "The lover-arguer cares enough about what he is arguing about to feel the tensions of risking his self, but he cares enough about his coarguer to avoid the fanaticism that might induce him to commit rape or seduction" (p. 5). The lover framework (whether it be with bosses, families, students, friends, or romantic lovers) provides the best possibility for productive conflict precisely because it requires adaptation to the interests of the other.

Do not misunderstand—you need not like, much less love, your co-collaborators. Collaboration, however, does require the language of "we" rather than the language of "I." And because parties mutually work together for desirable outcomes for all and protect their own as well as each other's interests, many times respect, caring, and admiration develop as by-products of the collaborative effort.

Refer to table 5.3 for the definitions of the following collaborative tactics. Here are some descriptions and dialogue examples of how the tactics might sound in conversation:

Description: People send messages, often unintentionally, all the time. Often we are surprised by behavior that might have been predictable if we had observed with care and insight. Here are some suggestions, adapted from Yarbrough (1977), for *descriptive observation.*

Describe without interpretation. Describe what you sense, feel, see, hear, touch, and smell instead of what your guess about the behavior is.

> *Example:* "You're so quiet. Ever since I said I didn't want to go out tonight and would rather stay home and read, you haven't spoken to me," *not* "You never understand when I want to spend some time alone!"

> *Focus on what is instead of what should be.*

> *Example:* "You look angry. Are you?" *not* "You shouldn't be angry just because I want to stay home."

> *Describe your own experience instead of attributing it to the other person.*

> *Example:* "I'm finding myself not wanting to bring up any ideas because I'm afraid you will ignore them," *not* "You are getting more critical all the time."

Qualification: "I'm interested in working out a way to keep our private conflicts from coming up in front of the staff. That is what I'd like to work out with you today. But I don't want to get into trying to solve our conflict about whom we should hire, just how to avoid involving everyone else in it."

Disclosure: "You may not have been able to tell, but I've been getting more and more unhappy each time we've brought this up. And now I feel very resigned and discouraged." *or* "This is going to be hard for me. My first boss asked for feedback and then used it against me, so I'm having to work at believing what you're asking me to do."

Negative inquiry: The boss says, "People aren't getting all their work done." Shirley responds, "Are you displeased with the quality of my work?" The boss replies, "Some, but I know you're working on it." Shirley inquires, "Would you tell me what part of my work is not up to standards? I want to improve my work." Negative inquiry invites others to give you negative information directly so that they don't have to hide the information in indirect comments or aggressive tactics.

Initiating problem solving: "Now that we have some idea of what went wrong, what could we do to keep from going through this again?" *or* "Have you thought of some solutions?" or "I think we're ready to work out some solutions together. I'd like to see us consider. . . ."

Conflict Directions and Tactical Patterns

As a conflict unfolds, its overall direction undergoes changes over time since each tactical move by a participant has some impact on the overall direction. At any point, a conflict is either *escalating, maintaining,* or *reducing* in intensity. Obviously, a conflict will often move through different directions before resolution. Conflict directions usually shift throughout the phases of a conflict (Rausch et al 1974). For example, in the beginning phase, one person may escalate and the other may avoid. By the time the middle phase is reached, both parties are escalating. The intensity is maintained at a high level because both parties use competitive tactics. Then one person begins avoiding the conflict, which produces even more escalation. At this point, both parties try to reduce the conflict and move toward maintenance of a reduced conflict. There is one last escalatory surge, then a reduction as the participants reach the resolution stage by using collaborative tactics. The parties reach agreement, and the conflict is further reduced and finally completed.

Conflict directions are set by the *patterns of tactical moves* made over time by the participants. No one party predetermines the directions a conflict will take because conflict directions are set by the joint tactical moves of the parties. To illustrate this, look at the hypothetical conflicts in figure 5.2. In those examples, Curtis makes identical tactical choices, but his sister Pam responds differently in the two cases. For purposes of comparison, the number

Figure 5.2. Tactical patterns and final conflict directions.

of tactical moves has been standardized for the two conflicts. In addition, the conflicts are artificially defined as starting with Curtis. The arrows show the sequencing of tactics.

In conflict A, after the tactics are enacted, the conflict is still escalated because Curtis' attempts at collaboration do not alter Pam's competitive tactics. In conflict B, Curtis' responses are identical to his moves in conflict A, but this time Pam concludes her moves using collaborative tactics, thus reducing the intensity of the conflict. The combination of these tactical moves determines the direction of the conflict.

Often tactics mirror one another, producing an interlocking or "chaining" of identical tactics. Sillars et al. (1982) found "there was a strong tendency for subjects to reciprocate avoidance, distributive, and integrative acts by their partners (p. 93)." For example, as we noted in discussing escalatory spirals in chapter 1, the use of coercion promotes coercion on the part of the other. Many a conflict participant has come away from a conflict with a feeling of "I wish I had not said that." Such reactions are usually the result of the escalatory spiral of threat-counterthreat. As Gottman (1982) notes, distressed marriages are often characterized by such tactical chaining.

The conflict direction needs to be monitored in the other direction as well. If the parties refuse to engage in a conflict, they can get into a *de-escalatory spiral* that results in the loss of relational vitality. As Cupach (1982) writes, "Avoidance behaviors constitute an effective temporary strategy. . . ." Carina, age nine, exemplifies this well. Once when confronted by her father about being "responsible" she said, "Who cares?" (with a giggle!). A good temporary tactic may, however, be counter-productive in the long run.

In any important relationship, whether formed within the family, in the work place, or in a social group, the long-term goals are important. If a conflict participant wants to preserve a good relationship while pursuing a goal that appears incompatible with that of the other person, collaborative tactics are needed. You may begin the conflict by avoiding or escalating, but at some point collaborative engagement is usually necessitated. Competent communicators are those who use constructive, pro-social, collaborative tactics at some stage of the conflict (Cupach 1982). As Schuetz (1978b) says "In situations of conflict, as in other communicative events, the competent communicator engages in cooperative interaction that permits both persons (factions) involved to achieve their goals" (p. 10). Sillars' work (1980a, 1980b) demonstrates that roommate conflicts characterized by collaboration, rather than by avoidance or competition, led to greater satisfaction with the roommate and greater likelihood of successful conflict management.

Collaborative tactical choices depend on a certain level of cognitive complexity (Applegate 1982; Delia 1977). Collaborative tactics involve supporting a positive, autonomous identity for the other while working for your own goals. Such multiple demands, while difficult to master, lead to productive results for both parties. For in the end, you are working with, rather than against the other for mutual collaborative gains.

Whatever tactical moves you make, the basic question is whether those choices lead to the effective management of the conflict over time. No one set of moves at any point will guarantee productive conflict, but collaborative tactics at least set the stage for the containment and management of the conflict if both parties move toward a problem-solution perspective. When in doubt, collaborate.

Summary

People act both spontaneously and in preplanned ways, and the difficulty and uncertainty present in most conflict promotes active strategizing—thinking about tactical moves. One can strategize in order to gain individual advantage or to serve collaborative goals as well. Once people are faced with a conflict, they make a basic choice to either avoid or engage the conflict. Either choice can lead to productive or destructive results, depending on the chosen tactics, the stage of the conflict, and the response of the other party.

Tactical moves can be classified according to whether they are forms of avoidance or engagement. Sample avoidance tactics are denial of the conflict, underresponsiveness, joking, and topic avoidance. Engagement tactics are either (1) competitive or (2) collaborative. Sample competitive tactics are faulting, hostile questioning, avoiding responsibility, and forms of prescriptions such as threats. Collaborative tactics involve searching for mutually favorable resolution by inducing the other party to cooperate with you by using disclosure, empathizing, accepting responsibility, and initiating problem solving.

People's tactical moves combine to affect the conflict in one of three directions over time, escalation, maintenance, or reduction. Often conflicts alternate among these three directions over time. One of the hallmarks of productive conflicts is entering collaborative phases, even if those have been preceded by cycles of escalation and maintenance. While collaborative tactics are not easy to enact, they can lead the conflict to a productive conclusion if matched by the other party.

Part 2 Conflict Intervention

Part 1 of this book discussed the components of conflict by examining the nature of conflict, conflict styles, power relations between parties, and participant goals. This second part incorporates conflict components into a comprehensive discussion of conflict assessment in chapter six. Whether you are a participant or third party, a full assessment of the conflict is a necessary prerequisite to intervention. Techniques for intervention in your own conflicts are presented in chapter 7, which centers on the skills of self-regulation. If you are a third-party intervener, or if you use intervention services, the principles and practices in chapter 8 will be useful.

6　Conflict Assessment

Have you ever been in a conflict in which you were so perplexed you asked, either silently or out loud, "What is going on here?" Or have you talked with a friend or work associate whose conflicts appear to be totally confusing and impossible to understand? If so, this chapter will help you "get a handle" on the structure of conflicts. The assessment guides are useful for describing conflicts whether you are a party to the conflict, a concerned third party such as a parent or friend, or a professional third-party intervener. Some of the techniques presented in this chapter and in chapter 7, "Self-Regulation," can be practiced as class or workshop activities. Later you might want to use the techniques for assessment and regulation as a manager, trainer, teacher, parent, or organizational consultant. If you are asked to perform an in-depth analysis of a conflict, either for one of your own or as a service to a group, you can choose several of the assessment devices in this chapter to help you describe the conflict with a minimum of bias.

Conflict assessment guides can help you understand your own conflicts, because most of us are notoriously inaccurate at describing our own behavior in a conflict. We develop blind spots about our own behavior and fail to "see" aspects of what is occurring. As Weick (1979) notes, people repeatedly impose on others that which they later claim was imposed on them. The person who believes the world is a competitive, win-lose place often doesn't see that this view sets those very processes in motion. Self-fulfilling prophecies are enacted over and over as we provoke the very behavior we accuse the other in the conflict of perpetuating. Then we each make ourselves out to be the other's victim (Warner and Olson 1981, 497).

Other people's conflicts can also appear confusing and unpredictable. As we have learned while working as consultants to families and organizations, each conflict at first appears new, different, and beyond comprehension. One city council is not like another, one family is different from the next, and the mental health agency down the street seems totally distinct from the one across town. As we become immersed in each conflict, diligently taking notes and interviewing the conflict parties, we often feel like Taylor (1979) that ". . . my ability to accumulate data often exceeds my capacity to integrate it. . . . I struggle to take in a mass of information that overloads me in some ways and leaves me in the dark in others" (1979, 479). The assessment approaches presented in this chapter can help with this kind of overload; they are "confusion-organizing tools" (Taylor 1979, 480).

As an assessor of conflicts, it is important that you identify some organizing scheme for reducing confusion before you begin the assessment. One such framework is systems theory, which offers a broadly based perspective on all social systems and is particularly useful when assessing an interpersonal conflict. With such an overall orientation, the specific assessment tools we present can be seen as parts of the whole picture.

Systems theory provides both macroscopic and microscopic perspectives on a system in conflict. Full assessment of a conflict can best be accomplished by (1) assessing the workings of the overall system, (2) determining recurring patterns inside the system that are associated with conflict, and (3) identifying individual contributions to the overall system functioning. A combination of the above, drawn from the different approaches discussed in this chapter, will provide you with data that can be used to provide a background for constructing helpful interventions. When multimodal and multilevel assessment is not used, one runs the risk of an undue focus on one's own area of concern or expertise, whether that be power structures, reduction tactics, improving the atmosphere, problem solving, negotiation, or any other facet of conflict.

Systems Theory: An Organizing Framework

General systems theory has provided the framework for a rich body of literature about the workings of entire systems and subsystems in organizations, small groups, and families. Many effective intervention techniques for productive conflict management derive from systems theorists who experiment with change. We will give suggestions for system change in chapters 7 and 8. In this section we will present systems concepts that have been the most helpful to us, our students, and our clients. The myriad approaches to assessment can be put in perspective by checking back to these principles to keep the mass of data organized in your mind as you devise change attempts. The genius of systems theory as a framework for assessment and intervention is that it provides a way to understand conflicts by giving information about patterns, interlocking sequences, functions of the parties, and methods of processing information. Conflicts are seldom managed productively by attention to blame or causality, seeking the truth, finding the initiator and responder, or detecting the persecutor and victim. If you do succeed in tagging someone with the "perpetrator" label, you have not managed the conflict; you have only created an enemy.

Extensive discussions of systems theory applied to various contexts have been published in the last decade. Gregory Bateson's two major works, *Steps to an Ecology of Mind* (1972) and *Mind and Nature* (1979), have become philosophical cornerstones of systems theory writing and research. The systems approach to describing normal family processes is discussed thoroughly by Galvin and Brommel (1982) and Walsh (1982). Overviews of systems theory and the change process helpful to counselors and therapists are provided by Minuchin (1974), Steinglass (1978), Neill and Kniskern (1982), Hoffman (1981), and Napier and Whitaker (1978). Systems theory applied to organizations and organizational change, helpful to consultants, workshop leaders, and organizational development professionals, are provided by Weick (1979) and Johnson (1977).

Selected principles derived from systems theory will help you understand the wholistic or systemic nature of any conflict. The following list is adapted from a practical and helpful article by Papp, Silberstein, and Carter (1973).

(1) *Systems operate as an interdependent unit with no villains, heroes, good and bad people, healthy or unhealthy members.* Rather than pinpointing one person as the cause of the conflict, look instead for predictable chain reactions occurring because what every person does affects every other person. *Study the chain reactions*—see who picks up what cues and identify the part each plays in the runaway spiral. Satir uses an image of a family as a mobile in which members respond to changes in each other. "As members respond to situations, certain other members may consciously or unconsciously shift to adjust to the quivering system" (Galvin and Brommel 1981, 27). The same kind of interdependence exists in organizations and small groups. One cannot *not* affect other members of a system.

Systems operate with *circular causality,* a concept that suggests that assigning beginning points is less important than looking at the sequence of patterns in the conflict process. Punctuation, interrupting a sequence of behavior at intervals, is important only for purposes of giving meaning to the behavior but not for assigning the "cause" of the behavior. Most of the time, conflict participants identify the other as the "cause," while portraying the self as innocent. The boy who runs home screaming, "Sara hit me" is clearly ignoring his part in the system (he threw dirt at her). All systems are characterized by circular causality—each one affects the other.

(2) *Each member gets labelled, or programmed, into a specific role in the system.* Labeling serves a function for the entire group. Most labels keep people from changing; however, the labeling process can be changed. For instance, the "watchdog" in an organization may be carrying too much of the quality-control function. Conflicts arise because the watchdog performs the function reinforced by the group, and if she stops being the "watchdog," others will try to pull her back into the role.

(3) *Cooperation is necessary among system members to keep conflicts going.* One person cannot carry on an interaction. Therefore, the cycle can be changed by any one person changing his or her behavior. Healthy systems are characterized by morphogenesis, or "constructive system-enhancing behaviors that enable the system to grow, innovate and change" (Olson et al. 1979). Conflict can be managed by one person initiating change or by members deciding together to initiate a change in their structure. A system that keeps conflicts going as a way to avoid genuine change is called a *morphostatic system,* one characterized by moves that members engage in designed to maintain the status quo, or no change.

If you are stuck in a system that does not change, one choice you always have is to change your own behavior, even if you cannot get others to change. In the Shepherd family, for instance, one of the five members usually felt left out. The family expectation was the four people together were enough but five people together were trouble, since each parent wanted to "take care of" one child. The family was able to change and make more room on the merry-go-round when Dad began sharing his time with all three children instead of paying attention to one child at a time.

(4) *Triangles* tend to form in systems when relationships are close and intense. When one person feels low power, the tendency is to bring in another person to bolster the low-power position. This maneuver forms an *alliance* if the resulting relationship is an open one or a *coalition* if the relationship is hidden. Since the person brought in to build up the position of the low-power person also maintains multiple relationships in the system, interlocking triangles that function over and over in predictable ways can be discovered. If these triangles lead to destructive behavior, they are termed *toxic triangles* (Satir 1972; Hoffman 1982; Minuchin 1973).

(5) *Systems develop rules for conflict* that, no matter how dysfunctional, are followed as long as the basic structure of the system does not change. What may develop is a prescriptive rule about conflict that states, "If we are a happy family, we do not have conflict" or "We have polite conflict." At work there may be a rule that "If you have conflict with the boss, you will be fired." Some departments only conflict in writing. Others require conflicts to happen only in meetings, while some postpone or "table" most potential conflicts. System rules often block collaborative conflict. At one time they served the system

well but not now. Parents may decide, for instance, never to fight in front of the children. When the children were infants, the rule protected them from angry faces and loud voices. But with children 12 and 16 years old, the rule makes little sense, as the children can always tell when Mom and Dad are in a conflict, and they are being brought up to fear conflict.

(6) *The conflict serves a function for the system.* The conflict may be substituting for other forms of intimacy and connection, for problem solving, or for expression of dissatisfaction. Never assume that members of a system want the conflict to be resolved. They may fear the vacuum in their interaction if they do not have the conflict for a particular function. While almost everyone in a conflict will say, "Of course we want this over and done with," the fact that people keep conflicts going, sometimes for years at a time, indicates that some system function is served by the conflict. One church congregation carried on a repetitive conflict at board meetings about the propriety of using the church buildings for partisan and special interest group meetings. A third party helped them discover that the debate was a substitute for a subgroup's dissatisfaction with the minister's involvement in social action projects. The board had been reluctant to confront the minister with their disapproval, so they always centered the discussion on "use of the building." The conflict allowed them to express their disapproval in an indirect way.

Identifying Conflict Patterns

One focus for assessing conflicts is the pattern of the conflict relationship between the parties. The conflict is composed of the system regularities such as patterns of communication, rules for behavior, and the characteristic dynamics of the system. Often the structure of the conflict is only expressed indirectly or implicitly so that assessment approaches cannot be constructed by asking the parties "What is the structure of your conflict?" Rather, the structure has to be derived from indirect approaches, a few of which we will overview. We include (1) metaphoric/dramatic, (2) sculpting or choreography, (3) conflict triangles, (4) system rules, and (5) microevents as indirect mechanisms to identify the structure of conflicts.

Metaphoric/Dramatic

Metaphors, discussed extensively in chapter 1, can be elicited by the third-party or conflict participants for the purpose of presenting an intuitively accurate description of a conflict. Haley (1976) notes that metaphors can be reflective of relational themes. Conflict parties can be asked to write or tell about the kind of novel, film, or television program their conflict is like. One group of nurses said they were like characters in a detective novel, looking for "who-dunnit." A family saw themselves as a pioneer family in a Western movie, circling their wagons against possible attack, pulling together on the trail, but scattering once they were not in danger. Some people can write poems about their conflicts or draw pictures of their conflict. Others can visualize disconnected images as they occur to them, then talk about what the images mean. One group elicited the following images for the divorce process: "drowning," "having the roadmap taken away," "playing cards with no rules," and "being in surgery and waking up to find that you're on an artificial heart." One foster child, when asking her counselor for placement in a different family, said, "They speak, I don't know, Spanglish or something, and they won't teach me the language." Children can look through magazines to find pictures that say how they feel in a conflict. Children also respond well to puppet shows in which they act out conflict roles, taking several parts at once. Your imagination can be your guide for helping conflicting parties find a way to express the feel and structure of their conflicts.

During interviews and observation, you can hear people spontaneously generate metaphoric ways of speaking of their conflicts. These expressions should be carefully noted and used in your overall analysis. You can ask people to explain how the metaphor works. For instance, a counseling center has a plaque labelling it as "The Little Mental Health Center on the Prairie" in the staff room. Values of neighborliness, assistance in times of trouble, and "pulling together" are evident in staff relationships. One structured technique for having people work with metaphors to manage their conflicts follows:

1. Ask parties to generate a metaphor for an important conflict, using one of the suggestions above. Write out the metaphoric image separately.

2. Ask one person to share the image with the group of conflicting parties or the discussion group. The group then asks clarifying questions of the person sharing the metaphor, using the images developed in the original metaphor.

3. The group then brainstorms, *still using the imaginary mode,* about ways to resolve the conflict.

4. The facilitator or leader then asks the group to translate these imaginary resolution ideas into practical steps for conflict management.

5. The primary party, or the group, then chooses the options that will most likely lead to collaborative conflict management.

6. After all the conflict parties have repeated this procedure, a contract is made for selected change.

Several examples of this exercise follow:

Case of Beth and Ted

Beth and Ted are a romantic couple who have been going out for one year. Beth has considered leaving on the National Student Exchange for one year at a school in Philadelphia, 2,000 miles away. She wants to continue the relationship with Ted while at school but also wants freedom to date others. Ted wants a more intimate relationship and feels that can be achieved only if he and Beth can see each other often.

Beth and Ted agreed together that the following image describes their current attempts to solve their conflict:

"We open a messy, heaping cupboard and upon seeing the disorganization and mess, Beth or Ted hurries to slam it shut before all the cans and bottles fall out, injuring one of us."

After following the discussion steps listed above, Beth and Ted agree that a new image will guide them to more productive conflict management:

"We open a messy, heaping cupboard. We roll up our sleeves, take all the items off the shelves, clean up, throw out the spoiled goods and put everything that is left back into a larger cupboard without doors—for easy reorganization."

The Case of the Dangerous Minefield

Margaret, a college student, writes:

"My father and I are in a mine field. The sky is blue, the sun is shining, there is green grass and sudden death underneath. Each of us is responsible for some of the mines underfoot, and we have to avoid our own mines as well as those planted by the other person. There are scattered trees and bushes around the field, which is quite large. They provide limited cover. We are each trying to get in close enough to the other to get a good look without being seen.

My father throws rocks at me to try to flush me out into the open. I back around a bush and meet him.

Boom! There's a big explosion—we both flee, wounded, only to begin the standoff over again."

Here are some metaphoric solutions translated into practical steps for conflict management:

Metaphoric Solutions	*Communication Possibilities*
1. Dig up my mines, or tell him where they are	Disclose myself
2. Get a metal detector, locate his mines, and—	"Psych him out" and
a. dig them up;	Confront him
b. throw heavy objects from a distance to set them off;	Backstab
c. avoid them	Avoid him or "be nice"
3. Wear explosion-proof armor	Decrease my dependence
4. Throw rocks at him	Attack or goad him
5. Abandon the field; leave	Don't communicate at all
6. Hold onto him when explosion goes off so we can't run from each other	Increase closeness and interdependence
7. Cut down the foliage	Describe our behaviors and feelings to each other
8. Use binoculars to see each other	Get information on him from other sources; focus carefully
9. Whistle as I go around the field	Let him know "where I'm coming from"
10. Stand in the open so he can see me	Give him the opportunity to get information about me; write him a letter

Options 1, and 7–10 seem to be moves that would help productively manage the conflict. Many more exist, but these are a good start.

Conflict Triangles

Conflicts can be structurally analyzed using diagrams. Several researchers note that the triangle is the basic unit of analysis for conflict communication (Satir 1972; Hoffman 1982; Minuchin 1973; Wilmot 1979). Why triangles? When people perceive that they are the low-power party in a two-person conflict, the typical response to the perceived low power is to try to form a coalition (hidden) or an alliance (open) with another person who can bolster the power of the low-power party. If another party joins the previously low-power party, that person then becomes part of the conflict, as you may have discovered if you have taken sides with a friend or coworker who was in conflict with someone else. "Three's a crowd" is a cultural cliche that has sound reasoning behind it. Three people find it difficult to stay in balance in a conflictual relationship. Usually they are structured as a "dyad plus one" (Wilmot 1979). However, three people may be able to interact with ease over a long period of time if they are not engaged in conflict. Triadic or triangular analysis can be used to study the relationships that make up an ongoing conflict of more than three people. The method is especially useful in conflicts involving five or more people. After interviewing and/or observing the conflict parties, follow these steps:

1. Ask about recurring experiences in the conflict system. Which are puzzling, painful, frustrating or triggering of conflicts? Note these by drawing and labeling them.

2. Draw triangles demonstrating all the different relationship combinations, including all the conflict parties. Mark conflicting dyads with ◄┼┼┼┼┼┼┼┼► . In a conflict consisting of many people, choose the most problematic triangles to work with first.

The following sample toxic triangles refer to Tom and Mary, a married couple in their second marriage. The word *toxic* (Satir 1972) was first applied to these kinds of relationships to describe the poisonous, dangerous, and potentially life-threatening nature of the relationships.

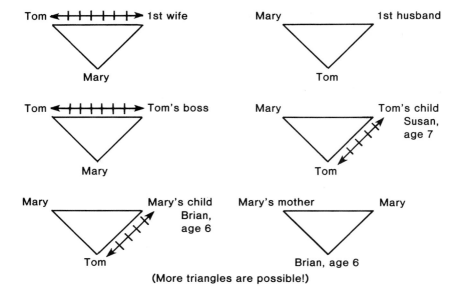

(More triangles are possible!)

3. Code high-power persons with a plus, (+), low-power persons with a (−). Power refers to this sample triangle only.

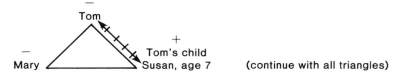

(continue with all triangles)

4. Identify alliances with a double arrow: ◄─► Identify coalitions with an arrow in parentheses (◄─►).

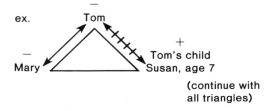

5. Identify isolates, or persons who are in few or no triangles. Can they be drawn in to productively restructure the conflict?

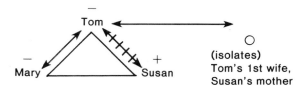

6. Identify persons involved in many or all the triangles. Can they withdraw from some toxic triangles?

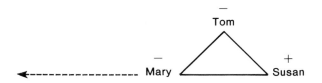

In this example, Mary could withdraw from active participation in Tom's and Susan's conflict, giving them the opportunity to communicate directly with each other.

Tom ◄────► Susan

This might accomplish two dyadic interactions with possibilities for collaboration:

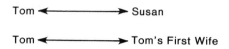

7. Discuss all toxic triangles (the ones that produce the most conflict), deciding how they might be productively restructured. (See chapter 3 for ideas on power balancing.)

8. Choose several options to begin management of the conflict.

9. Each person keeps a list of agreements for change made during the session. These agreements are negotiated by the parties involved and the trainer, and involve self- (not other-) centered action.

Diagrammatic techniques are not limited to personal relationships; they can also be applied to conflict in small groups, work groups, or subunits of an organization.

Sculpting or Choreographing

Sculpting, or choreographing, is a nonverbal method of demonstrating the structure of a conflict by having each member of the conflict "arrange the other members in a tableau that physically symbolizes their emotional relationships with each other" (Papp et al. 1973). Each party creates a live portrait, placing other parties together in postures and spatial relationships that show the essence of one's experience of the conflict. This "picture is literally worth a thousand words" (Papp et al. 1973). Confused feelings are given form. This art of representing family roles spatially comes from Papp and her colleagues, Duhl, Kantor, and Duhl (1973) and Satir in her many training films and workshops. The sculptor is in the creative position of acting in a scene while explaining his or her actions at the same time. In addition minature figures can be used to facilitate sculpting (Howard and Hocker 1981; Hocker and Bach 1982). Such sculpting techniques can also be used with less intimate conflict parties than families, such as staff persons who work together daily. Triangles, alliances, and coalitions, as well as rules about who may talk with whom, are dramatically displayed.

After each party to the conflict gets a chance to place members in relationship to each other, the parties are directed to slowly move in the direction they usually do. The incompatible goals, scarce resources, and other structural elements of the conflict usually become quite evident. Sculpting is a technique that has even more potential for clarifying conflict as the method receives refinement.

One recent example of how sculpting can illuminate conflict patterns was provided by Fred in a workshop. His parents, Joe and Patricia, were having recurring conflicts that were drawing in Fred and the other family members. Joe and Patricia were retired; Patricia's mother was elderly and living in the same town in her own apartment. Every day Patricia visited her mother and assisted her with small tasks. The mother had a part-time caretaker paid for by Joe and Patricia. Each time Fred would visit his parents, Joe complained bitterly that "Patricia is spending all her time with her mother." Patricia was avoidant; she did not openly discuss the issue with Joe and tried to deflect any discussion of it. Over time, Joe became more isolated from Patricia, and Patricia's alliance with her mother became closer. When Fred sculpted this conflict, he represented Patricia and her mother standing close together, Joe a long distance from them and slowly moving farther away. Joe was also far from the other family members such as Fred—his complaining drove them away from him. The emotional gap between Joe and Patricia was represented by their being spatially distant from one another in the sculpture.

Patricia, recognizing that she did not want Joe to be so far away, began the following dialogue:

Patricia: "But I don't want him so far away!"

Facilitator: See if you can get closer to him.

(Patricia walks closer to Joe, the woman playing Patricia's mother pulls her back. Patricia is pulled in the middle.) After discussion, Patricia decided she could set aside time when she and Joe could be together so that she did not feel pulled in the middle. Joe helped her decide when would be the best time for her to visit her mother each day. Joe reported that he had begun to think that Patricia did not care about him and had not realized that she felt the pulls on both sides so strongly.

Choreographing conflicts works best when the parties are present together, each has a chance to choreograph the movements of the system, and they work together to solve their joint problem.

System Rules

Rules that limit change and morphogenesis in any conflict system can be discovered and discussed. Since a conflict always reflects an underlying rule structure, the conflict is always more fundamental than the specific triggering event. As Bateson says, "The meaning or function of an event is not contained in itself but in its relation to the context" (1972). Each communicative behavior performed in a conflict is not an isolated event—it both reflects and reinforces an underlying structure. Or, put another way, all communication events and conflicts display sets of "rules" that are operating. Shimanoff (1980) defines a rule as *"a followable prescription that indicates what behavior is obligated, preferred, or prohibited in certain contexts"* (p. 57). System rules may be explicitly stated, or they may be implicit.

Implicit rules are not stated but must be inferred from behavior (Shimanoff 1980, 54). The following are some examples of rules that conform to this definition:

1. *Rules are prescriptions for behavior* stated in the following form: "When in context X, Y must/must not occur."

   "When Father shows sadness or anger, Mother must soothe him."

   "When the program director decides to assign a case to a counselor, the counselor must accept the case or convince the program director to reassign it."

2. *Rules are stated in prescriptive, not evaluative, language.*

   "When brother and sister fight, Dad must intervene to stop it."

   not

   "Dad feels responsible for stopping brother and sister's fights even though they can handle them without interference." (This is interpretive and evaluative.)

   One of the characteristics of important rules in a system is that usually some implicit message against knowing or stating the rule directly is present. It's almost as if people must follow the rules but they can't say what they are. For that reason, listing rules for the way a certain system of people engages in conflict may not be easy. The kinds of rules we are discussing may be stated openly, such as "When coming to a staff meeting, all teachers must be prepared to give a weekly progress report on the special students." The rules that are likely to cause difficulties in conflict situations, however, are the implicit rules, such as "When the family picks a campsite for their vacation, all members must express pleasure at the campsite or a decision is not considered final." When Bill joined Joyce's family to go camping for the first time, the campsite decision took hours. Since he just said sites were "OK," members kept finding new spots, looking for approval from the newest member of the family. The more he said "I really don't care," the less able the members were to settle on a site!

Rules may be elicited from conflict parties by following these steps:

1. Each party makes a list of explicit and implicit rules that prescribe behavior in conflicts.

2. If you have trouble thinking of rules for your system, think of times when the rule was broken. How did you know the rule was broken? How was the violation communicated?

3. Make sure you generate rules for both behavior that must and must not be performed.

4. Go back over your list. Make each rule simple and prescriptive. Write rules even for "obvious" communication patterns. They may prove to be important as possibilities for change.

   Example: New staff members in the staff meeting must not express opinions unless they have a sponsor who is an older staff member.

5. Code each rule as to—
   a. Whose rule is it?
   b. What keeps the rule going?
   c. Who enforces the rule?
   d. Who breaks the rule?
   e. What function does the rule serve?

6. Discuss how the rules help or harm the productive management of conflict. Make decisions for change.

   Example: Old rule—when Dad is angry at younger brother, older brother must protect younger brother from Dad's disapproval.

   Result—Older brother and Dad engage in conflict often, reducing effect of the protection (a toxic triangle).

   New rule—When Dad and little brother get into a conflict, they must talk about their conflicts without big brother (a new affiliation).

Many groups are amazed at the complexity of their conflict rules. A first step in collaboration can be to generate the list of rules together, adding to the suggestions made by each member in a brainstorming fashion at first, then refining the rules for accuracy. Often groups and families can decide together which rules get in the way of collaborative conflict management.

Microevents

Microevents are repetitive patterns that carry information about the underlying conflict structure. The identification of such recurring episodes can lead to morphogenesis or system change. Microevents are "repetitive loops of observable interpersonal behaviors . . . with a redundant outcome . . . (Metcoff and Whitaker 1982, 253). The microevent reinforces the structural patterns of relating to one another by supplying a repeatedly experienced interaction. As such, they are similar to rules but are clusters of behaviors organized into structurally repetitive episodes.

Perhaps the clearest keys to the nature of an underlying structure are the "substitutable communication events that reveal the structure" (Metcoff and Whitaker 1982, 258). Metcoff and Whitaker (1982) give an example of such repeatability. This is a family in therapy; it is composed of father, mother, and the children.

Every time the husband $\begin{cases} \text{scratched his ear} \\ \text{rubbed his nose} \\ \text{tapped his right foot} \end{cases}$ during

an argument with his wife, one of the children

would $\begin{cases} \text{ask to go to the bathroom} \\ \text{slap a sibling} \\ \text{begin to cry} \end{cases}$ so that the

husband-wife dispute was never resolved" (1981, 258–259).

The implicit, unstated structure underlying these repetitive conflicts can be summarized as follows: "When the husband and wife begin to initiate a conflict, one of the children makes a move to gain their attention, and the husband-wife conflict is not resolved" (p. 259). Each system will, of course, have a different structure underlying the observable conflict. The microevent serves to define the conflict because it "embodies themes of stability and change within the family system" (Metcoff and Whitaker 1982, 263).

Once the underlying structure is decoded, one can begin to predict where, when, or how conflict will erupt. Emily and Gordon are a married couple in their sixties whose children are all grown and living elsewhere. Before each vacation, he decides alone where a good place would be to go, then tries to persuade Emily of the wisdom of the choice. Emily won't agree to go, but neither will she say no. Then, the night before the trip, Gordon stays up most of the night packing and reluctantly Emily goes with him. Their repetitive conflicts are structured in the following manner:

1. He always initiates.

2. She always is convinced (reluctantly) to go.

3. No discussion of their relationship is engaged, all issues are handled through content.

4. Neither receives positive results from their respective stances.

5. Neither one can solve nor escape the conflict.

Their next conflict, over whether and when to go somewhere for Christmas, will repeat a similar structure.

In decoding the structure underlying a microevent, one can focus on these questions as a starting point for analysis.

1. Who inititates and in what way?

2. Who responds and in what way?

3. Who else is present but does not stay identified as a party to the conflict?

4. Does anyone "speak for" someone else? If so, does this keep them embroiled in the conflict?

5. If there were no conflict, what would be missing?
   a.) Who would not be connecting to whom?
   b.) How would the parties structure their time?
   c.) Would conflicts continue with new parties entering into the fray?

6. Is the conflict serving to fill up emotional space so other parties cannot fight?

The communication patterns created in a conflict often serve to cycle back and imprison the players. Take Beverly and her son, Randy. Beverly went through a divorce two months ago, and Randy is having difficulty at school. At least twice a week, Beverly and Randy get in a conflict about his poor work in the fifth grade. He has been labeled as a "troublemaker" at school and has been sent home from school three times in the last month. This is embarrassing to Beverly; she also gets very angry at Randy for his "stupid behavior." The repetitive microevent that Beverly and Randy enact has the following features:

1. Beverly initiates each conflict by being distressed about his school performance or that he was sent home again.

2. Randy responds by being sullen, pretending he is deaf and can't hear requests, and withdrawing.

3. The older brother is present in the house but serves as a bystander (and is unemployed).

4. Randy and Beverly both are singular parties—neither has anyone come to her or his aid during the conflict.

5. If there were no conflict, mother and son would find it difficult to have any common interests. Beverly can't "think of things" that might be interesting for the two of them to do together.

This recurring conflict both illustrates and crystallizes the family structure. Here are some ways you can discover and describe microevents.

1. Act as a qualitative researcher who performs observation and interviewing to determine patterns.

2. Provide a professional third-party description of common conflicts (consultant, organizational development specialist, therapist).

3. Keep a journal of conflict episodes that seem repetitive—those that have a "here we go again" theme.

4. Ask newcomers to a system, such as new employees, new family members, or new committee members, to describe what they have experienced so far

The microevent on p. 146 was written by a student who kept a journal for several months. It isolates clearly the repetitive patterns.

Microevents can provide information about changing the conflict structure just as rules can. In this instance, Melissa decided to give her schedule to her grandparents each time as soon as she got there so her grandmother would not be left wondering, and Melissa could be open about her plans.

Quantitative Assessment

The above assessments of conflict patterns have concerned gathering information from real-life conflicts via retrospective or third-party observation reports. Quantitative approaches, on the other hand, have been developed for conflicts in a variety of contexts ranging from real-life to laboratory-induced conflicts.

For purposes of research or teaching, one can tap real-life conflicts retrospectively or create a conflict in a laboratory or classroom for observation and coding. Two of the most useful techniques for highlighting past conflicts are the Revealed Differences Technique (Strodtbeck 1951) and the List of Problem Areas for Spouses (Weiss et al. 1973). In addition, the "Structured Family Interview" (Watzlawick 1966) has some useful subparts. While used primarily for spouses, these basic techniques can be adapted to a variety of contexts such as the work setting.

If one wants to observe a conflict rather than rely on retrospective self-reports, the conflict parties can be asked to replay a conflict they have had (Knudsen et al. 1980), or they can be given a conflict scene and asked to improvise a conflict (Raush et al. 1974). Structured game approaches to conflict have been used for both research and teaching purposes. In these games, the rules produce conflict situations of the win-lose variety, which may be useful for observation purposes. The most widely used and known is the Prisoner's Dilemma, described in many sources, including Swensen (1973), Rubin and Brown (1975), and the first edition of this book (1978). In addition, the Parchees Coalition Game (Vinacke and Arkoff 1957), Acme-Bolt Trucking Game (Deutsch and Knauss 1960), and Bilateral Monopoly Game (Siegel and Fouraker 1960) are available. Rubin and Brown (1975) provide an overview of the above structured approaches. The Color Matching Test (CMT) promotes conflict because it requires a dyad to reach a joint decision about matching a color presented to them. Unknown to the participants, the charts they are using are

The Broken Plans

Every time there is a break from school and work, I go down to Medford to visit my relatives. I usually begin by staying at my grandparents' house and then spending a night or two at my brother's house and visiting my cousin or aunt. The following communication patterns are repeated the first morning of every visit at my grandparents'.

When I get up, Grandma has already fixed my breakfast and has it set out on the kitchen table—cereal, toast, juice, fresh fruit, etc. Grandma always goes to great lengths to have everything perfect. "Would you like an egg, dear?" she asks.

"No thank you, Grandma; this is fine. You really don't have to fix me breakfast. I could do it fine."

"Well, we don't get to see our girl very often; you don't mind being spoiled a bit, do you?" She and Grandpa then bring their coffee into the kitchen and sit down and drink it while I eat my breakfast.

"What are your plans for this time?" asks Grandma. I have already told her that I only have three days, but I haven't mentioned what I am doing.

"Well, I'm not really sure. I hadn't really decided," I answer. At this point I am stalling a bit because actually I have already decided that I am going to leave later this evening and go over and visit my brother. However, I don't want to hurt my grandparents' feelings, so I stall.

"I hope you will be able to spend a little more time with us," says Grandma. Her hopeful look melts my strong will about sticking to my plans.

"Let her do what she wants," says Grandpa. "Must be pretty boring for a young girl like her hanging around with a pair of old fogies like us," says Grandpa, but I get a sly wink or pat on the knee. "You know we love having you dear, but there are other people who want to see you too."

"She has plenty of time to see everyone else!" argues Grandma. "For once, I would like her and I to have a nice visit without worrying about her running off to visit someone else."

"We will have a nice visit, Grandma," I say. By this time I am even more reluctant to mention my plans because I don't want to hurt her feelings. "Remember over Christmas I spent nearly a week with you, and the rest of the family only got a few days." I attempt to rationalize.

"Oh, that was months ago," she answers. "Can I get you something else for breakfast?"

"Grandma, I'm fine," I answer.

"I just want to make sure you're not hungry or anything. Whenever you are at our house, you just get whatever you need. You don't have to ask; you just get what you want," Grandma says. "Grandpa and I really enjoy having you, even though we don't get to see you that much." I can sense her watching me while I concentrate on my dish of shredded wheat which has gone soggy during our conversation. Breakfast usually ends with me deciding that it is better to spend an extra day with my grandparents instead of having guilty feelings during the rest of my visit. The repetitive patterns of "We love you and will do nice things for you if you please stay with us," win out over my initial plans for the break.

(Courtesy of Melissa Price)

coded differently, which sets the stage for a conflict (Goodrich and Boomer 1963). A similar technique of presenting slightly different information to the conflict parties and asking them to reach agreement is used in the Olson-Ryder scenario method. In this simulation, two disparate descriptions of a "conflict" between spouses are given to the players, and they decide which person described in the scenario is "primarily responsible" for the conflict (Olson and Ryder 1970). The added "real world" nature of the scenarios makes it particularly useful.

If one wishes to create more lengthy conflict interactions, three longer simulations are useful. Both *Powerplay* (Peabody and Dietterich 1973, appendix) and *Starpower* (appendix) structure the participants into conflicts and produce intensive involvement through strategic bargaining. Any approach, whether relying on retrospective self-reports, asking for a replay of a conflict, creating a script for improvisation, or putting participants in a highly structured simulation, has advantages and limitations. One needs to take care to have experienced leaders available for debriefing any intensive conflict experience created by structured games or simulations. For an overview of the validity and representativeness of games and simulations to real life, see Knudson et al. (1980), Glick and Gross (1975), Ryder and Goodrich (1970), Barry (1970), and Raush et al. (1974).

A variety of instruments are available for the quantitative assessment of conflict. Some are used for workshops and discussion groups and are not intended for research, while other instruments have been specifically formulated for research purposes. Many research instruments, however, are also useful in workshops and training sessions because of their specificity and validity. In this review, when a scale has not been researched extensively, it will be labeled as a "discussion starter." Citations to instruments will specify the articles that detail the instrument and its uses. Some of the instruments can only be obtained by writing to a specific address listed in the appendix. Sometimes, after consulting a particular article, it is obvious that the instrument is only available from the first author of the article, and, in almost all the published articles, the author's institutional affiliations are listed.

Conflict parties' global overall reactions to conflict can be solicited by a variety of means. The "Conflict Attitudes Questionnaire" (appendix) constructed by Hocker and Wilmot is a helpful discussion starter used to sensitize people to their own and other's attitudes toward conflict per se. It can be used in class and workshops to allow for exploration of advantages and limitations of a variety of orientations to conflict. Similarly, general "predispositions" toward conflict can be gathered by using the "Predispositions toward Conflict" scale generated by Yelsma (1981) and Brown, Yelsma, and Keller (1981). Global assessments of family systems can be specified with the FACES scale (Olson, appendix; Olson et al. 1979, 1980), which quantifies the degrees of cohesion and adaptability in a family. Other self-reports can be used for identifying the areas of change desired in one's spouse, which corresponds to content areas where conflicts are likely to have occurred (Patterson 1976; Weiss and Perry 1979; Weiss and Buchler 1975; Weiss, Hops, and Patterson 1972). This particular thirty-four item questionnaire is called the Areas of Change questionnaire.

Conflict parties' communication behavior can be rated on either global or specific bases by using the inventories developed by Bienvenu (1970), Hobart and Klausner (1959), or the more lengthy 400–item Spouse Observation Checklist (Patterson 1976; Weiss et al. 1973; Weiss and Margolin 1977). The latter has been shortened to 179 items and retitled the Marital Observation Checklist (Christensen and Nies 1980). Extensive reviews of these two instruments are available in Gurman (1981), Gurman and Knudson (1978), and Margolin (1981). One instrument specifically designed for use with spouse disagreements is the Problem Inventory (Gottman et al. 1976). All of these instruments are self-reports by spouses on a variety of behaviors, including conflict.

Coding schemes that external observers can use for conflict behavior are the MICS—Marital Interaction Coding Scheme—(Hops et al. 1972) and the shortened MICS revised version by Resick et al. (1978) and Welsh-Osga (1979). In addition, the widely cited Coding Scheme for Interpersonal Conflict (Raush et al. 1974) is particularly comprehensive for coding conflict behaviors. A shortened version revised for observation of small-group conflict appears in Baxter's work (1982).

Conflict styles have received considerable attention for both workshop use and research. Many of the scales essentially duplicate one another, especially those based on the Blake and Mouton Managerial grid. But for training use, the instruments by Hall (appendix), Roberts (1982), Lawrence and Lorsch (1969), and Kilmann-Thomas (1975) are useful. Research on their dimensions, however, has been limited or insufficient. Putnam and Wilson (1982) have provided the best researched and most versatile instrument. While it was designed for assessing personal styles in organizations, it has utility in other conflict settings. Also, it can be adapted for use with both self and other conflict styles (and so can most other instruments). Finally, one other instrument measures perceptions of the spouse's style, but there is some doubt as to the generalizability of its a priori dimensions (Rands, Levinger, and Mellinger 1981). All of these above devices are self-reports on typical conflict styles as the *parties* perceive them.

Power in conflict can also be measured. The work by Cavanaugh et al. (1981) is a beginning attempt to specify individual values about power, and it provides information similar to "attitudes toward conflict" approaches. Power per se is a difficult concept to measure, and before selecting any one approach, the reviews by Berger (1980), Cromwell and Olson (1975), Turk and Bell (1972), Galvin and Brommel (1982), McCall (1979), McDonald (1980), and

Gray-Little and Burke (1983) should be consulted. Basically, power is multidimensional, and the separate components are not necessarily similar to one another. Further, assessments have tended to specialize in either (1) process (interaction) or (2) outcome (decision-making) approaches. Process approaches are represented by the work of Rogers and Farace (1975), Rogers-Millar and Millar (1977), Ellis (1979), Aldous (1977), and Mishler and Waxler (1968). Outcome stances are represented in the work of Blood and Wolfe (1960), Safilios-Rothschild (1970), Heer (1962), Kenkel (1975), Olson and Strauss (1972), Olson and Rabunsky (1972), and McDonald (1980).

Tactical options can be measured quantitatively through self-reports or observational methods. Some self-report methods are provided by Brown and Levinson (1978), who organize tactics according to whether they support or attack the other's presentation of "face" or self. For a typology of "Compliance-Gaining" tactics (which are limited by their one-way view of social interaction), consult Marwell and Schmidt (1967) and additional sources cited in the Conflict Tactics chapter in this book. In addition, Kipnis (1976) discusses "Means of Influence" from a similar one-way perspective. The self-report styles instrument of Putnam and Wilson (1982) can be modified to apply to a particular conflict instead of for predominant stylistic choices. Finally, the Strauss (1978, 1979) Conflict Tactics Scale is noteworthy for its inclusion of a physical violence index as part of the scale.

For observational coding of tactical choices, one can choose between the work of Rausch et al. (1974), Chafetz (1980), and Sillars (1982). For tactics used in negotiation settings, Donohue's (1982) approach is useful.

Conflict assessment always involves some choice making. If you wish to get a clear sense of the overall pattern of a conflict, a broad view of the place of rules and repetitive patterns in the system are needed. Such a "macro" view provides richness of description and creativity at the expense of quantitative specificity. The quantitative approaches, while providing reliable specificity in a given area, do not place those specifics within a comprehensive framework. We conclude this chapter by providing two overall assessment guides that can be used as organizing schemes for probing conflicts. These guides supply perspectives, not answers, and they need to be adapted for your particular purposes.

Comprehensive Assessment Guides

Conflict assessment is the process of systematic collection of information about the dynamics of a conflict. The guides stress open-ended, participant-based data as the path to specifying conflict processes. Such approaches are particularly useful for third parties such as intervention agents and students wishing to study a particular conflict. As a party to the conflict, one can use the guides to collect information from himself or herself and the other party about the conflict. In either case, one needs to use primary information from the parties—for they are the ones who created and maintain the conflict.

Two assessment guides are (1) the Wehr Conflict Mapping Guide and (2) the Hocker-Wilmot Conflict Assessment Guide. Depending on the purpose of the assessment, the guides can be combined or altered to specifically address one's assessment goals. All conflicts change over time, and an assessment is limited to the time period in which it was collected—one might obtain different information by assessing earlier or later in the conflict process.

Wehr's Conflict Map

In his book *Conflict Regulation,* Wehr (1979) provided a "Conflict Mapping Guide" to give "both the intervener and the conflict parties a clearer understanding of the origins, nature, dynamics, and possibilities for resolution of conflict" (19). The map should include the following information:

  I. *Summary Description* (one-page maximum)

 II. *Conflict History.* The origins and major events in the evolution both of the conflict and its context. It is important to make this distinction between the interactive conflict relationship among the parties and the context within which it occurs.

III. *Conflict Context.* It is important to establish the scope and character of the context or setting within which the conflict takes place. Such dimensions are geographical boundaries; political structures, relations, and jurisdictions; communication networks and patterns; and decision-making methods. Most of these are applicable to the full range of conflict types, from interpersonal to international levels

IV. *Conflict Parties.* Decisional units directly or indirectly involved in the conflict and having some significant stake in its outcome.
   A. *Primary:* parties whose goals are, or are perceived by them to be, incompatible and who interact directly in pursuit of those respective goals. Where the conflict parties are organizations or groups, each may be composed of smaller units differing in their involvement and investment in the conflict.
   B. *Secondary:* parties who have an indirect stake in the outcome of the dispute but who do not feel themselves to be directly involved. As the conflict progresses, secondary parties may become primary, however, and vice-versa.
   C. *Interested third parties;* those who have an interest in the successful resolution of the conflict.

Pertinent information about the parties in addition to who they are would include the nature of the power relations between/among them (e.g., symmetrical or asymmetrical); their leadership; each party's main goals(s) in the conflict; and the potential for coalitions among parties.

V. *Issues*. Normally, a conflict will develop around one or more issues emerging from or leading to a decision. Each issue can be viewed as a point of disagreement that must be resolved. Issues can be identified and grouped according to the primary generating factor:

   A. *Facts-based:* disagreement over *what is* because of how parties perceive *what is*. Judgment and perception are the primary conflict generators here.
   B. *Values-based:* disagreement over *what should be* as a determinant of a policy decision, a relationship, or some other source of conflict.
   C. *Interests-based:* disagreement over *who will get what* in the distribution of scarce resources (e.g., power, privilege, economic benefits, respect).
   D. *Nonrealistic:* originating elsewhere than in disparate perceptions, interests, or values. Style of interaction the parties use, the quality of communication between them, or aspects of the immediate physical setting, such as physical discomfort, are examples.

With few exceptions, any one conflict will be influenced by some disagreement emerging from each of these sources, but normally one source is predominant. It is useful not only to identify each issue in this way but to identify as well the significant disparities in perception, values, and interests motivating each party. (*Values* are here defined as beliefs that determine a party's position on any one issue [e.g., economic growth is always desirable]. *Interests* are defined as any party's desired or expected share of scarce resources [e.g., power, money, prestige, survival, respect, love]).

VI. *Dynamics*. Social conflicts have common though not always predictable dynamics that if recognized can help an intervener find the way around a conflict. The intervener must seek to reverse some of these and make them dynamics of regulation and resolution. They include the following:

   A. *Precipitating events* signaling the surfacing of a dispute.
   B. *Issue emergence, transformation, proliferation.* Issues change as a conflict progresses—specific issues become generalized, single issues multiply, impersonal disagreements can become personal feuds.
   C. *Polarization.* As parties seek internal consistency and coalitions with allies, and leaders consolidate positions, parties in conflict tend toward bipolarization that can lead both to greater intensity and to simplification and resolution of the conflict.
   D. *Spiraling.* Through a process of reciprocal causation, each party may try to increase the hostility or damage to opponents in each

round, with a corresponding increase from the latter. Also possible are deescalatory spirals, in which opponents reciprocally and incrementally reduce the hostility and rigidity of their interaction.

E. *Stereotyping and mirror-imaging.* Opponents often come to perceive one another as impersonal representations of the mirror-opposite of their own exemplary and benign characteristics. This process encourages rigidity on position and miscommunication and misinterpretation between conflict parties.

VII. *Alternative Routes to Solution(s) of the Problem(s).* Each of the parties and often uninvolved observers will have suggestions for resolving the conflict. In conflicts within a formal policymaking framework, the options can be formal plans. In interpersonal conflicts, alternatives can be behavioral changes suggested to (or by) the parties. It is essential to identify as many "policies" as possible that have already surfaced in the conflict. They should be made visible for both the conflict parties and the intervener. The intervener may then suggest new alternatives or combinations of those already identified.

VIII. *Conflict Regulation Potential.* In and for each conflict situation are to be found resources for limiting and perhaps resolving the conflict. The mapping process notes these resources, albeit in a preliminary way. They may include the following:

A. *Internal limiting factors* like values and interests the conflicting parties have a common, or the intrinsic value of a relationship between them that neither wishes to destroy, or cross pressures of multiple commitments of parties that constrain the conflict.

B. *External limiting factors* like a higher authority who could intervene and force a settlement or an intermediary from outside the conflict.

C. *Interested or neutral third parties* trusted by the parties in conflict who could facilitate communication, mediate the dispute, or locate financial resources to alleviate a scarcity problem.

D. *Techniques of conflict management,* both those familiar to the different conflict parties and third parties and those known to have been useful elsewhere. Such methods range from the well-known mediation, conciliation, and rumor control to fractionating issues and extending the time range to encourage settlement.

IX. *Using the Map.* The conflict map is most useful (and quite essential) as the initial step in conflict intervention. Mapping permits an informed judgment about whether the intervention should continue. The map is also helpful in assisting conflict parties to move back from and make sense out of a process to which they are too close. If the mapper decides to further intervene, sharing the map can loosen up the conflict, making it easier to resolve. Finally, the map helps demystify the process of conflict that, for so many people, seems a confusing, unfathomable, inexplicable, and thoroughly frustrating phenomenon.

The Hocker-Wilmot Conflict Assessment Guide

This guide is composed of a series of questions designed to focus on the components of conflict discussed in part I of this book. It can be used to bring specific aspects of a conflict into focus and serve as a check on gaps in information about a conflict. The guide is best used in toto so that the interplay of conflict elements can be clearly highlighted.

I. **Nature of the Conflict**
   A. What are the "triggering events" that brought this conflict into mutual awareness?
   B. What is the historical context of this conflict in terms of (1) the ongoing relationship between the parties and (2) other, external events within which this conflict is embedded?
   C. Do the parties have assumptions about conflict that are discernable by their choices of conflict metaphors, patterns of behavior, or clear expressions of their attitudes about conflict?
   D. Conflict elements:
      1. How is the struggle being expressed by each party?
      2. What are the perceived incompatible goals?
      3. What are the perceived scarce rewards?
      4. In what ways are the parties interdependent? How are they interfering with one another? How are they cooperating to keep the conflict in motion?
   E. Has the conflict vacillated between productive and destructive phases? If so, which elements were transformed during the productive cycles? Which elements might be transformed by creative solutions to the conflict?

II. **Styles of Conflict**
   A. What individual styles did each party use?
   B. How did the individual styles change during the course of the conflict?
   C. How did the parties perceive the other's style?
   D. In what way did a party's style reinforce the choices the other party made as the conflict progressed?
   E. Were the style choices primarily symmetrical or complementary?
   F. From an external perspective, what were the advantages and disadvantages of each style within this particular conflict?
   G. Can the overall system be characterized as having a predominant style? What do the participants say about the relationship as a whole?

    H. From an external perspective, where would this conflict system be placed in terms of cohesion and adaptability?

    I. Would any of the other system descriptions aptly summarize the system dynamics?

III. Power

    A. What attitudes about their own and the other's power does each party have? Do they talk openly about power, or is it not discussed?

    B. What do the parties see as their own and the other's dependencies on one another? As an external observer, can you classify some dependencies that they do not list?

    C. What power currencies do the parties see themselves and the other possessing?

    D. From an external perspective, what power currencies of which the participants are not aware seem to be operating?

    E. In what ways do the parties disagree on the balance of power between them? Do they underestimate their own or the other's influence?

    F. What impact does each party's assessment of power have on subsequent choices in the conflict?

    G. What evidence of destructive "power balancing" occurs?

    H. In what ways do observers of the conflict agree and disagree with the parties' assessments of their power?

    I. What are some unused sources of power that are present?

IV. Goals

    A. How do the parties clarify their goals? Do they phrase them in individualistic or system terms?

    B. What does each party think the other's goals are? Are they similar or dissimilar to the perceptions of self-goals?

    C. How have the goals been altered from the beginning of the conflict to the present? In what ways are the prospective, transactive, and retrospective goals similar or dissimilar?

    D. What are the content goals?

    E. What are the relational goals?

    F. What is each party's translation of content goals into relationship terms? How do the two sets of translations correspond or differ?

V. Tactics

    A. Do the participants appear to strategize about their conflict choices or remain spontaneous?

    B. How does each party view the other's strategizing?

    C. What are the tactical options used by both parties?

    D. Do the tactical options classify primarily into avoidance, competition, or collaborative tactics?

    E. How are the participants' tactics mutually impacting on the other's choices? How are the tactics interlocking to push the conflict through phases of escalation, maintenance, and reduction?

VI. **Assessment**
    A. What rules of repetitive patterns characterize this conflict?
    B. Can quantitative instruments be used to give information about elements of the conflict?

VII. **Self-Regulation**
    A. What options for change do the parties perceive?
    B. What philosophy of conflict characterizes the system?
    C. What techniques for self-regulation or system-regulation have been used thus far? Which might be used productively by the system?

VIII. **Attempted Solutions**
    A. What options have been explored for managing the conflict?
    B. Have attempted solutions become part of the problem?
    C. Have third parties been brought into the conflict? If so, what roles did they play and what was the impact of their involvement?
    D. Is this conflict a repetitive one, with attempted solutions providing temporary change, but with the overall pattern remaining unchanged? If so, what is that overall pattern?
    E. Can you identify categories of attempted solutions that have *not* been tried?

    The Conflict Assessment Guide can be used in a variety of contexts. Students who are writing an analysis of a conflict can use the questions as a check on the components of conflict. Using extensive interviews with the conflict parties or constructing a questionnaire based on the guide enables one to discover the dynamics of a conflict. The guide can also be used for analyzing larger social or international conflicts, but without interviewing or assessing the conflict parties, one is restricted to highly selective information.

    A consultant to organizations can also use the guide by modifying it for direct use. Similarly, an intervener in private conflicts such as those of a family can solicit information about the components of a conflict in an informal, conversational way by referring to the guide as an outline of relevant topics. In either case, care should be taken to modify the guide for the particular task, for the conflict parties, and for your intervention goals.

    If one is a participant in a conflict, the guide can be used as a form of self-intervention. If both parties respond to the guide, you can use it to highlight what you and the other party perceive about your conflict. Usually, we recommend that a questionnaire be constructed for both persons to answer, and once the data are collected, the parties can discuss the similarities and differences in their perceptions of the conflict.

Whatever your preferred assessment technique, or combination of approaches, the assessment devices in this chapter can enable you to see some order and regularity in conflicts that at first appear confusing and overwhelming. With careful assessment, the dynamics of conflict can come into focus so you can fashion creative, productive options for management.

Summary

Conflicts are often perplexing to both participants and outsiders. Usually, however, an interpersonal conflict is operating as a system of relations, complete with repetitive behavior, rules, and other identifiable dynamics. There are many possible ways to assess conflict patterns. Metaphoric/dramatic approaches search for the images of the process held by the participants and use those as a stepping stone for creative management options. Diagramming triangular relations also provides useful information about system dynamics. Sculpting is a nonverbal, spatially-based technique for identifying patterns of communication within a larger system. One can also focus on system rules, the prescriptions for what one ought to do in a given situation. Microevents are observable, recurring patterns of behavior that can be analyzed for underlying conflict structure.

If one wishes a quantitative assessment of conflict components for either (1) conflicts produced by simulation or games or (2) real-life conflicts accessed through self-reports of the parties, many options are available. For example, one can measure general orientations toward conflict, code behaviors enacted in an episode, identify conflict styles, assess power balances, or isolate the tactics used in a conflict.

Finally, two overall assessment guides are presented. The Wehr and Hocker-Wilmot guides are useful ways to generate information about the dynamics of specific conflicts; they can be used by either participants or outside observers.

7 Self-Regulation: Changing Conflict from the Inside Out

The young father, in his early twenties, was busy at the childrens' slide in the city park. He was keeping track of two other young children plus his own daughter, aged two years. She kept heading for the ladder on the slide to go up by herself, and each time he said, "Cristy, if you don't wait for me, I'll spank you." Then, he would join her and they would slide together. After one particular trip, she left and went to their small black puppy who was off to the side. When she picked him up by the neck, the father came running, spanked her four hard swats, and said in a loud voice, "Dammit, you shouldn't hurt animals smaller than you."

While disclaiming otherwise, the father was teaching his child to relate in conflict by using force. In the half hour he was sliding, he hit the youngster on the rear end three times, each time saying something like, "Now, listen to your dad." One thing is abundantly clear—the father could profit from mastering techniques for dealing with conflict with his daughter other than falling back on threat and physical force.

Options for Change

Parties to conflicts, like the father above, have three basic options for altering the conflict:

1. *Try to change the other party.* This is a "natural" response, usually highly unsuccessful. Just as you take your stance and choose your options for good reasons to you, the other party does the same. You will appear as unreasonable to the other as the other does to you— and your efforts to change the other will be met with efforts on his or her part to change you.

2. *Try to alter the conflict conditions.* If you can increase scarce resources, alter the nature of a problematic interdependence, change perceptions of incompatible goals, or make some other alteration in the conflict elements, you will be able to change a conflict.

3. *Change your own behavior.* This is usually the most difficult and, paradoxically, the most successful way to alter a conflict. A true change in your orientation to the other, your interpretation of the issues, reaction to power, or alterations in your own conflict process will have profound effects on the conflictual elements in the relationship. Self-change is the most successful focus for energy expenditure if you want to alter the course of a conflict.

This chapter highlights the philosophy that regulation of conflict "from the inside out," through *self-regulation,* is an effective technique for making conflicts productive. Further, we supply specific information on skills useful for changing behavior in conflicts. We discuss regulation generated by the individual instead of by rules imposed by someone higher up—you can regulate yourself and your own conflict behavior. Just as the Environmental Protection Agency regulates the amount of toxins in air and water, individuals may discipline themselves to regulate the intensity of conflict, the use of destructive tactics, displays of unequal power, unfair goals, or demeaning and unproductive styles. After you have assessed your conflict, self-regulation techniques can be used.

Our basic premise is that the conflict parties are responsible for the direction of their relationship. If you are in an unproductive or destructive conflict with another, you have the responsibility to put restraints on your own choices that feed the destructive spiral. People create the systems of interaction that later encircle and entrap them into repetitive rounds of destructive conflict. As noted in the discussion of systems theory in the last chapter, change in an individual changes the entire system. Some interesting research on teacher-student interaction pointed out this fact in a particularly graphic way. Marginal students in an elementary school were identified and given special training to modify the behavior of the teachers who were most hostile to these students who often did not do their work, disrupted class, acted arrogantly, and engaged in other behavior considered unacceptable by the teachers. The students were taught to verbally reinforce the teachers for any positive attention and to point out to them in socially acceptable ways what teacher behaviors were harmful and helpful to the students. For instance, the children were taught to say things like, "I'd appreciate it if you would warn me about talking before sending me out of the room." The results, of course, were astonishing, with many of the students being socialized back into their classrooms, with large changes in their self-esteem, and with the teachers feeling much more positively about the students (Gray, Graubard and Rosenberg 1974).

Self-change in a conflict, since it is difficult, usually has some prerequisites. If you are going to alter your own behavior, rather than just assert that your actions are "natural" or "only in response to what she did," you usually have to care about the relationship. If the relationship is of no consequence to you, then you feel little impetus to change. In addition, you have to be willing to accept the notion that your own choices are most assuredly having some influence on the conflict process—even if you cannot identify the effects.

Finally, people get something from a conflict interaction even if they claim they do not; recognition of what you are gaining from the ongoing conflict may free you up for change. Some possible "gains" in the midst of trauma are—(1) the relationship keeps going, though destructively; (2) pleasure is gained by proving to family or friends how wrong the other is (and how innocent and purely motivated you are); and (3) you are able to exert overt power. Each party to an ongoing conflict receives some gain from the conflict, even in the midst of the negative consequences.

Midrange Conflict

Moderated conflicts have the greatest potential for productive management. Suppressed or unacknowledged conflict and unrestrained runaway conflict spirals are equally unproductive. Figure 7.1 illustrates the potential for productive conflict, depending on the conflict degree (for similar treatments see Walton 1969, Brown 1983).

Low productivity occurs when interpersonal conflicts are not identified or openly expressed to the other party. The unexpressed frustration prevents you from working through the conflict, gives you the entire burden of negative feelings, and precludes the other from joining with you to create solutions to the difficulty. You neither share the pain nor experience the release of pent-up feelings when it might do some good. Choosing to engage the other in conflict can enable you to—

1. assert yourself as a legitimate party;

2. verbalize the content issues of which the other may be unaware;

3. recognize mutual dependence and importance of the relationship; and

4. create solutions that can emerge from both parties.

At the other extreme, with few restraints on conflict expression, a runaway destructive conflict spiral damages all. Two businessmen who have no restraints on their competition would logically end the conflict by burning down one another's business! Similarly, the lack of regulation in personal relationships is damaging. For instance, a divorced couple attempted to share the custody of their two children and were close to agreement when the ex-wife

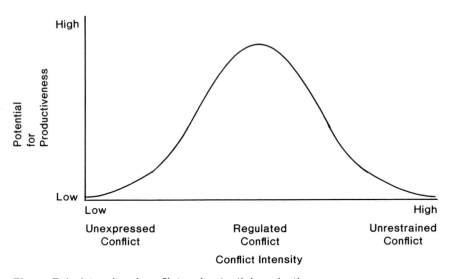

Figure 7.1. Intensity of conflict and potential productiveness.

exploded in the mediation session, saying, "He's selfish! He always was and he always will be!" Her unregulated outburst ruined the chance for collaboration on their problem. Regardless of the specific conflict, after an episode has passed, the other person will recall what you did during the conflict. This, in turn, sets the stage for the next enactment of the conflict in your relationship. People have long memories for poor treatment. Keeping a conflict in the midrange through self-regulation will mitigate these long-term effects.

If people are successful at keeping their conflicts in the midrange or bringing them up into midrange from avoidance, they can expect some distinct advantages from their efforts at conflict regulation. Conflict regulation—

1. alters the escalatory conflict spiral and halts destructive behavior;

2. allows self-discovery; when you use restraint, you have the time to understand sources of power you can use, and you can understand your own needs and goals for this particular conflict;

3. allows for more creative conflict management options than either party could generate singly; each individual is induced into innovation (Walton 1969);

4. prevents you from taking actions that you will later have to justify or feel remorse for using; and

5. releases energy for productive uses that was being diverted into frustration.

Changing oneself to engage in midrange conflicts brings these advantages; for the rest of the chapter we discuss techniques useful for engaging in regulated conflict.

Types of Self-Regulation

Regulation through Belief in Nonviolence

The peace tradition in the United States and elsewhere continues to contribute a religious and philosophical perspective on the limitation of conflict behavior. Groups and individuals in the historic peace churches, persons who identify themselves as pacifists, conscientious objectors to the draft system, proponents of nonviolent social change, and advocates of the nuclear freeze movement and other disarmament movements all support, to varying degrees, the principles of nonviolent change. The basic principles of nonviolence will be discussed in the context of interpersonal rather than international conflict.

Power and violence were treated at length in chapter 3. Proponents of nonviolence often support the idea that "power is abused as soon as a man can with impunity impose his will upon another" (Tournier 1978, 116). While different views of violence are proposed, most pacifists define violence as more than physical force or coercion. Tournier warns of the "mutual and fatal interplay between the unseen violence of the powerful and the open violence of those who oppose them" (1978, 114). Carefully balanced power, which may be based on a balance of fear and threat, often suddenly amplifies into aggression or violence that no longer serves the forces of life and growth, but acts against life, sowing the seeds of death (Tournier 1978, 6). A death can be the physical death of a person, the death of a relationship, or the death of creative struggling toward peaceful management of conflict.

Nonviolent principles warn against the buildup of arms in the service of ultimate peace. C. Wright Mills calls the policy of arming in order to disarm the exercise of "crackpot realism." Kurt Adler (quoted in Tournier 1978, 10) notes that "the word deterrence may be new, but the fact is as old and as universal as the human race. The Romans said: *'Si vis pacem, para bellum*— if you want peace, prepare for war'." We have already discussed the problems with threats and power balancing based on fear of the other. In interpersonal relationships, building up arms might be characterized by practices such as developing private coalitions, keeping secrets to use against an opponent when needed, telling only part of the truth in the hope of not having to play all your cards, using the threat of blackmail against enemies, and engaging in various other "dirty tricks." Indeed, the conflict style of too many persons is directed toward developing "first-strike capability" even in close relationships. Energy and personal resources are used in the stockpiling of personal power rather than in the building of new possibilities for the people working through their problems.

Peace in interpersonal relationships is not simply the absence of conflict. Rather, "Peace is the process of working to resolve conflict in such a way that both sides win, with increased harmony as the outcome of the conflict and its resolution" (McGinnis and McGinnis 1981, 23). Consistent with the notions of midrange conflict expressed above, the nonviolent approach to conflict does not try to stop conflict, but tries to keep conflict at a moderate, manageable level (Arnett 1981). As Arnett aptly says, "Nonviolent peacemaking values the other and attempts to encourage each person's growth. The peacemaker needs to build up the other and seek a creative end to conflict that does not tear down people or cultures" (Arnett 1980, 27).[1] The goal for nonviolence is to develop effective nonviolent means of resolving conflict (Frank 1978).

Our language lacks a precise term for the kind of peacemaking advocated by pacifists. The usual terms such as nonviolence, passive resistance, pacifism, and so on, according to Frank, conjure up images of a person "standing by with a holy look on his face while a soldier runs a bayonet through his sister" (1978, 194). Actually, of course, the aim of nonviolence is to keep such situations from arising in the first place. The terms used for such activity do a disservice to the high degree of initiative, activity, resourcefulness and courage required by the approach. Gandhi in India and King in Alabama, for instance, actively trained followers in the creative uses of nonviolence—training that included physical reactions to violence as well as philosophical principles about nonviolence. Even the phrase "nuclear freeze" is not reflective of the activity required for disarmament and the persuasive campaign for changing public opinion. Nonviolence as a movement awaits a more accurate term to describe its process.

We will give one final explanation of what nonviolence is *not*. It is not a simple, global solution to world dangers. The chant of the demonstrators of the sixties, "All we are saying is give peace a chance," was a beginning wish, not a solution to put in practice. Nonviolence is extraordinarily difficult, incurs grave risks, and demands the development of a wide variety of measures tailored to meet the specific requirements of different types of conflicts (Frank 1978).

Interpersonal Nonviolence

Nonviolence has been developed over many years, and as a tradition it draws from different religious and philosophical sources. Some common principles useful to interpersonal conflict follow.[2]

1. For a comprehensive discussion of nonviolent principles applied to interpersonal relationships, see Ron Arnett's book, *Dwell in Peace: Applying Nonviolence to Everyday Relationships* Elgin, Ill.: The Brethren Press, 1980.

2. For a brief but comprehensive exposition of nonviolence, see: *Speak Truth to Power* (Philadelphia: American Friends Service Committee, 1955), Hinshaw, C. E. *Nonviolent Resistance: A Nation's Way to Peace* (Wallingford, PA: Pendle Hill, 1956), and King, M. L. *Stride Toward Freedom* (New York: Ballantine, 1961).

Dialogue

One's communication both indicates and creates the level of conflict intensity (Waln 1981). Dialogue differs from the usual kind of conversation because while you may dislike what the other person advocates, you still listen and work to value the person. While "you can't value all human behavior positively, . . . you can value each human positively" (Stewart 1978). Dialogue is possible only between two persons or two groups whose power relationship is more or less in balance (Tournier 1978). In dialogue one constructively confronts the other so that". . . the answer to a conflict emerges 'between' the conflicting parties" (Arnett 1980, 113). In this dialogical view of conflict, neither party alone possesses truth; truth emerges during the struggle with one another (Buber 1972; Stewart 1978). The concept centers on the nature of the struggle between the parties. As you can well imagine, dialogue is not easy. As Keller says, "The true test of dialogue is in conflict, not in casual conversation" (Arnett 1980, 124). Engaging in dialogue requires an "immense toughness of self," demanding that we confirm the opposing party while doing conflict (Brown and Keller 1973). Engaging a person in dialogue is an act of commitment to the relationship and to one's own principles at the same time. If a person can find the courage to meet aggression with calm friendliness, this may have a powerful inhibiting effect (Frank 1978). Dialogue taken seriously leads toward collaboration.

Self-restraint

Another principle of nonviolence is that of self-control, or maintaining belief in an internal locus of control (Elliott 1980). Since "conflict resolution is largely the discovery of a means to break into escalatory reciprocal causation and reverse its direction (Wehr 1979, 63), self-restraint and self-control do create change in the conflict system. Proponents of nonviolence maintain that one always has a choice about how to respond to provocation. Even if the choice (at an extreme) is to submit with grace to coercion and to feel pity for the person perpetrating the violence, a choice remains. One may experience a flash of anger but choose to take actions that reflect a different feeling. For instance, parents often are furious with their children. They report to counselors that they have fantasies about hurting their children, abandoning them, or wishing them dead. Yet most parents are able to restrain their occasional outbursts of destructive feeling. They exercise self-control in the interest of the larger, loving relationship. *We do not have to act the way we feel.* Persons such as Gandhi and others who developed nonviolence as a cornerstone of their personal orientation to life were apparently able to control not only the action but the feelings as well.

Joining

If you follow the nonviolent philosophy, your goal is to join with your opponent in forming a team of persons struggling together to find a solution to a common problem. In some mediation sessions, the mediator requests that the "opponents" sit side by side while they focus attention on a chalkboard on which the problem is written. Early Quakers asked potential conflict partners, such as American Indian chiefs and colonists who did not want them to settle in their midst, to join with them in a period of silence. The purpose of the silence was to await wisdom about how to speak with each other. Agreeing to join with each other in this step was actually a first step in resolving their conflict. The Senoi tribe in Malaysia, a tribe that until recently experienced little poverty or social disruption, taught their children to walk toward monster figures in their dreams—to ask the scary figures what they wanted, and to ask for a gift from the threatening figure (Garfield 1974). There exists a pressure toward symmetry (Capella 1981); one is likely to act in like manner to the initiator. Moving toward enemies as if they were friends exerts a paradoxical force on them and can bring transcendence of the enmity relationship (Schroer 1981).

Refusal to Compromise One's Deepest Principles

Nonviolent confrontation is not a move toward compromise. It is, instead, a gently stubborn insistence that principles of right and fairness cannot be compromised, along with the insistence that former enemies working together can produce a better solution than presently exists through coercion. Gandhi's *satyagraha* movement exemplified this pacificist stance through the objective of waging conflict without violent means or consequences (Wehr 1979, 5). As Wehr outlines, Gandhi's conflict style, which resulted in the freeing of millions of Indians from control of the British, supplied a strategy for each force that might escalate into destructiveness.

The fifth dynamic, emergence of extremist leadership, pertains more to large social movements. Gandhi met it by retaining leadership and continually applying the brakes of nonviolence (Wehr 1979). The essential elements of a pacifist, nonviolent approach to conflict management are especially applicable to interpersonal conflict situations. The refusal to engage in physically or psychologically violent behaviors can pave the way for a continued relationship with the other party, bypassing destructiveness for both.

The nonviolent conflict management perspective can be an effective approach. Boulding (1977) notes that nonviolence is as effective as violence. Recent work on interpersonal negotiation demonstrates that collaborative, integrative solutions come from "vigorous discussions or mild arguments" (Pruitt 1981, 192) rather than competitive orientations toward conflict management. Of course, limitations to a pacifist strategy exist. When there are no restraints on the other party, nonviolence may fail (Reychler 1979). When the power balance is seriously disparate, it is not likely that the low-power person

Gandhian Responses to Destructive Conflict

Destructive Conflict Forces	Gandhi's Strategy
1. Movement from specific to more general issues and from original to new issues	Tie each campaign to a single issue and in a sharply limited arena.
2. Movement from disagreement to antagonism as the conflict develops	Reduce threat by stressing the maintenance of good personal relations with opponents while pressing the issue, simultaneously providing for confrontation and maximizing the potential for conciliation.
3. Distortion of information	Openly discuss tactics; eliminate secrecy and misinformation to reduce the perceived threat to opponents.
4. Mutual reinforcement of response (escalatory spiral)	Use positive reciprocal causation; nonviolent action promotes a nonhostile response.

(adapted from Wehr 1979, 60–62)

can maintain effective change through nonviolence. However, as discussed in chapter three, people usually have more potential bases for power than they recognize. Often the leap into violence is made in ignorance of nonviolent possibilities.

A program for interpersonal nonviolence is not a list of techniques that, if followed, will lead to nonviolent solutions. You will need to devise your own way of incorporating nonviolence into your approach to conflict if the principles are ones you already hold or wish to adopt.

Nonviolence is a highly personal, involving way of acting, dependent upon firmly held beliefs. One way to start is to keep track of the times you feel coerced or violated—your feelings, your plans for revenge, your stored-up anger. Then ask those close to you to tell you when they have felt the same way. If you have a friend who will tell you when you were coercive, you are fortunate indeed, since most of us are blind to our own use of interpersonal violence. Reading further in the literature of nonviolence may be a step you want to take. The techniques that follow in this chapter, while not drawn directly from the literature on nonviolence, can all be used to follow principles of nonviolence. They all require self-control, restraint, and a planned approach to the reduction of conflict while not giving in too quickly to the wishes or demands of another person.

Techniques for Self-Regulation

When an interpersonal system spirals into escalation, the conflict parties need some mechanisms for altering the destructive conflict dynamics. Numerous ways exist to escape the encompassing traps of mutual escalation. Etzioni (1964) writes of "encapsulating" conflict, Osgood (1962) of "reciprocal concessions," and Kipnis (1979) of "inhibiting the power act." Whatever your preferred label, these techniques will help you escape from the seductive trap of continued escalation and intensity (Rubin 1981).

Fractionation

The basic reduction tactic is usually some form of the device known as fractionating, a phrase coined by Fisher in his seminal essay, "Fractionating Conflict" (1971). He suggests that conflict can be reduced by focusing attention on the *sizing* of disputes. Conflicts can be broken down from one big mass to several smaller, more manageable conflicts. Fractionating conflict does not make it disappear, of course; it simply makes component parts of large conflicts more approachable by parties who are trying to manage their disputes. Even though we often forget the idea, conflicts "do not have objective edges established by external events" (Fisher 1971, 158). Conflicts are more like a seamless web, with indistinguishable beginnings and endings. Choices are almost always available as to how the conflicts are sized for management. A group of ten townspeople recently met at the instigation of one of the members to determine what should be done about the deteriorating quality of the town's air. They were determined to do something to improve the air quality after the recent inversion caused several persons to be hospitalized and other residents suffered from respiratory problems, allergies, and asthma attacks. In the group's opinion, the major culprit was the town's large paper mill, which had, they suspected, been violating air quality standards. One way to size the conflict would be to mount an all-out attack on the very existence of the plant, contacting everyone they could think of to try to get the plant closed down. One step down from that mode of attack would be to conceptualize the conflict as being between the citizens of the town and the management of the company. Defining the parties in this way suggests a negotiation device to try to resolve the conflict. An even smaller sizing might be to conceptualize the conflict as being between some concerned citizens and city council and the county commissioners who enforced the air quality standards. If the conflict were conceptualized in this way, yet another plan of management would be appropriate. The smallest sizing of the conflict would have been one between the committee of ten and the engineers who monitor the air quality machinery at the plant. The group succeeded in reducing the conflict by defining the conflict carefully, assessing their resources, talking to the "other side," and carefully planning an incremental campaign to get more citizens involved in the issue. By fractionating the conflict for purposes of analysis, they were able later to manage

Fractionating with Neighbors

While writing this chapter on self-regulation, an opportunity for using fractionation and nonviolent principles presented itself. We were on sabbatical, living in an apartment in a large city, writing late at night, and working to meet publication deadlines. As the deadlines approached, one or the other of us was up typing much of the time. One night, the neighbor, a woman from downstairs, knocked on the door at midnight. The exchange follows:

Neighbor: I can't sleep with all that stomping around! I have to get up at 5:30, and you stomp all night.

Bill: I'm sorry. I didn't know we were disturbing you.

Neighbor: You stomp all the time. I can't sleep!

Bill: You mean our walking bothers you? We didn't know that. We'll be as quiet as we can.

Several nights later, a knock on the ceiling below notified us, we thought, that the typewriters were disturbing the neighbor. We stopped typing and started building up resentment.

Finally, one night, Joyce decided to try to fractionate. By this time she was rehearsing in her mind all the reasons that the neighbor was unreasonable, "How can I get my work done if I can't even type," etc. She went down to speak with the neighbor after reflecting on nonviolence. . . .

Joyce: Hello. I'm your neighbor from upstairs. We are aware that we've been disturbing you and wanted to ask if the typing is a problem late at night.

Neighbor: No, it's *not* the typing it's the stomping and taking showers at all hours.

Joyce: We don't want to disturb you. We have been trying to walk softly, and now we know that showers are a problem too. We can change that. Here's a card with our phone number on it. We'd appreciate a call if you're being kept awake by our noise.

Neighbor: Well, after hours is after hours! If you could just keep the stomping and showers down. Walk softly!

Joyce: We will try, but we may need your help. I'm relieved to know the typing doesn't bother you. We'd rather get a phone call and stop whatever we're doing than disturb you. Will you do that?

Neighbor: Maybe you didn't know anyone lived here. The apartment was empty for a while. It's just the walking, not the typing.

Joyce: OK. We'll watch it for sure. And I'm glad you're going to help us. Thanks.

Neighbor: (Smiles.) Good luck on the writing.

The outcome for Joyce and Bill was that they felt responsible for keeping their part of the agreement, and not asserting their "right" to do what they pleased, which would have led to escalation. We can only guess at the outcome for the neighbor. We hope she slept well and was relieved of anger at her upstairs neighbors.

it to fit their purposes. After all, closing the plant would have had negative consequences for the town, too.

Fractionation also implies making small conflicts out of larger ones. This simple idea remains one of the most useful tactics. Almost all conflicts can be made smaller than they are without, we might add, trivializing or devaluing them. In a student-teacher conflict, for instance, the students might come into the classroom one day and ask for the abolition of all the grading in the course. The teacher could escalate the issue by becoming defensive and polarizing the issue or resorting to rules or external authority. But the issue could be reduced in size by the teacher's asking the students what they most objected to in the tests and then talking about those features. Or the teacher could look for other subissues in the "Let's don't have tests" statement and might find that the tests were misscheduled, unexpected, unclear, or too long. Then the parties can handle their small issues instead of expending their relational power by fighting an issue that is too extreme and probably would not be resolved satisfactorily.

Some phrases that help in the process of fractionation follow:

- "What part of that problem is most important to your group right now?"

- "Who are the people most immediately involved?"

- "Whom could we go talk to about this?" (This approach personalizes instead of stereotypes the other side.)

- "Maybe we'll have to go to that, but let's see what we might try first." (This statement acknowledges the possibility of escalation but expresses a preference for sizing the conflict.)

- "I want to hear more about your objections. Please tell me what is not working for you." (This statement joins with the other party, inviting dialogue rather than setting up a competitive stance.)

- "You probably know I cannot accept what you are saying. That approach would violate what I hold most dear. I want to know what makes that decision your first choice. Then I can work with you to meet both our needs." (This statement reiterates that certain principles cannot be breached but that you are continuing the dialogue.)

GRIT

The "Graduated Reduction in Tension" technique (originally labelled "Graduated Reciprocation in Tension Reduction") was developed by Osgood (1972). The GRIT approach stresses the importance of unilateral action and its potential induction of reciprocation in the other conflict party. One controls the tension in a conflict relationship as the leverage for reducing the conflict intensity. The GRIT technique was designed for the arms race, but the principles apply to interpersonal conflict as well. It is similar to fractionation in its conceptual base.

The technique involves a small, step-by-step reduction in tension, announced at each stage. Further, one person tells the other party where he or she is going and makes an explicit invitation to come along. You then take the graduated reduction regardless of the other's reaction and do it in such a way that the step is unambiguous. Put briefly, if two people "keep on behaving *as if* they trusted each other, their beliefs and attitudes tend to fall in line with their behaviors" (Osgood 1972, 525). One uses the GRIT technique because it (1) maintains some degree of security for the initiating party and (2) induces reciprocations from the other party because of the expectation of fairness and reciprocity.

Stuart's Conflict Containment Model

Stuart's (1980) model provides an overall outline for conflict containment based on his work with married couples. He notes that issue expansion (Raush et al. 1974) and personal attacks accompany destructive conflicts, thus his model offers guidelines for containing and regulating the exchange. It involves three primary foci (Stuart 1980).

1. Emphasizing a *present orientation*—The focus is on the present, not the past. The "search for roots of conflict in the past should be abandoned in favor of the quest for solutions in the present." *Why* questions are replaced by *how* questions.

2. *Adopting a "conciliatory set"*—This requires (1) labelling the behavior of the other in the most positive light and (2) planning moves to "resolve the issue equitably" rather than by winning. For instance, Margaret arrives home for dinner an hour late. Burt decides that she has no regard for his feelings, so he gets mad and labels her "selfish." He could have labelled Margaret's behavior differently; for instance, "She has trouble managing time," or "She gets really involved in her work." Either of these relabelled attributions would allow him to have a different response to the trigger event (pp. 292–293). Labelling one person as the villian merely sets off counter attacks.

3. *Seeking solutions in small steps*—Address issues one at a time and sequentially. Sometimes using writing as a way to slow the process down is helpful. One complaint is dealt with at a time, and each person takes a turn.

These basic techniques are adapted to the various stages of conflict. The following conflict stages can be usefully responded to by using the three techniques listed above. Note that conflict containment techniques are necessarily adapted to the specific stage the conflict is moving through.

Stuart's Conflict Containment Stages

1. *Trigger stage* (the first recognition of the conflict involving emotional reaction)

   Pause before responding and use that time to ask yourself these questions.
   a. Exactly what is the issue?
   b. Exactly what would satisfy me?
   c. Is the goal important?
   d. Have I tried to get what I want through problem solving?
   e. How much conflict am I willing to risk to get what I want?

2. *Reflex stage* (when you respond to the other; often with the expression of anger)

   You can put your threatening messages into focus by asking yourself these four questions.
   a. Have I qualified my statement by accepting my anger?
   b. Have I expressed respect for the other person although communicating my displeasure with his or her actions?
   c. Have I made a threat that is modest and therefore credible?
   d. Have I asked for a specific and reasonable change?

3. *Reflex fatigue* (the reaction from having expressed one's anger)

   A useful two-step approach can move the interaction from conflict to problem solving.
   a. Express recognition of his or her anger.
   b. Refocus it by asking what he or she would like you to do in the future.

4. *Commitment stage* (in which the persons maneuver for relationship gain, "generally in the form of greater power in future exchanges." People harden into positions temporarily.)

   You can assist the other by announcing your intentions before the fact; "I am going to sit and tell you how frustrating this has been for me." If you are the recipient, listening quietly, and respecting the other's anger as legitimate will assist in its reduction.

5. *Reconsolidation stage* (in which the problem mode is engaged)

   You can learn to signal the other when you are ready to problem solve, e.g., "OK, I'm ready to begin working on how to stop this from happening again." People develop private signals to communicate, "Let's work on it."

6. *Reapproachment* (summarizing what you have learned, acknowledging the lesson, and making agreements to change)

   Obviously, without this "learning" stage, the conflict will be left to simmer and erupt again. You need to take action to demonstrate to the other your willingness to alter elements of the conflict.

   (from Stuart, *Helping Couples Change*, 1980, 295–300)

The stages listed above may be useful to you in several ways. People might use them as a guide to help them understand conflicts or to pinpoint the stage at which their present conflict gets bogged down. Observers can help with the three approaches that Stuart suggests (emphasizing the present adopting a conciliatory set, and seeking solutions in small steps.) Application of these three suggestions, as well as others made throughout the book, will help parties move quickly through these stages. People may, of course, have developed different stages of conflict that characterize their relationships. These three approaches are an amalgamation of many couples with whom Stuart has worked. Finally, one person can employ self-limitation with an eye toward productive conflict even if the other person does not. Such an example follows:

Brenda and Gerry

(The following is a shortened version of a conflict in which Brenda tries to self-limit and Gerry does not.)

Gerry: You never have understood how important my work is to me. Now you're trying to get me to stop working on my computer program for the new game. Somebody has to take work seriously.

Conciliatory Set

Brenda: I want to work this out. It's not working for me to constantly ask for more time from you and for you to feel guilty and lock yourself in your study.

Gerry: You didn't want me to go into programming from the beginning.

Present Set

Brenda: I don't want to change your profession at all. I want more time from you this year—I don't want to wait until vacation to spend time alone with you.

Gerry: I guess I should quit doing creative work and just punch the old time clock. Would that make you happy?

Small Steps Conciliatory Set

Brenda: No, it wouldn't. I can't be happy if you're doing something you hate. We ought to be able to work out time together and some time for your new game. I miss you.

Gerry: What is it you want to do so bad?

Small Steps

Brenda: I want to spend good time with you. We can work out how and what together.

Negotiation: Agreeing to Rules of Process

Negotiation is a means for regularizing conflict processes so that agreements can be reached between the conflict parties. We have all heard of contract negotiations between labor and management, collective bargaining for employees in the public sector, and international negotiations over troop withdrawals and related issues. Negotiation occurs in any conflict arena; it is the process of parties' interacting to arrive at the settlement of some issue (Rubin and Brown 1975, 2). Stated technically, "Negotiation is a process by which a joint decision is made by two or more parties" (Pruitt 1981, 1).

The negotiation process serves to regulate an exchange between the conflict parties. If you agree to negotiate, you are signalling a desire to work with the other party, though the process itself may involve intensive work, extensive maneuvering, and many trips to the bargaining "table." But the conflict parties, by agreeing to negotiate, are placing limits on their conflict relationship—they open themselves up for an exchange with the other. Whereas coercion in a conflict is "characterized by two negative interests connected by a threat," bargaining is "characterized by two positive interests connected by a promise" (Rummel 1976, 179). The promise is to continue working to reach accommodation and agreement on the issues.

Through communication, the process of waging midrange conflict unfolds. There are numerous ways to study the processes per se (Zartman 1971; Spector 1977; Putnam and Jones 1982; Donohue 1981, 1981b; Hale 1982; Tedeschi and Rosefeld 1980; Schuetz 1975) and a wide-ranging literature on negotiation is available (see, especially, Rubin and Brown 1975; Pruitt 1981; Gulliver 1979; Walton and McKersie 1965; Duckman 1977; Strauss 1979, and Raiffa 1982). Rather than summarizing that diverse literature, most of which focuses on contract negotiations, we will discuss negotiation concepts that are useful across a variety of interpersonal settings.

The very term "negotiation" seems offensive to some; it may connote a "game-like" posturing by the parties, a mechanism that can be misused to drag out a conflict, or a process that brings a sharp distinction between the parties in which each is totally self-motivated. However, if parties agree to cooperate in conducting a conflict via negotiation, they already reduce the potential intensity of the conflict. *Tacit negotiations* occur continuously in most ongoing relationships. One person agrees to something if the other will likewise agree ("I'll pick you up at 8:00 tonight if you'll take me to the airport tomorrow"). Sometimes, it is easier for people to classify their tacit bargaining as an "agreement" or "informal understanding," rather than to say, "I will negotiate with my neighbor tomorrow about where to put the fence." Many prefer to not call attention to the process, and they say something like "We are going to chat tomorrow about the fence."

   In marital and other close relationships, the nature of the negotiation exchanges are often symptomatic of relationship distress. These ongoing dynamics, made especially clear during conflicts, are characterized by more negative exchanges, less problem solving, more blaming, and the placing of "you go first" on requests for change (Weiss, Hops, and Patterson 1972; Vincent 1975; Margolin 1982; Ferreira and Winter 1968). The "silent bargains" (Strauss 1979) of the conflict parties keep them embroiled in classic unproductive exchanges—blaming the other, taking extreme stands, and engaging in repetitive conflicts that are not solved. The "implicit substratum of negotiation" (Morgan 1975) keeps the relationship distressed by continuing the destructive conflict cycle. These cycles can be altered by changing the communication during the conflict so that, over time, the relationship can improve. Communication skills training, contracting, and negotiation and problem-solving skills can improve even the most intimate type of relationship (Hocker 1984; Baucom 1982; Patterson, Hops, and Weiss 1975; Margolin 1982). Such approaches have also been applied to conflicts between youths and their parents (Kifer et al. 1974). We discussed earlier the Fisher and Ury (1981) approach to negotiation that applies across settings ranging from interpersonal to international. Some specific techniques for negotiating interpersonal conflicts follow. These skills can be used in a variety of settings, ranging from organizational to intimate contexts.

Negotiating Interpersonal Agreements

Gottman et al. (1976) constructed the "Family Meeting," used by families, work groups, roommates, or any intact system that is small enough for all the parties to convene. The meeting is usually facilitated at first by a third party as an external check on the process as it unfolds; groups can also conduct such meetings without third-party assistance. The purpose of the meeting is to increase the number of positive behaviors and break out of deadend destructive spirals through the use of (1) gripe time, (2) agenda building, and (3) problem solving. The stages are outlined on p. 174.

   The family meeting outlined above is useful for making specific plans for change, especially if the family or group has tried to change before but has failed because the members tried to "have a better attitude" or "show love more" or made other kinds of nonspecific change attempts. Some feel the format of the negotiation meeting is too rigid, that it does not allow for feeling expression. Yet for the group that needs help in learning that they can indeed change, and that small steps need to be taken, the method works very well. We have used this step-by-step procedure with small children who can follow pictured symbols on a chart to help them keep up with the steps. Some families use the meeting on a weekly basis, thus assuring that problems do not build up over a long period of time. Care needs to be taken to help more reticent members participate and to encourage more assertive members to take their turn fairly.

The Family Meeting

Stage	Your Job
Gripe time	1. State clearly the gripes you have about your spouse, parent, or child.
	2. Follow the rules for constructive leveling.
	3. Listen and accept others' gripes as legitimate feelings.
	4. Work to understand gripes by summarizing and paraphrasing what was just said.
	5. Help to turn negative nebulous gripes into specific negative gripes. (Nebulous gripes are fuzzy and nonspecific.)
Agenda building	Decide on one or, at most, two gripes you feel are the most important to work on right now in the problem-solving stage. Other members do the same. Reach consensus about which gripes to solve.
Problem solving	1. Together with spouse or family member, turn the specific negative gripes (chosen in the agenda building) into positive suggestions for increasing the frequency of a positive behavior that will answer the gripe.
	2. Form a contract in which you agree to increase a positive behavior. Determine the reward you will get for increasing your behaviors.

In one family meeting, Mom stated a "negative nebulous" gripe to son Dan, a 14–year-old boy, by saying, "I wish you would show respect to your father and me." The family agreed to work on this gripe, which was in Dan's interest to negotiate, since he had just been grounded by Mom for "not showing respect." The younger siblings were helpful in specifying exactly when Dan and Mom got into a negative spiral over "respect." All made suggestions for how Mom and Dan could change their behavior. Not surprisingly, Dad and the younger brother and sisters had suggestions that involved them, too. They were able to agree on several suggestions made by the family, on a form that looked like the example on p. 175.

Note that the agreements negotiated are *noncontingent,* that Dan and Mom do not wait to see whether the other will comply before they are obligated to follow their part of the agreement. Noncontingent contracts work well if there is a basic level of trust; if the group or family is seriously distrustful, a contingent agreement may have to be negotiated at first. When a negotiated

---

Negotiation Agreement

Dan	Mom
1. I will call home if I'm going to be more than thirty minutes late.	1. I will call around to see if our curfew is similar to that of Dan's friends.
2. I will tell Mom and Dad where I am going.	2. Dan may go see friends in the neighborhood before dinner without telling us where he is.
3. I will not use sarcasm when I'm asked about my plans.	3. I will ask Dan privately what his plans are instead of in front of his friends.

The reward I will receive for this behavior at the end of a week is _____ (Dan)

_____(Mom)

Signed _____   Date _____

---

agreement is contingent, it is usually a quid pro quo (Lederer and Jackson 1968). A quid pro quo means "getting something for something."

Each party offers to alter some behavior if the other will also. For example, if two roommates are continually arguing over their apartment chores and each is angry at the other for "not doing her share," they can negotiate on a contingent basis. Susan might say, "OK, if you will take out the garbage during the week, I'll shovel the snow off the walk." This principle could be extended into other areas as well, with each person specifying what she will do in exchange for the other's efforts. The key to a successful quid pro quo is treating one another as equals in order to consummate the trade. It is the process of activating equal power that makes the quid pro quo work, regardless of the specific agreements. If both parties are full participants, the agreement will be of like value to both of them.

Handling Crises (Editing)

In a family (or other groups as well) the participants will often find themselves continually in crises, tempers flaring, and negative communication behaviors rebounding with increased frequency. Gottman et al. (1976) suggests that in such a crisis, you should—

1. *Stop action*—Halt the destructive exchanges.

2. *Be active*—Take action toward some solution. Imperfect solutions are better than none.

3. *Be agreeable*—Even if you feel hurt and wronged, both of you have to be agreeable to some solutions to reach accommodation.

In addition, the following seven suggestions can be used to tip the balance of interaction to the positive end. Usually, these are utilized after conflict participants are out of a crisis.

1. *Set up ground rules*—For example, agree on "no more behavior X" (screaming, stomping out of the room, etc.)

2. *Define structure*—"Set rules for behaviors and interaction both inside and outside of the home (p. 129)." Avoid actions that typically produce high conflict.

3. *Stop action*—If undesirable behaviors occur, stop them immediately.

4. *Shaping*—Once you and the other begin to act more positively, give praise, rewards, and concrete attention to each other.

5. *Stop acting out*—As Gottman et al. say, "No acting out, just talking out." Acting out is any desperate behavior—threatening to run away or leave, threatening to kill oneself or harm others.

6. *ABCD analysis*—Antecedents: What led up to the crises? What were the precipitating events?

   Behaviors: How did each person act in coping with the crisis?

   Consequences: What were the consequences from these behaviors?

   Do differently: What can be done differently now?

7. *Negotiate a temporary agreement*—After the problematic behaviors are identified, specify the changes each person can make. Put these in a written contract.

The analysis, recording, and alteration of specific behaviors on the part of the participants points the way to more productive patterns of communicating. Parents, especially, can teach these self-limiting steps to themselves and their children.

Leveling

Leveling is a device for clarifying complaints. As we have discussed, in conflicts in which parties launch into generalized attacks ("You are a lousy husband"; "You are ridiculous at parties"), it is useful to specify the nature of the complaint while taking responsibility for one's own reaction. Leveling can be used to increase the intensity in conflicts that are underground and not openly expressed. Instead of saying nothing to the other, or saying something like "You're a failure," try the X-Y-Z skill. It is simple to describe, hard to master, and can have profound effects on relationships with others.

When you do X
In situation Y
I feel Z

(Gottman et al. 1976, 37)

The secretary who says, "When you give me three separate requests (X) when I am on the phone (Y), I feel really overburdened (Z)," is clarifying her reaction. Her statement will have a better chance of leading to some constructive solution than if she says "I don't get any respect around here!" The XYZ skill has the advantage of working both to clarify the issue of concern for the recipient of the anger, and to urge the sender of the message to take responsibility for his or her emotional reaction. While XYZ does not prescribe the desired change, the complaint is lodged in specific, descriptive form so that the hearer might be able to reduce defensiveness and respond appropriately. Some additional examples of the technique follow:

Example #1.
Roommate to roommate:

> When you leave all your clothes from the day on the floor (X) And I have people in after my night class, (Y), I feel embarrassed (disappointed, angry, put out, or disgusted) (Z).

> *but not*

> I feel like burning them! (This is an action, not a feeling. State the feeling; then work on the solution later.)

Example #2.
Coworker to peer:

> When I'm required to come to meetings (X) and the meeting is cancelled after I've shuffled my plans, (Y), I feel unimportant (or disregarded, furious, disappointed) (Z).

The coworker might respond with an XYZ statement:

> Well, when I don't have your schedule to work with (X) and I must call a meeting quickly (Y), I feel irritated with you, and I don't worry about your schedule (expanded Z statement).

The coworkers can continue clarifying the problem and then work toward resolution of future difficulties.

A Postscript on Further Education

The techniques we have discussed in the preceding section are oriented toward individual use in conflicts, although many require some level of cooperation from the conflict partners. Further education about effective communication can serve a regulating function for lifelong training in effective conflict management. Destructive conflict sometimes grows from ignorance or lack of practice in growth-producing communication. When we know only destructive tactics, those are the tactics we use. If you are interested in further study in conflict management techniques specifically applied to individuals, families, and groups, many such opportunities exist. Human relations and management workshops or short courses are offered around the country every month. The couple and family enrichment movement has grown greatly in the last ten years (see a partial review in Galvin and Brommel 1980). Some excellent couple communication skills improvement programs are the Couple Communication Program (Miller et al. 1981) (formerly the Minnesota CCP) and various marriage enrichment programs (Mace and Mace 1976). Many counselors and therapists are trained in systems or behaviorally oriented skills training programs such as those by Carnes (1981), Lederer (1981), and Gottman (1976). University Associates in San Diego has for years provided management-oriented human relations training of high quality. The teacher using this text may be able to provide you with current information on such communication skills training, which might be of interest to you, your family, or your work group.

If you become aware that certain kinds of conflict continually create tension and create destructive outcomes, you might want to seek further training in the kinds of skills addressed by these programs. You might want to take further courses in communication at your college. We venture this personal note because we have seen people change their conflict approaches hundreds of times, often after believing that they had few options except to continue in a destructive pattern. Conflict regulation is an activity that depends on people who are educated into humane and intelligent ways of approaching this difficult process. Learning about the process is one way to regulate conflict.

Summary

This chapter has discussed self-regulation of conflicts through the creation of midrange, potentially productive conflicts. Nonviolent philosophical beliefs often predispose one to regulate the intensity of conflict expression. Specific techniques for self-regulation are fractionation, GRIT, and the Conflict Containment Model. Negotiation as a process of self-limitation by agreeing to process rules was explored, along with specific kinds of negotiation processes especially useful in interpersonal conflicts (contracts, editing, and leveling). Finally, the need for further education in conflict and communication skills was stressed. Conflict depends on individuals who are willing to regulate their own communication and continue to grow in options for productive management.

8

Third Party Intervention: Changing Conflict from the Outside In

Intervention is appropriate in situations such as these:

- Your sister is going to file for divorce; she asks you for a recommendation for an attorney.

- Two neighbors dispute constantly about their property line; their conflict affects the entire neighborhood with its bitterness.

- A father calls the police after his son's fourth runaway attempt.

- A store owner argues with a customer who wants to return a vacuum cleaner the customer believes to be defective.

- Two motorists collide, then stand in the street in a face-off; each accuses the other of fault.

- Your labor union and management call off contract talks.

- Three individuals in a department receive a raise; criteria for the decisions are unknown. The rest of the employees meet to decide how to protest against the apparent inequity.

Parties in all the above incidents could use the services of a third party. You may become involved in conflict intervention by (1) serving as a third party yourself, (2) assisting your work associates, family members, or friends to find qualified third parties, or (3) asking for third-party assistance for your own conflicts. Third-party intervention is part of many professional jobs, such as hotline counseling, drug abuse treatment, therapy, social work, juvenile and adult probation, law, dormitory counseling, police work, politics, teaching, ministry, and management. A congressman recently intervened on behalf of a veteran who lost his benefits; front page news resulted from the successful intervention of the politician with the veteran and the Veterans' Administration officials. You may have intervened, as Mark did, when two roommates reached an impasse due to different work and study schedules. Mark suggested that they go to the resident assistant to work out some settlement, since they each had escalated to the point of unplugging each other's alarm clocks, hiding stereos, refusing to take messages for the other, and other desperate tactics.

Many conflicts require the use of a third party, competent but without a vested interest in a specific outcome. Most people function as an intervener at some time or another. *The choice is not whether you will be involved in others' conflicts, but how competently you will serve as a third party.* Likewise, if you use third parties, you will be more satisfied with the intervention if you choose a qualified person to help you.

Whether formal or informal, *the goal of all intervention is to assist in a transformation of the conflict elements.* The transformation may take many forms. For example, intervention may alter the power balance, change the expression of conflict, help parties change their goals, or change perception of scarce rewards, interdependence, or interference. After a third party helps conflict parties, coworkers may be able to speak to the boss directly instead of forming coalitions, and the boss may agree to give negative feedback in person instead of in writing. Parents may agree to help their 18–year-old daughter go to college in a different state; a conflict over a scarce parking space may be redefined so that coworkers can talk about their relational conflicts instead of the content conflict. Competent intervention transforms the conflict so parties can solve it.

The Intervention Continuum

Interventions come in many forms ranging from formal to informal. Conflict parties can be served by different types of intervention at different points. For example, in the early stages of a family conflict between a teenager and his parents, informal assistance may be given by a friend or other family member. If these attempts do not move the conflict to productive ends, formal intervention by a counselor or representative of the law may be forthcoming. We will overview the two ends of the continuum, formal and informal, then present the intervention process in detail.

Formal Intervention: Consultation

Conflict intervention in businesses, agencies, and organizations is a form of consultation, a field of endeavor now recognized as a distinct profession (Gallessich 1982). Two vantage points define the consultant's perspective. Intervention is performed from within the organization or from outside the organization (Brown 1983; Van De Vliert 1981). Persons inside the organization, popularly called "in-house" consultants, are employed by or are members of the organization they serve as consultant. For instance, the director of training consults with three departments that because of budget cutbacks, must merge. In-house consultants are especially prone to the problems of bias mentioned previously; their consultant roles must be clarified during each separate instance of consultation. The director of training must separate any evaluation of conflict parties from attempts to help them merge their activities into one department; otherwise, the warring parties will simply withhold important information and try to make the other parties look less competent.

In-house consultants can use Walton's (1969) checklist for criteria for third-party intervention when one is a member of the organization. Consultants serve best who have—

1. high professional expertise in social processes;

2. low power over the fate of the principals;

3. high control over confrontation setting and processes;

4. moderate knowledge about principals, issues, and background factors; and

5. neutrality or balance with respect to substantive outcome, personal relationships, and conflict-resolution methodology.

(Walton 1969, 139)

Dr. Winter, a professor of communication at a large state university, was asked by the training director of a state natural resources agency to intervene in a conflict between the director of the agency, who required department heads, at the direction of the legislature, to implement a new system of cost accounting. Previously, department heads were able to juggle money from one budget area to another as long as they did not spend more than their department had been allocated by the director. The change required "line item accounting," meaning that if a certain sum had been allocated by the director to be spent for professional training and travel, only that amount and no more could be spent for training and travel. The training director was satisfied that Dr. Winter was competent in conflict processes; he had taken a course from her in the continuing education department. Dr. Winter did not know the principals in the conflict. She required that no report about individuals be given to the director. She negotiated a conflict management process that gave her control over the time of meetings, who would be there for the three-day period, and the kind of meeting environment that would be provided by the agency. She interviewed the principals prior to the meetings, being certain to spend equal amounts of time with them, using the training director as a consultant to her about specific content. Dr. Winter's conflict management goal was that the participants would be able to collaborate toward a creative solution; she entered without specific opinions about kinds of alliances to be formed, whether training and travel should increase or decrease, whether line-item accounting is the best way to run an agency, or about the management style of the director of the agency. The meetings centered more specifically on content than process, but the principals appeared to make better progress using this mode than they did discussing the relational issues directly. Dr. Winter was able to assist in the process since she acted as a conflict management facilitator, not as an expert on management style, resource development, training needs, or legislative process.

Further cautions apply to outside consultants. They must avoid developing a stake in the specific outcome, remain experts on conflict processes instead of juvenile probation, rapid market growth, legislative lobbying, land-use planning, student-teacher relationships, classroom practices, curriculum development, wildlife management, or other specific content areas. If the outside consultant becomes a real or imagined expert in specific content, the primary focus on processes of conflict management may be forgotten.

The overall intervention process has been outlined by many authors in detail. Consult, for instance, Friedman and Yarbrough 1984; Gallessich 1983; Sundberg, Taplin, and Tyler 1983; Varney 1978; Ottaway 1983, Argyris 1970; and Goldhaber 1983. After we overview the nature of informal intervention in conflicts, we will discuss the steps in the intervention process that apply equally to formal and informal intervention.

Informal Intervention

Many well-functioning relationships occasionally require assistance from someone other than parties in the ongoing relationship. Married couples who come to a clinic for counseling often function quite well at other times (Vincent 1972); labelling them as distressed may be only temporarily accurate. Many everyday conflicts are settled out of court or without the aid of a professional helper, using the assistance of informal mediators such as friends, neighbors, and others (McGillis 1981). These interveners serve the same objective as more defined agents, that is, "to interrupt a self-maintaining or escalating-malevolent cycle in one way or another and to initiate a de-escalating-benevolent cycle" (Walton 1969, 89). In some circumstances, third parties serve restricted roles such as passing messages back and forth (Brown and Rubin 1975). You may have informed a friend when her angry boyfriend was ready to talk over a conflict or told your brother that his younger sister was upset and needed to talk.

Informal third parties enter conflicts through diverse routes. Parties may ask for help indirectly, without making a direct request. Children, for instance, seem to sense that parents will step into the role as a third party when they get beaten up on the playground, when "Jill won't give me back my teddy bear," or when big brother picks on little brother behind the parents' back. The complaint, accompanied by anger or tears, serves as a request for help. A friend may call to discuss a potential romantic breakup. You may guess that he wants you to carry a message, or come over to talk with the unhappy couple. A staff person may say, "What would you think about coming to the meeting Tuesday with Julie and Chris? I think we could use your level head."

Indirect cues indicating that your help may be needed are ones such as these:

1. The person spends more time with you than usual, asking for advice and sharing feelings.   *Sensory*

2. Private information is shared.

3. Your acquaintance indicates that a decision is impending and that the decision is crucial.

4. The person makes you understand that life is not smooth, distress is present, or that things seem out of control.

5. Friends may make dramatic, noticeable changes.

A teacher may notice that a student, usually happy and in love with life, talks more and more of negative feelings and events. Accounts of events may shift from balanced to blaming. A student who says, "They won't hire me. They don't think I have any useful experience" may be indirectly asking for the teacher's intervention in the form of a phone call or letter of recommendation.

Excuses and justifications, two ways of accounting for one's behavior, may indicate that a friend feels low power. *Excuses* are socially approved ways to relieve oneself of responsibility when one's conduct is questioned (Scott and Lyman 1968). Constant use of excuses may indicate the desire for third-party help. Chuck, a student assigned to a small group, made excuses for his lack of participation in the group ("I'm just lazy, I guess," "You guys never tell me when you're going to meet," "I forgot") until Pat, the teaching assistant, called a meeting of the group and helped the group determine that Chuck felt railroaded to do a project he did not believe in. They shifted the topic slightly to accommodate Chuck's feelings; in the process the group gained an enthusiastic member.

Justifications offer socially approved words asserting that the act performed had a positive value even though others see the act as negative. Justifications come in many forms; all indicate unsatisfactory relationships. Examples of typical justifications are a denial of injury to the other person, denial that anyone rational could disagree, asserting that others do it, too, so it cannot be seen as bad, or an appeal to a person's good feelings about the injured party ("I really did it for his own good"). One manager announced that a grant, written by one of the staff members, had been denied by the funding agency. The announcement was made in the general staff meeting; when the writer of the grant later protested that he wanted to be told privately, the manager asserted that "I have no secrets from my staff." He justified the action but denied the relational consequences of the action.

It is important to determine what the parties are communicating about their conflict by constant use of excuses and justifications. This kind of communication may be an indirect request for assistance, since excuses and justifications seldom are used in well-functioning, collaborative conflicts. A third party may be able to change the structure of the conflict informally after attending to cues that help is wanted and needed. Many people are shy about asking for help directly, so they indicate their needs nonverbally, indirectly, and with negative communication.

The Intervention Process

Intervention processes for both formal and informal intervention agents share some commonalities. The process proceeds from an identification of the intervention needs, encompasses a decision to intervene, involves a negotiation of your role, necessitates a conflict assessment, utilizes an intervention design, activates actual intervention tactics, and finally, ends with an assessment of the intervention.

Identify Intervention Needs

Third parties are employed or asked to intervene on a voluntary basis for many reasons. Church congregations, for instance, may ask for outside help under the following conditions, a list equally applicable to other kinds of organizations:

1. The conflict is urgent and time is short.

2. Everyone is either an advocate or has declared for one side or the other.

3. No one can be found who will function as referee.

4. The scale or complexity is beyond the range of resources available.

5. No trust exists in internal resources.

(Leas and Kittlaus 1973, 76)

Similarly, a family or business group might conclude that "We've been over this a million times and we aren't getting anywhere." In industry, the financial stakes may be high when conflicts are unresolved; strikes result, time is spent on fighting instead of production, or departments duplicate efforts in a costly way because they cannot agree to work together. Third parties intervene when a large percentage of persons are fired, when a company grows quickly, or when layoffs are likely to occur. Families and couples ask for help when they feel their abilities to solve their problems without help are small and when the stakes are high.

Some third-party situations are forced upon one of the parties. One person files a lawsuit without the agreement of the other, police intervene in crime or domestic violence, or a judge makes a decision affecting a party who sought no judgment. If a manager hires a conflict management expert to mediate a conflict between two factions in the organization, the parties have no choice but to cooperate, at least at some level. Optimum intervention occurs, however, with the support of all the parties, but sometimes parties cannot exclude third-party involvement.

The point at which people recognize the need for assistance varies. "Conflict situations are frequently allowed to develop to almost unmanageable proportions before anything is done about them, by which time it is often too late to resolve them by peaceable and procedural means" (Boulding 1962). Some people will not, under any normal circumstances, open their personal or professional relationships for impact by others. Diagnostic aids for the appropriateness of intervention follow. Intervention is especially crucial when—

- a relationship is stuck; no productive change occurs, and one or more of the participants feel dissatisfied;

- one person feels wronged, mistreated, or unduly coerced by another; intervention balances the power enough so the situation can be assessed;

- repetitive, destructive conflict cycles characterize the relationship to the point that one or more of the parties (or all) want to harm or injure the other; or

- outside observers see damaging patterns and call for formal intervention to save someone from abuse, physical harm, or other life-threatening experience.

Some third-party intervention necessitates an agreement by all parties before it can be used; this may involve calling in a mediator in a labor strike, seeking personal counseling, teaching families or work groups problem-solving skills, or involving a friend in intimate conversation with two or more parties. Conflict management intervention between any two or more equals requires equal say in asking for help. Interveners frequently fail when they are invited by only one party. Divorce mediation is a striking example of a situation in which both parties must agree to the use of a third party or the procedure will surely fail. Good intentions of a third party result in nothing except frustration and wasted time unless parties desire a more productive process of conflict.

Decide to Intervene

In formal intervention situations, the consultant and client explore the appropriateness of intervention, suitability of the consultant, and expectations of both the conflict parties and the consultant. Such explorations usually take more than one meeting and cannot be taken lightly. Keep in mind that "the interventionist and client will have discrepant worlds" (Argyris 1970); this early stage, if performed carefully, brings common understanding to the process. Sometimes a client feels pressured to "fix" a conflict fast, the consultant is eager to sign a contract, or the client and consultant assume that they will work out the details as they go along. Such shortcuts often result in a conflict between consultant and client, and this may become large enough to subsume the original conflict the consultant was supposed to help solve. Quick commitment on the part of the client or the consultant usually backfires. One state utility company hired a consultant to find out why the customer service personnel were dissatisfied with their jobs and why so many complaints were being registered by the public against the customer service personnel. After the consultant designed a training program oriented toward solving conflicts to the customers' satisfaction, he found to his chagrin that top management personnel held a belief that their employees were right and the public was wrong. He rushed into working on the "problem," but they wanted him to bring back a verdict of "no problem."

Potential intervention may be terminated when the conflict parties decide to seek other help or to seek no help at all or when the consultant decides not to intervene for a number of reasons (Sundberg, Taplin, and Tyler 1983). The decision to continue the potential intervention requires a fit between the conflict parties and the intervener. If such a fit is found to be lacking, all parties are better off not pursuing the relationship.

Negotiate a Role

If you have decided to offer to help people resolve their conflict; you must now choose when to intervene, what your role will be, what your intervention style will be, and what skills you bring to this conflict. Before you make a commitment to help, answer the following questions:

1. Are they ready for a third party? What evidence do you have to indicate such readiness?

2. How certain are you that your help has been requested? If the request has been indirect, clarify your understanding of the request.

3. How do you know that they want *you* to help?

4. What skills prepare you to help them? Can you help best by referring them to someone else?

5. Is your role free and flexible enough so you can help, or are you biased, committed to one of the parties, grinding your own ax, or unable to help because of time, position, or other matters?

6. Can you say no? If not, then you are probably too involved in the conflict to be an effective helper.

If you are satisfied with answers to these questions, take the time to think about the consequences of your intervention. Remember, someone else's problem is not necessarily your problem—you have a choice. If you think you have no choice, you cannot be useful as an informal or formal intervener. You have the right to not be the solution to someone else's conflict (Smith 1975). Many adults get involved in conflicts between their parents only to discover the futility of trying to solve marital problems not of their making. If you do not want to get involved in a conflict but think that you should, the lack of enthusiasm for the role results in lessened energy and creativity, a lack of sensitivity, and ineffective intervention. If you don't want to help, don't.

If you choose to take a role in the conflict after all, even if the role is informal and nonspecific, take special care to retain your neutrality. Informal third parties often take sides (Van De Vliert 1981). If one of the parties succeeds in allying with the helper, the resulting alliance restructures the power, invalidates the other side in the conflict, and creates a new issue in the conflict—that of unfair bonding. Consultants to organizations are trained to avoid such biased behavior, but friends and relatives may slip into taking sides only to find that their help has made the conflict worse. The following result from siding with one party:

- Siding implies that the outsider adopts the win-lose thinking of the principal parties, reinforcing the destructive effect.

- Siding creates a winner (the party chosen) and a loser (the rejected party), which precipitates escalation by the rejected party.

- Siding increases the number of conflict participants.

- By adding views, siding complicates the conflict issues and the conflict behavior.

- The siding outsider invests energy, increasing the stake of the parties in the conflict outcome.

- The outsider exhibits behaviors supportive of the choice made.

(adapted from Van De Vliert 1981, 497–8)

Siding with one conflict party, while not wise for an intervener, does have its place. If, for example, your close friend is in the middle of breaking off a relationship with her fiance, you may choose to side with her to give her support. Anything else would be unrealistic. However, you should be aware that siding with one of the conflict parties precludes you from being an effective helper; you will become a new party to the conflict.

Refusing to take sides can result in (1) your not being involved in the conflict or (2) your preparation to be an effective change agent. One new employee of a hospital was approached by persons on opposite sides of a conflict over whether the assignment of nursing shifts should result from seniority only or from seniority and experience. The new nurse found herself being pushed toward the middle—both sides wanted her to persuade the other side of the rightness of their position. She wisely told all parties, "I am too new to have an informed opinion. Besides, I value my relationships with all of you. I choose not to help with this problem."

In a case on a university campus, a faculty member's neutrality set the stage for an effective intervention. The faculty member heard from a student who wanted to graduate early that another faculty member refused to consider a petition to waive or substitute a required course. She offered to intervene by privately asking the resistant faculty member to discuss the issue in a meeting. The resulting discussion removed the issue from what had become a two-party conflict to a discussion based on principles of fairness and desirability of such requests. The intervening professor did not take sides; she provided a forum for handling the matter creatively.

If you are going to intervene, clarify any change in your role from your habitual role with the conflict parties. If you have been a buddy, boss, romantic partner, coworker or casual acquaintance, any change in that role needs to be overtly communicated. An example of such a successful change occurred recently. A fourteen-year-old girl, Toni, lived with a couple in their mid-fifties who cared for her as foster parents. The state childrens' service worker, Anne, functioned in the past as a person who found placements for Toni, certified the home, and provided ongoing counseling for Toni. Mr. and Mrs. Black began to quarrel about whether to continue providing care for Toni, since their own children were out of the home and they were beginning to want time without children. Mrs. Black wanted to wait until Toni graduated from high school to request another placement, while Mr. Black wanted Toni to be moved during the summer. Anne was able to act as a third party to their conflict, after making clear that her first loyalty was to Toni's best interests. Since all three people agreed on the interests, they were able, with Anne's help, to find a solution to the conflict. Unless Anne had clarified her role, which was one of not taking sides with either parent, and keeping Toni's interests prominent, both parents would have tried to elicit Anne's support for their side.

Several cautions are relevant to the friendly intervener. Be certain the parties want to bring in someone to help them manage their conflict. Any time a third party enters into an existing relationship, the relationship is changed. Be careful that their successful conflict management is not built at the expense of the third party—they may cast you as the enemy, thus finding a temporary bonding with each other and excluding you. Remember, you are entering an already existing system, whether it is two friends, two employees, or any greater number of persons interdependent with each other. Your client, even if you are taking an informal role, is the relationship. If you become a common enemy by pushing the parties too hard, they will not solve their problem and you will lose two friends. Additionally, remain constantly aware of the attempts to convince you of the rightness of each side. Once you coalesce with one person, you lose your helpful role and weaken their relationship. While you cannot predict ahead of time exactly what will happen when you involve yourself, you do need to monitor the interactions to watch for shifts in coalitions or destruction of the original bond. If you begin thinking "No wonder he is struggling with her; she is completely unreasonable," you have formed a coalition and lost your effectiveness.

Honest and helpful assistance can serve the process of healing conflicts and furthering the ongoing relationship. Just remember to intervene for the people who want your help and not just for your own purposes.

You may be in the position of needing to request the help of an outside consultant for your organization, family, or personal relationship. You can be helpful to the consultant by asking for what you want and clarifying what you do not want. If you want someone to train your staff in conflict management, that is a different process from asking for mediation. Helping the third party clarify his or her role can be greatly facilitated by someone inside the system who knows how to ask for help in a clear and specific way.

Assess the Conflict

Once the intervention needs have been identified, the decision to intervene has been made, and you have negotiated a role, the conflict should be assessed. The guides for assessment presented in chapter 6 can be used at this stage. Assessment often serves a concurrent function as a form of intervention. In an intervention with a community agency, as part of the intervention decision, the consultant and staff agreed that individual interviews with all nine staff members would be conducted. The consultant spent an hour and a half with each member for the purpose of understanding the primary conflict issues, the communication used so far, and the elements of the conflict. The interviews doubled as intervention since they also provided a forum for each staff member to ventilate feelings in a safe manner and to build rapport and trust with the consultant, as well as gave the intervener enough knowledge and power in the system to change the dynamics of communication in the agency.

Assessment provides information so the formal or informal consultant can decide whether to reduce conflict if there is too much or to promote conflict if there is too little (Brown 1983). Detailed information provides a data base about the nature of the conflict and the possible ways one might intervene to change the system. The following generic issues characterize this phase.

1. *Tractability.* Does the conflict offer some hope of success, given the intervener's time, energy, skill, and the funds available?

2. *Divisibility.* Can one intervene in only one issue or segment that might be the most manageable?

3. *Timing.* Is it too early—are the parties hurting enough to welcome intervention? Or is it too late—has it gone too far? (Wehr 1979)

4. *Intervention Options.* What possible approaches could be used for this particular situation?

The design of intervention options follows assessment, with the most helpful options flowing from specific assessment.

Design the Intervention

Intervention techniques should be matched to the needs of the conflict parties and should suit the training and expertise of the third party. The use of just one way of solving conflicts limits effective management. Some consultants develop one style of conflict intervention that they always use, whether that approach be team building, small group discussion, mediation, listening training, or many other techniques. Just as a physician would not treat every disease with penicillin, each conflict requires separate treatment in the form of a new intervention design. When the parties' needs do not match the intervener's skills, referral to other professionals is the best move.

Intervention designs are numerous, ranging from mediation between parties, arbitration, training workshops that teach conflict management skills, and coaching managers to function as problem solvers. One helpful approach is to help participants change the contextual factors that encourage the conflict rather than working on personal change of the participants (Wehr 1979). For instance, if two people who share an office get into constant conflict, perhaps a different work space might be found. Training workshops, even those that focus on conflict skills, do not function specifically as conflict intervention. Intervention occurs *within* a given system, not between individuals who have no interdependency with one another. For that reason, training and intervention are treated separately in the consultation literature. For an overview of the varieties of consultation models available, see the discussion in Thomas (1976).

Intervention Tactics

We have already overviewed the entry phases in the intervention process— ranging from identifying needs to designing the intervention. Once these are completed, the intervention agent proceeds with the intervention, by formal contract with an organization or an informal understanding with the conflict parties.

The following discussion of intervention tactics does not apply to adjudication and arbitration, which are processes in which a third party decides the outcome to the conflict. The following suggestions are limited to cases of formal and informal consultation, whether that be in the form of organizational development, mediation, paid facilitation, or informal intervention.

Effective intervention necessitates (1) excellent third-party communication skills, (2) third party control of the process, and (3) transformation of the elements of the conflict.

Communication Skills

The success of intervention depends on one's abilities to communicate. An ineffective communicator who enters a conflict produces more damage and complicates the conflict so it cannot be productively managed. A complete listing of all the necessary skills would be long; we suggest you consult any basic interpersonal communication skills book for more extensive treatment of the necessary skills. However, the following skills are needed as a minimum requirement for any person wishing to be either a formal or informal helper of conflicts.

Third parties need skills in empathic understanding, congruence, openness and genuineness, nonverbal sensitivity, active listening, and persuasive ability. Empathic understanding involves seeing the world from the frame of reference of the conflict participants (Carkhuff 1969; Rusk and Gerner 1972; Brammer 1973; Arnold 1977). The effective intervener knows that "only the parties themselves have experienced the full complexity of their situation, and only they know most of the determinants of their behavior" (Fisher 1972). No one wants to be judged, evaluated, or misunderstood—especially by someone who changes the communication system by his or her presence. The participants should be able to "tell their own story" without evaluation or undue hurry. If an intervener is able to be empathic with the participants, then each conflict party will begin to have confidence in the third party. The intervener can be effective only if the parties feel he or she understands their sides and has their best interests at heart, even if the process of reaching agreement is difficult.

The third party's congruence, openness, and genuineness are also important (Carkhuff 1969; Rogers 1951; Brammer 1973; Combs 1969). What the third party says has to ring true with the participants; any attempts at deceit or manipulation will likely boomerang and produce additional difficulties for managing the conflict. For instance, a friend might ask you if you will come over to help her and her roommate work out some way to share responsibilities for the upkeep of the apartment. You have been a close friend of both of them, and they have a conflict over what each sees as the other's taking advantage of her. If you are uncomfortable about intervening, you need to tell them. If you feel you can intervene but know that one of them is making tentative plans to move out, you might say, "I'm not comfortable with your level of commitment to each other. I want to help, but I've noticed a lot of energy going elsewhere. Maybe you should decide on your commitment to each other before we decide on how to divide up chores."

Nonverbal sensitivity helps the third party infer the reality of a conflict from the "cues" the participants emit. For instance, tension shown in body posture, orientation away or toward each other, territorial markers, and dozens of other nonverbal cues may be more important than what the participants say is wrong. One of us intervened in a personnel issue involving a secretary who had been given a raise by her boss, who had not gone through the personnel system of the organization. In a meeting, which involved seven active and vocal participants, the boss sat slightly in front of the secretary. He answered for her, explaining "their" position. He challenged the personnel officer, saying, "You don't know her work. Don't you think I'm competent to judge my own people?" From the man's defensive posture and choice of seating, it became obvious that he was more of a party to the dispute than was the secretary. In fact, the secretary constantly tried to soften her boss's statements with a shrug of the shoulders, a smile, and a gesture of self-derogation. The mediator was able to separate the issues starting with the boss's identification with the conflict—for him it was a personal challenge of authority. Without the mediator's nonverbal sensitivity, the entire process might have been sidetracked with an incorrect issue focus on the secretary.

Active listening involves a sequence of steps so the third party becomes clear about what the parties are saying, and helps the parties listen to each other. When used effectively, it also helps the parties to be congruent; the nonverbal messages and verbal messages agree with one another. The steps of active listening are easy to describe and difficult to perform but can have a positive impact on the conflict process. Consult a basic communication skills text for more extensive material on listening skills. A brief summary of active listening steps is as follows:

1. *Reflect the feelings* of the participants before you paraphrase or ask questions about the content they are communicating. Conflict parties often escalate until they feel heard. One of the functions of the third party is to help in the constructive expression of anger and ventilation of feelings.

Example:

Head resident: No one working for me goes behind my back and stays on my staff! That's it!

Facilitator: You feel really strongly about what you're saying. This is important to you.

> After feelings are acknowledged and clarified without evaluation, possible solutions can be generated. Until then, the unexpressed feelings will distort the thinking processes of the conflict parties.

2. *Restate or paraphrase* what you hear without adding new material of your own. Third parties help slow down escalating conflict so people can think about what they are saying. Rephrasing helps parties clarify for themselves and each other what they think and feel. This

is not the time, however, for you as a third party to add helpful suggestions or interpretations. Your role at this point is to help the parties communicate accurately.

Example:

Head resident: I can't trust John. He went behind my back before and he will again. I want him replaced.

Facilitator: Your trust in John is so low right now that you don't think you can work with him. (Notice the facilitator does not say "Your bottom line is that you want John replaced," which would add information the head resident did not communicate.)

   3. *Ask open-ended questions* to clarify the communication. Open-ended questions are genuine questions for which the answer is unknown, and cannot be given with a simple "yes" or "no." Open-ended questions give parties a chance to expand and clarify what they are saying in a nonthreatening atmosphere. The questions should not be probing, leading, manipulative, or phony.

Example:

John, the resident assistant: He's (the head resident) never around. Somebody has to take charge.

Facilitator: How do you decide when you need to check with the head resident and when you act on your own?

Notice that the facilitator assumes that John has good reasons for doing what he did and that the charge about the head resident not being available is not addressed at this time.

   4. *Clarify options the parties express.* Another function of the third party is to help highlight creative options the parties express. These potential solutions are often lost because of the strong feelings in the meeting or because no one is taking notes. Again, the third party does not add suggestions of his or her own at this time.

Example:

Head resident: I can see that if I'm gone, he has to do some things without checking.

Facilitator: Maybe you're saying that John could make certain kinds of choices without checking with you if you are gone. What might those be?

5. *Make suggestions, give information or advice when warranted in the process.* Parties need to work through their own solutions to their own conflicts with your process help. Information and advice given about specific content often is premature unless considerable attention has been given to the active listening steps above. Carl Rogers is reported to have said, "Never give advice to anyone unless it's asked for three times." That is helpful advice!

The third party also has to persuade the conflict parties. Sometimes clear communication will open up new options and provide new avenues for management. More often, however, the third party must work actively with the parties to get them to change. The mediator affects the behavior of the parties, molding and nudging them to change (Bartunek, Benton, and Keys 1975). If the third party establishes a solid relationship with all parties, he or she can persuade them to alter their positions in order to reach agreement. Persuasion should be limited to advice on coming up with a different solution, or more solutions, rather than a specific solution. If interveners offer specific solutions, they must be careful not to get invested in their adoption.

Process Control

An intervener *intervenes*—alters the process of the conflict. The effective third party does not let a conflict spiral into destructiveness; rather, he or she limits the exchanges between parties and focuses on the problem at hand. Of course, the parties need to be heard, yet the third party controls the process of participation.

Process control is exercised by a third party in two forms, *overall structure of meetings* and *specific communication exchanges.* In controlling the overall process, the intervener sets the meeting times. Usually, an effective intervention cannot be accomplished in just one session. With multiple meetings, the parties have time to reassess their positions, new intervention tactics can be adapted to the specific changes in the conflict, and external forces impinging on the conflict can be altered.

Once the third party meets with the participants, an interrelated series of process tasks needs to be accomplished. The intervener needs to limit the agenda so the parties will discuss the issue at hand. Getting agreement ahead of time on the agenda is a safeguard against later subversion of the management process. For example, in formal intervention one can put the agenda on a flip chart or blackboard and the participants can be guided through the topics they have agreed to discuss.

The intervener balances the participation of the participants. Whether informally helping two roommates or serving as a formal intervention agent, the intervener needs to bring all parties into the discussion. If one conflict party dominates the discussion, then joint solutions to the conflict will not arise; one party will feel "run over." Participation can be balanced by calling on the more reticent party in a nonthreatening way while restraining the more vocal party. Saying something like "Thanks for your contributions, Jon; now we need to hear from Jan who is equally involved so we can get a complete picture of what has transpired in this conflict" will often serve to set the stage for balanced participation.

The third party also alters the quality as well as the quantity of communication. This can be done by restating what parties say and checking for the other's understanding. Sometimes the communication process is kept productive by spotting internal conciliators—members of either side who are restating, emphasizing, using active listening, initiating problem solving, or making other conciliatory moves. Here is an example. One of us was empanelled to be on a formal board to hear a dispute among transportation interests, in this case two taxicab companies in a small, wealthy resort town. Each principal presented its case, point out that the other side was totally without redeeming virtue and was wrong in every way. But one side consisted of three men, two of whom attended but did not speak. The mediator noticed that the vice-president of the company winced and grimaced when the president presented some of the more inflammatory statements about the impossibility of negotiating with the other side. When asked if all members of the company agreed, a discussion followed among the three officers, who then softened their position. Pinpointing the potential helpers toward conciliation is a wise move; the third-party process is difficult and all available help needs to be called upon.

Quality of communication is greatly facilitated when the consultant or friend directs the feedback process. The conflict participants are usually engaging in communication practices that make agreement difficult—derogatory statements, not listening to the other side, and other forms of uncooperative communication. The following list of rules for feedback can be shared with the participants; the third party intervenes in the process to assure that they will happen (adapted from the National Training Laboratories 1968 and Filley 1975).

Be descriptive rather than judgmental.

Encourage specificity.

Deal with things that can be changed instead of "givens."

Encourage parties to give feedback when it is requested.

Give feedback as close as possible to the behavior being discussed.

Encourage feedback whose accuracy can be checked by others.

Speak only for yourself.

Transformation of Conflict Elements

The intervener uses his or her communication skills in order to perform one overall function: *transformation of the conflict elements*. Any of the conflict components treated in part I of this book can be altered to change the course of the conflict. For example, one may transform the way the parties express their struggle, thus improving communication, stopping defensive reactions, and promoting listening between for the first time. Maybe the intervener will equalize the power of the participants or alter their perceptions of one another's power and stop an escalatory spiral of moves and countermoves. Or parties' perceptions of their and the others' goals may change, thereby moving the conflict to a productive phase.

The third party may help participants to work for *superordinate goals* that transcend the individual interests they brought to the conflict. If a married couple, for instance, is involved in a series of conflicts, some possible superordinate goals might be appealing to "the marriage," "the children," or "your need of one another during these difficult times." Just as nations have a superordinate goal of not destroying the human race, interpersonal conflict participants may be convinced not to destroy the good elements of their relationship.

One final admonition. The intervener should be eclectic. He or she should not get stuck using one particular tactic or approach to intervention, for just as it is perfected, there will be a conflict in which its use is not appropriate. The creative third party needs to have a repertoire of skills available for use as the situation demands. For example, if the intervener has a fine ability to restate positions and listen actively, he or she may be involved in a conflict between two friends in which what is needed are persuasive skills. Similarly, a fine ability to analyze conflicts may not help move the conflict to productive ends if shared with the parties.

One should be prepared to utilize any of the approaches we mentioned in this book. The GRIT technique listed in the chapter on self-regulation and the steps for principled negotiation discussed in the goals chapter are two noteworthy avenues for intervention techniques. All the techniques of self-regulation are potentially useful, but none is magic. In a conflict in which neither party is able to fully engage the issues, escalation may serve to clarify the issues. It is important to remain flexible and always keep an eye on assisting the parties so that they reach some agreement with one another. If the intervener's job is done well, the parties will move their relationship to a new level of cooperation and understanding.

Assess the Intervention and Exit from the System

At the conclusion of an effective intervention, the third party assesses the utility of the intervention. If it has been a formal intervention, the clients are asked about their satisfaction with the process and the outcome. Likewise, in informal intervention one would turn to the friends or coworkers and ask, "Is this a decision that you can live with?" or related questions. In both cases, the intervener should summarize the agreements made and check them with the parties, either orally or in written form, depending on the formality of the management role.

Assessing an intervention should also be done at a later time. If a work group reaches a decision, the last "check" on its utility should not be during the same meeting in which it was made. At the very least, a follow-up meeting helps add a realistic component to any solution. Parties use the time between meetings to cool off, to reassess their goals, and to try out bargains made in previous meetings. Multiple meetings also allow for alterations in the intervention plan so the consultant can remain flexible and responsible to changing conditions. Following the principle of helping people argue from interests, not positions, necessitates a constant check on the changing interests and goals of the parties. Conflict intervention centered around prospective goals only is to be avoided. Intervention is a living contract; a changing design.

Once the work is completed, the third party exits from the system. In both formal and informal intervention, the goal is to set the parties free so they can manage their own relations. An intervener who does not work himself or herself out of a job is not doing the job properly; the parties must become independent of the third party. In one conflict we mediated recently, the leaders of two departments agreed to set up weekly meetings to discuss ongoing conflicts or potential conflicts. A three-month follow-up meeting with all the original conflict parties was scheduled to assess how the weekly meetings were working—and to make sure the meetings were occurring. An effective third party trains people in the process of conflict management so that the clients

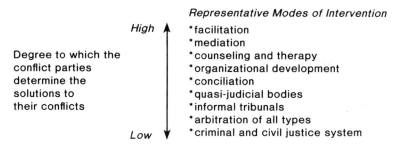

Figure 8.1. Intervention modes and party involvement in determining solutions to conflicts.

will not need further services. In either formal or informal roles, an intervener who provides the impetus for altering the party's relations over time has contributed a valuable and reusable resource to the system.

Formal Intervention Modes

Formal and informal intervention modes differ according to the *degree to which conflict parties determine the final outcome*. In some forms of third-party intervention, the intervener serves as a facilitator to the parties who make their own decisions, whereas other forms impose a resolution to the conflict upon the parties (see figure 8.1).

The intervention types listed in figure 8.1 are pure types, whereas in many interventions, combinations of approaches are used. For instance, some forms of conciliation use both mediation and arbitration, usually decided by the third party who is assisting the parties to reach agreement (Buzzard and Eck 1983). Contracts between labor and management often specify a sequence of steps such as (1) negotiation, and, if necessary, (2) mediation. If that fails, (3) arbitration of the contract terms begins. Divorce mediators often specify that if the mediation breaks down on a specific issue, that particular issue is taken to an arbitrator, thus allowing mediation to continue (Coogler 1978).

The most popular forms of intervention will now be discussed. Each mode will be defined; then the uses and limitations to each type will be specified.

Adjudication

Adjudication is a process in which parties go before a judge or jury. Adjudication assumes that parties are unable to solve their own conflicts. It is similar to arbitration in that a third party decides, but the judgment can be put into motion without mutual consent. Each citizen has the right to sue another for a variety of wrongs. Additionally, the officials of the criminal justice system can initiate charges. Adjudication further assumes that the full exposition of each side to a conflict will allow a judge or jury to make a just decision.

Court processes are fairly well known. One party files charges, suit, or a petition in court and the other is charged to appear to respond. Between the time of the filing and the court date, the lawyers usually negotiate with each other regarding the case. For example, a landlord charges a tenant with violation of a lease agreement. The tenant signed a one-year lease and moved after four months. The landlord filed suit to recover the rent for the eight months the person was not living there. The two lawyers typically begin negotiations, calling and writing back and forth. If they are not able to reach settlement, the case goes to court; a judge or jury, after hearing testimony and evidence from both sides, decides that the tenant must pay the eight months' rent, plus attorney fees. If no appeal is filed, the resolution process ends with the enforcement of the action.

Adjudication brings a number of positive features to conflict management. It gives access to a resolution process to all; as such, it serves as a power-balancing mechanism. For example, individuals can sue large corporations. "Equal protection of the law" allows access for all people in need of the legal system. In the case of abused or neglected children, for instance, a state agency can bring the parents before a court to determine their suitability for continued parenting. The children's representative acts as their agent. One does not have to get agreement of the other party for participation in the court system. As Wehr (1979) notes, "Asymmetrical conflict is best resolved through intervention that empowers the weaker party" (p. 37).

A second positive feature of adjudication is that it provides rules for fairness such as the admission of evidence. In some interpersonal conflicts, one party may monopolize the process, with no restraints. Process restraints are, however, built into the legal system. Each party has equal protection of the right to speak. The process rules provide for one's position to be fully explicated.

Third, use of professionals to speak for the conflict parties is an advantage for people who need assistance in preparation or presentation of their case. The trained legal expert can develop the best case for the client, watch procedures to ensure fairness, and set forth the case with vigor.

Finally, adjudication serves as a backup for other processes of conflict management. When arbitration, mediation, conciliation, and negotiation fail to produce agreement, the dispute can go to court. The appeal process allows people to go to a higher court to present their case if they dislike the earlier judgment. The moral as well as physical power present in our judicial and criminal justice system provides a last-resort option when necessary. Many conflicts reach resolution on the courthouse steps prior to the hearing. The parties decide under the pressure of going to court. Thus, the very existence of the court system can motivate settlement.

The judicial system has some limitations in dealing with conflict. First, it has been overutilized and, as a consequence, is overburdened and misused. Chief Justice Warren Burger, referring to the legal profession, said, "The obligation of our profession is to serve as healers of human conflicts," (Ray 1982), but "suing has become an American parlor game" (Marks 1981). As a result, there is an "unprecedented demand upon the judicial system, leading to considerable frustration and delay . . ." (Sanders 1977, 2).

The guarantees of speedy justice are difficult to receive, with delays such as two years between filing and first court appearances being common. As Judge Evans of the Court of Civil Appeals says, ". . . there are certain elements . . . that are inappropriate. They are not efficient, they are not effective" (Ray 1982, 52). Finally, because the judicial system has been used and talked about so much, many individuals automatically think of it as the way to "get even" for some wrong. They often do not realize they have made a choice for a mode of conflict resolution until "they find themselves caught up in it with apparently no way out" (Coogler 1978, 6). One legal scholar concludes, ". . . it seems clear that it is simply too cumbersome and expensive for most (minor) disputes . . ." (Sanders 1977, 24). A continuing round of court battles in order to "win" can deplete almost anyone's finances.

The second disadvantage of using the legal system for conflict resolution is that conflict parties no longer make their own decisions. For example, in a dispute involving a community (such as an environmental issue), "litigation takes the decision out of the hands of the communities who must live with its consequences" (Wehr 1979, 123). Similarly, if two people are involved in a protracted domestic dispute such as a contested divorce, the parties stop dealing directly with one another and the attorneys take over the negotiation process. Figure 8.2 portrays the lines of communication when professionals are used to speak for the parties.

As figure 8.2 illustrates, once a suit or petition has been filed with the court, lawyers negotiate with one another, often instructing the litigants to not talk with one another. In this structure, it is easy for the litigants (the conflict parties) to set into motion a struggle that the lawyers act out. The original conflict metamorphoses into a conflict between the two lawyers (Irving and Bohn 1978). The prime players become the attorneys, who negotiate with one another, trying to estimate what the judge (or jury) will do with such a case. Each lawyer's estimate of the judge's or jury's probable response becomes the base of the negotiation strategy, and they often try to persuade the other attorney about their view.

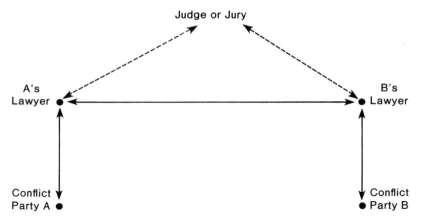

Figure 8.2. Lines of communication with professional advocates. (Solid lines indicate heavy communication; broken lines signify that the judge or jury is used as a reference point for the attorneys, often without direct communication; absence of lines signifies no direct communication.)

A specific reaction to this structure of communication is illustrated in the case of Sharon and her ex-husband, Ted. They had been divorced for three years and were having difficulties agreeing on child visitation arrangements. They lived in different towns, and each had consulted an attorney about their options regarding visitation. One day in April, Sharon flew to Ted's city and called him, only to discover that his attorney had told him, "Don't talk to her, and hold out for all you can get." Sharon told Ted that she had received the same advice from her attorney. They realized that if they both followed their lawyers' advice, they would be in for a protracted court battle. The two of them wisely decided to empower themselves. They met the next day and amicably worked out an agreement—though the process was difficult for them. They were the original parties to the dispute and are the ones who have to live with the long-term results of a decision. Therefore, turning over the responsibility for the decision to their representatives did not seem a desirable option.

The third, and related, disadvantage of adjudication is that the adversary system operates on a win-lose set of conflict assumptions that encourages escalation tactics. Often the lawyer is seen as each client's only champion in a hostile world. This belief promotes escalation when, in fact, it might not be necessary. In order to file an action, one has to blow up the magnitude of the conflict to a "You owe us" or "We'll get you" frame of mind; one tries to win at the other's expense. Filing an action is a signal of seriousness in the conflict, but unfortunately, filing sets an escalatory process in motion. Because attorneys are usually charged with representing solely the interests of their client,

"The client's interest is always perceived as being in opposition to the interests of the other party. The lawyer cannot and does not regard the parties as having a common problem which he or she will help resolve" (Coogler 1978, 7). The gathering of evidence for one side of the conflict disregards the relational, common interests of both parties. Parties cooperate in following rules of procedure, but this level of commonality does not open up many potentially creative outcomes. The escalatory, win-lose atmosphere often is difficult to disengage from, once it has been set into motion. Suits and countersuits often reflect a continual escalation, with each "loser" trying again on some other basis until resources or options are exhausted.

Arbitration

Arbitration comes into use when the conflict participants mutually empower a third party to decide the outcome of their conflict. They assume that they cannot resolve their conflict unassisted and that a neutral third person is needed (Blake, Shepard, and Mouton 1964). As a result, they mutually empower an arbitrator to solve their conflict.

The arbitration process varies according to the type of dispute and the needs of the parties. For example, a grievance procedure initiated by a worker who feels unfairly treated may be long and involve numerous others in testifying. An *interest arbitration* focuses on a simple, limited contract issue such as benefits or seniority (Clark 1974). Contract disputes are a common form of interest arbitration; many managers and line workers routinely sign contracts with a clause calling for arbitration in the case of disagreement. For instance, if you buy a car, have difficulty with repairs, and cannot get satisfaction from the dealer, you can ask for arbitration. The arbitrator listens to both sides of the dispute, questions you and the car dealer's representative, and renders a judgment. When the parties contractually agree to arbitration, the results of the arbitrated judgment are enforceable in court. This process is called *binding arbitration;* the judgment is final. Voluntary or *nonbinding arbitration* is sometimes used when the parties will not agree to binding arbitration. It often allows for further arbitration or the freedom for parties to initiate a court case if they still cannot accept the judgment.

Arbitration has some distinct features that make it useful as a form of third-party intervention. First, unlike adjudication, both parties enter into arbitration voluntarily. Neither party can force the other into the process, and as a result, neither party will feel coerced into a settlement situation. Second, it keeps one party from using passive aggressive or impasse tactics on the other—sooner or later the issue will be resolved (Coogler 1978). Third, in many cases the arbitrator has special training in the content area of the dispute, such as in contract arbitration. When the arbitrator has special expertise in the content of the arbitration, he or she can often offer creative solutions.

Fourth, arbitration is readily available for use in situations in which the participants experience a communication breakdown and are no longer able to solve their own problems. Finally, arbitration is a process that can be used for a wide variety of content areas, ranging from contract disputes, medical malpractice, or landlord-tenant conflicts to domestic relations (Alper and Nichols 1981).

Arbitration does have some limitations. First, it tends to resolve conflicts solely on a content basis; typically arbitration does not address the relational aspects of the dispute. Often, if the parties can reach some accord on their relationship, the content issues can be worked out. Second, arbitration reinforces the assumption that the parties are not capable of learning to manage their own difficulties—that a third party has to manage any solution. Third, it reinforces a win-lose style of thinking in which escalation is used as a legitimate tactic since intransigence automatically brings in an outsider (Blake, Shephard, and Mouton 1964).

Even with these disadvantages, arbitration is still a widely used conflict management alternative because it places boundaries on parties' choices, thus binding them procedurally for purposes of resolution. The prerequisite that parties agree to arbitrate (either contractually before the dispute begins or voluntarily once they are in conflict) enhances the chances for productive conflict managment.

Mediation

Mediation is a process in which an intervener helps parties to change their positions so they can reach agreement. In more elaborated form, mediation is the "art of changing people's positions with the explicit aim of acceptance of a package put together by both sides, with the mediator as listener, the suggestor, the formulator of final agreement to which both sides have contributed" (Alper and Nichols 1983, 31). As Keltner (1983) says, "Your job is to *facilitate* the parties to the dispute to reach an agreement *themselves*." The mediator confers with each party before the first meeting, gains the confidence of each party, and learns about the nature of the dispute. The mediator is in charge of the arrangements for the meeting and controls the process of negotiation between the parties. The mediator is not just a "note-taker"; rather, he or she is active in the process, constantly persuading the parties toward agreement. Of course, sometimes one party is facilitated or listened to, then the other, and the mediator has to be a good listener at all times (Keltner 1983). The mediator is really working for the relationship—trying to bring the parties into accord, saving face for all sides so they can move toward agreement (Pruitt and Johnson 1970).

The process of mediation assumes that conflict is inevitable and resolvable and that parties can be moved to agreement. It further assumes a conflicted relationship has enough common interests for bringing about an agreement and that the parties are ultimately responsible for settling their conflict. It assumes that agreements between parties will be more responsive to their needs than will a settlement imposed by a third party.

Mediation brings three distinct advantages to the managment of conflict. First, because it relies on the parties' active negotiation and involvement, it promotes a mutual stake in the resolution; solutions derived through the process are more likely to be carried out by the parties. The agreement is theirs, not imposed, and as a result there is no "loser" who feels compelled to strike back. The parties created the conflict, and they work for its management. Their active involvement is a source of mutual empowerment; they take ownership of the conflict and, with the mediator's assistance, keep some limits on the process. Mediation recognizes that the parties "have had some sort of prior relationship that will continue long after the dispute has been resolved" (Alper and Nichols 1981, 13).

Second, since mediated agreements represent work on the part of all concerned, the solutions have a higher probability of being integrative and containing elements of creativity. Rather than choosing between two discrete choices of interlocked, non-negotiable positions, new solutions can be generated (Pruitt 1981). As Fisher and Ury (1982) suggest, behind each specific position are more general issues. A mediated agreement can focus on interests rather than on particular positions. Often, someone who is holding out for a monetary reward is more satisfied with an apology than with a sum of money!

Finally, mediation is a flexible process that is equally adaptable to many types of conflict. It has been used successfully in such diverse arenas as family disputes, labor-management impasses, and international conflicts (Wall 1981; Kochan and Jick 1978; Kolb, 1983; Young 1972). For example, family mediation can be used for problems such as runaways, living arrangements of unmarried couples, custody and visitation, family disagreement over estate planning, and other matters (Vroom, Fassett, and Wakefield 1981, 1982). The application of mediation principles and processes to a host of domestic problems may well keep conflict management focused on the "patterns and relations" as the realities to be dealt with (Weick 1979, 79) and lead to more creative management. As Wehr (1979, 34) says, "This process of creative intervention to facilitate voluntary settlement is the most promising and least developed sector of the conflict regulation field." The wide adoption of divorce mediation, by itself, would reduce the amount of acrimony present in society.

One very poignant example of a creative use of mediation cited by Alper and Nichols (1981) for minor crime, is as follows:

An example taken from the files illustrates the constructive use of mediation to achieve both symbolic and actual restitution. An elderly woman returned to her home one afternoon to find her television set gone. The youth who had stolen it was apprehended and admitted that he had sold the set to a fence. Rather than face a fine or continuance under probation supervision, the defendant, in the presence of the mediation board and of the victim, sat down to work out a non-punitive resolution of the case for submission to the judge for his approval. The woman began to describe her life and broke down in the course of telling the boy, "I watch television all day. This is all I do. I watch sixteen hours a day. You have taken the heart of my life away." Confronted with the direct result and personal implications of his act, the youth agreed to accept a job in order to buy the widow a new set. In addition, he agreed that he would accompany her to the bank to cash her weekly check and also escort her to the market for her shopping. A postscript to the case reports that the woman invited the boy to have coffee with her, and she learned from him that his mother had died and that he lived in an uncongenial relationship with his father and brother. Thereafter these Saturday morning coffee hours became a weekly feature. The closing entry reports that the boy had volunteered to paint the woman's kitchen (pp. 146–147).

Early evidence on the effectiveness of mediation suggests that about 70 percent of the cases brought before community-based forms of resolution like the above are settled successfully (Alper and Nichols 1981, 137). Of course the training and expertise of the mediators will have a substantial impact on the success rates. In order to be effective, a referee or mediator should approach the task with this set of assumptions:

1. Conflict is inevitable and resolvable.

2. Conformity is not required.

3. Few situations are hopeless.

4. One part affects another.

5. Each side probably has a piece of the truth.

6. There is some similarity between opponents.

7. Present problems are the ones to solve.

8. The process is of great importance.

9. There is no right answer.

(Leas and Kittlaus 1973, 65–72).

Limitations to the use of mediation as a settlement option do exist. First, not all conflict parties will agree to work through their conflict with the "enemy." They may either not want to talk openly about their difficulties with the other or may have an intense desire to not be in the presence of the other person. In addition, many conflicts escalate to the point where conjoint constructive work is not possible. For example, in one study of couples who did and did not choose mediation for their divorces, the man's perceived chances of winning in the adversarial system affected his willingness to try mediation (Pearson, Thonnes, and Vanderkooi 1982). If someone, in this case the man, thinks he or she can win by going to court, that person is less likely to want mediation. The conflict may be so protracted and the trust level so low that the only basis for solution is a win-lose structure in which an outside party decides.

Second, mediation may not be appropriate for certain types of relationships. Mediation involves considerable commitment to work on the conflict, and some relationships cannot respond to such work. Many parties are not prepared to reinvest in a relationship that has been problematic for them; they would rather try other routes to settlement or just continue the conflict. For example, Kressel *et al.* (1980) discovered that enmeshed couples were so intertwined in their dynamics that mediation was not successful with them. Similarly, couples who are autistic (the relationship bonds are so weak as to be almost nonexistent) were not good candidates for mediation. Too much involvement and too little involvement with the other both work against mediation.

Finally, the dispute may be a type in which involvement in mediation is not worth the effort. Many small disputes may be more efficiently handled with third-party adjudication than with the disputants trying to work with one another. The conflict may not be serious enough to warrant "working through" by the conflict parties.

The three primary formal intervention modes—adjudication, arbitration, and mediation—all have uses and limitations. There are other modes, such as conciliation, that derive their processes from these basic forms. Conciliation, for example, is often a hybrid between mediation and arbitration, with the third party changing roles as he or she deems necessary (Buzzard and Eck 1983). Some forms of conciliation maintain a prearranged goal, such as preserving a marriage. For instance, some marital conciliators will always work for relational preservation rather than see negotiation or a separation or divorce relationship as a viable option. Other forms of conciliation, such as that used by many conciliation courts, use mediation as a process for possible agreement on the issues of support and custody so that a judge does not have to decide. Most alternative forms of conflict management use combinations of mediation, arbitration, or adjudication, depending on the dispute and the dynamics involved.

We have stressed throughout this book a more extensive view of conflict than is offered by looking for winners and losers. Conflict parties who create their difficulties can often untangle those very difficulties with outside assistance supplied either formally or informally. Our own preferences are to stress the modes of management that are least polarizing, that are less win-lose in structure, and that empower the parties to manage their own conflicts. Obviously an intervener has a distinct advantage if he or she enters a dispute before it has escalated to a court appearance (Goldman 1980; Musetto 1982). Polarization of family members, former spouses, or work associates does little to bring ongoing peace to all concerned. Working with them so they can be active agents in the management of their conflicts will yield long-term advantages.

Summary

Many conflicts can be turned into productive experiences with the assistance of either formal or informal third parties. Formal and informal intervention processes share some similarities. The process begins with an identification of the intervention needs, making a decision to intervene, and negotiating a role as intervention agent. If one still feels comfortable with taking on an intervention after these initial steps are taken, the next step is to assess the conflict. The approaches on conflict assessment suggested in chapter 6 can be used for this task. Once you understand the dynamics of the particular conflict, you can design intervention tactics that might be helpful.

Third-party intervention involves use of excellent communication skills, control of the process, and a transformation of the conflict elements. The most common formal intervention modes are adjudication, arbitration, and mediation. Formal modes differ to the extent that the conflict parties have a hand in the final solutions. Any successful intervention will alter the relationship between the parties and settle content issues so that the conflict will not continue unabated.

Epilogue

At the beginning of this book, we discussed the need in our world for creative forms of conflict management. Conflict reduction and peacemaking have emerged in this age as necessities for survival. We are convinced that effectiveness in all arenas of peacemaking contributes to meeting the needs of the world community. Peacemaking at home and at work contributes to an overall atmosphere of lessened hostility, anger, and defensiveness. As we noted at the beginning of this chapter, Kenneth Boulding said that humankind must change its way of thinking more in the next twenty-five years than in the last 25,000. He made that prophetic statement in 1962. May a new dawning of human consciousness about possibilities for living in peace rise in our lifetimes. We invite you to join in the search for peace—in your personal lives and in the family of humankind.

Appendix

Conflict Resources Directory

This directory lists sources for (1) measurement scales, (2) exercises, and (3) simulations that can be used for assessing and learning about conflict. Many of the sources cited in the text are not listed here—we have selected those we think will be more useful. If you wish to secure a particular scale mentioned in the text and not listed here, consult the original article cited.

Some of these resources require a fee; a letter to the person listed will provide you with particulars. Others, such as games and simulations in publications, require only that you have the book available.

I. Measurement scales

1. FACES Scale	Bell, R. Q., Olson, D. H. and J. Portner, "Family Adaptability and Cohesion Evaluation Scales (FACES)," Clinical and Research instrument, Family Social Science, University of Minnesota, St. Paul, MN, 55108
2. Kilmann-Thomas Conflict MODE Instrument	Xicom, Inc. Sterling Forest Tuxedo, NY 10987
3. Jay Hall's Conflict Management Survey	Teleometrics, Inc. P.O. Drawyer 1850 Conroe, TX 77301
4. Diagnosing Organizational Conflict-Management Climates	Bob Crosby and John J. Sherer, in Jones and Pfeiffer (eds.) *1981 Annual Handbook for Group Facilitators,* pp. 100–109, University Associates, San Diego CA

5. Putnam/Wilson Conflict
Behavior Scale

Linda L. Putnam and Charmaine
E. Wilson, "Communicative
Strategies in Organizational
Conflicts: Reliability and Validity
of a Measurement Scale," in
Michael Burgoon (ed.)
Communication Yearbook VI.
Beverly Hills, CA: Sage Publishing
Co., 1983, or write to Dr. Linda L.
Putnam, Dept of Communication,
Purdue University, West Lafayette,
Indiana 47907

II. Exercises for classroom and training use

1. Various exercises

Fred E. Jandt and Mark Hare,
Instruction in Conflict Resolution.
Speech Communication
Association, 5105 Backlick Rd, #E
Annandale, VA 22003

2. Various exercises

Lois B. Hart, *Learning From
Conflict, A Handbook for Trainers
and Group Leaders.* Addison-
Wesley Publishing Co., 1981,
Reading, MA 01867

3. Conflict Attitudes
Questionnaire (for
facilitating discussion
about attitudes toward
conflict)

Either author of this text at
Department of Interpersonal
Communication, University of
Montana, Missoula, MT 59812

III. Simulations

1. Starpower

Lansford Publishing Co. P.O. Box
8711 San Jose, CA 95155

2. Powerplay

George Peabody and Paul
Dietterich, 1973, Powerplay, Inc.,
Naperville, Illinois 60540

3. Parker High School
Simulation

Paul Wehr, *Conflict Regulation,*
Westview Press, 1979, Boulder,
CO pp. 185–189

4. "Controversial Issues: Case Studies in Conflict #224"

1978 Annual Handbook for Group Facilitators, J. William Pfeiffer and John E. Jones (eds.) University Associates, San Diego, CA

5. "Win as Much as You Can: An Intergroup Competition

Vol II of *Structured Experiences for Human Relations Training,* 62–67, Pfeiffer and Jones (eds.), 1974,

6. Prisoner's Dilemma: An Intergroup Competition

Vol III of *Handbook of Structured Experiences,* #61, pp. 52–54, Jones and Pfeiffer (eds.), University Associates, San Diego, CA

7. High Iron: Collaboration and Competition (an adaptation of the Deutsch and Krauss Acme-Bolt Trucking Game)

1980 Annual Handbook for Group Facilitators, Pfeiffer and Jones (eds.), #280, pp. 78–83, University Associates, San Diego, CA

8. Conflict Styles: Organizational Decision Making

1979 Annual Handbook for Group Facilitators, Pfeiffer and Jones (eds.), pp. 15–19, University Associates, San Diego, CA

9. X-Y: A Three-Way Intergroup Competition

1976 Annual Handbook for Group Facilitators, Pfeiffer and Jones, (eds.), pp. 141–146, University Associates, San Diego, CA

10. Win What, Lose What? An Intergroup Conflict Intervention

1975 Annual Handbook for Group Facilitators, Pfeiffer and Jones (eds.), #145, pp. 51–55, University Associates, 8517 Production Ave, San Diego, CA 92126

11. A variety of collective bargaining and mediation cases that can be used for analysis and/or simulation. Some sample cases are—

   Rolling Donut Metal Truck Case

   Midwest Telephone Case

   The Case of Sue Fox

   Silvers and Super City Public Schools

   The Corn Valley Lumber Co. Case

   The Graduate Student Union Case

   The Case of Hernando Cortez

   The Case of Minni Minutchka

John W. Keltner
Consulting Associates
P.O. Box 842
Corvallis, OR 97339

References

Aldous, J. "Family interaction patterns." *Annual Review of Sociology* 3 (1974):105–135.

Alper, B. S., and L. W. Nichols. *Beyond the Courtroom.* Lexington, MA: Lexington Books, 1981.

Altman, I., and D. Taylor. *Social penetration: the development of interpersonal relationships.* New York: Holt, Rinehart and Winston, 1973.

Altman, I., A. Vinsel, and B. B. Brown. "Dialectical conceptions in social psychology: an application to social penetration and privacy regulations." *Advances in Experimental Social Psychology.* Vol. 14. Edited by L. Berkowitz. New York: Academic Press, 1984.

Apfelbaum, E. "On conflicts and bargaining." *Advances in Experimental Social Psychology.* 7 (1974):103–156.

Applegate, J. L. "The impact of construct system development on communication and impression formation in persuasive contexts." *Communication Monographs* 49 (December 1982):277–286.

Argyris, C. *Intervention theory and method: a behavioral science view.* Reading, MA: Addison-Wesley Publishing Co., 1970.

Arnett, R. C. *Dialogical foundations of conflict resolution.* Paper presented to the Speech Communication Association Convention, New York, Nov. 16, 1980.

Arnett, R. C. *Dwell in peace: applying nonviolence to everyday relationships.* Elgin, IL: The Brethren Press, 1980.

Arnold, W. E. "Crisis communication." In *Communicating through behavior.* Edited by W. E. Arnold and R. O. Hirsch, St. Paul, MN: West Publishing Co., 1977.

Bach, G. R., and H. Goldberg. *Creative aggression: the art of assertive living.* New York: Avon Books, 1974.

Bach, G. R., and P. Wyden. *The intimate enemy: how to fight fair in love and marriage.* New York: Avon Books, 1968.

Bardwick, J. M. *Psychology of women: a study of biocultural conflicts.* New York: Harper & Row, 1971.

Barry, W. A. "Marriage research and conflict: an integrative review." *Psychological Bulletin* 73 (1970):41–54.

Bartunek, J. M., A. A. Benton and C. B. Keys. "Third party intervention and the bargaining behavior of group representatives." *Journal of Conflict Resolution* 76, no. 3 (1975):535–555.

Bateson, G. *Steps to an ecology of mind.* New York: Ballantine Books, 1972.

Baucom, D. H. "A comparison of behavioral contracting and problem-solving/communications training in behavioral marital therapy." *Behavior Therapy* 13 (1982):162–174.

Baxter, L. A., and J. Philpott. *Preplanned and emergent strategizing in everyday interaction.* Unpublished manuscript, 1983.

Baxter, L. A. "Conflict management: an episodic approach." *Small Group Behavior,* 13, no. 1 (February 1982):23–42.

Baxter, L. *Contemporary measurement devices: assessing change in conflict relationships.* Paper delivered to the Instructional Communication Division, International Communication Association Convention, Portland, OR, April 1976.

Bell, J., and A. Hadas. *On friendship.* Paper presented at Wyotana Conference, University of Montana, June 1977.

Berger, C. R. "Power and the family." In *Persuasion: new directions in theory and research.* Edited by M. E. Roloff and G. R. Miller. Beverly Hills: Sage, 1980.

Berne, E. *Games people play.* New York: Grove Press, Inc., 1964.

Berscheid, E. and E. H. Walster. *Interpersonal attraction.* 2nd ed. Reading, MA: Addison-Wesley, 1978.

Bernstein, L. *Disarmament.* Address to Johns Hopkins University, 1981.

Bienvenu, M. J. "Measurement of marital communication." *The Family Coordinator* 19 (1970):26–31.

Bienvenu, M. J., A. Shepard, and J. S. Mouton. *Managing intergroup conflict in industry.* Houston, TX: Gulf Publishing Co., 1964.

Birchler, G. R., R. L. Weiss and J. P. Vincent. "A multimethod analysis of social reinforcement exchange between maritally distressed and non-distressed spouse and stranger dyads." *Journal of Personality and Social Psychology* 31 (1975):349–360.

Blake, R. R., A. Shepard, and J. S. Mouton. *Managing Intergroup Conflict in Industry.* Houston, TX. Gulf Publishing, 1964.

Blau, Peter M. *Exchange and power in social life.* New York: John Wiley & Sons, 1964.

Blood, R. O., Jr., and D. M. Wolfe. *Husbands and wives: the dynamics of married living.* Glencoe, IL: Free Press, 1960.

Bochner, A. P. "Conceptual frontiers in the study of communication in families: an introduction to the literature." *Human Communication Research,* 2, no. 4 (Summer 1976):381–397.

Bochner, A. P. "On taking ourselves seriously: an analysis of persistent problems and promising directions in interpersonal research." *Human Communication Research,* 4, no. 2 (Winter 1978):179–191.

Boulding, K. *Conflict and defense: a general theory.* New York: Harper Torchbooks, 1962.

Boulding, K. "The power of nonconflict." *Journal of Social Issues* 33, no. 1 (1977):22–33.

Bowers, J. W. "Beyond threats and promises." *Speech Monographs* 41, (1974):ix-xi.

Bowers, J. W., and D. J. Ochs. *The rhetoric of agitation and control.* Reading, MA: Addison-Wesley Publishing Co., Inc., 1971.

Braiker, H. B., and H. H. Kelley. "Conflict in the development of close relationships." In *Social exchange in developing relationships.* Edited by R. L. Burgess and T. L. Huston. New York: Academic Press, 1979.

Brammer, L. M. *The helping relationship.* Englewood Cliffs, NJ: Prentice-Hall, 1973.

Brockriede, W. "Arguers as lovers." *Philosophy and Rhetoric* 5 (Winter 1972):1–11.

Brown, C. T., and P. W. Keller. *Monologue to dialogue.* Englewood Cliffs, NJ: Prentice-Hall, 1973.

Brown, C. T., P. Yelsma and P. W. Keller. "Communication-conflict predispositions: development of a theory and an instrument." *Human Relations* 34, no. 12 (1981):1103–1117.

Brown, L. D. *Managing conflict at organizational interfaces.* Reading, MA: Addison-Wesley Publishing Co., 1983.

Brown, P., and S. Levinson. "Universals in language use: politeness phenomena." In *Questions and politeness: strategies in social interaction.* Edited by E. Goody. New York: Cambridge University Press, 1978.

Buber, M. *Between man and man.* New York: MacMillan Co., 1972.

Bullis, C. *Conflict behavior: an inductive examination of deductive measures.* Paper presented at the Western Speech Communication Association Convention, Albuquerque, NM, February 1983.

Bullis, C. B., M. C. Cox, and S. H. Bokeno. *Organizational conflict management: the effects of socialization, type of conflict, and sex on conflict management strategies.* Paper presented to International Communication Association Convention, Boston, MA, May 1982.

Burke, K. *Language as symbolic action.* Berkeley: University of California Press, 1968.

Buzzard, L. R., and L. Eck. *Tell it to the church: reconciling out of court.* Elgin, IL: David C. Cook Publishing Co., 1982.

Cahill, M. *Couples' perceptions of power.* Paper for Interpersonal Communication 595: Advanced Conflict Management, University of Montana, 1982.

Capella, J. N. "Mutual influence in expressive behavior." *Psychological Bulletin* 89 (1981):101–132.

Carkhuff, R. *Helping and human relations.* 2 vols. New York: Holt, Rinehart & Winston, Inc., 1969.

Carnes, P. J. *Family development I: Understanding Us.* Minneapolis: Interpersonal Communication Programs, Inc., 1981.

Cavanaugh, M., C. Larson, A. Goldberg, and J. Bellow. *Power and communication behavior: a formulative investigation.* Unpublished manuscript, Dept. of Speech Communication, University of Denver, 1981a.

Cavanaugh et al. "Power." *Communication* 10, no. 2 (May 1981b):81–107.

Chafetz, J. S. "Conflict resolution in marriage: toward a theory of spousal strategies and marital dissolution rates." *Journal of Family Issues* 1 (1980):397–421.

Christiansen, A., and D. C. Nies. "The spouse observation checklist: empirical analysis and critique." *The American Journal of Family Therapy* 8 (1980):69–79.

Clark, R. T. *Coping with mediation, fact finding, and forms of arbitration.* Chicago, IL: International Personnel Management Association, 1974.

Cody, M. J. and M. McLaughlin. "Perceptions of compliance-gaining situations: a dimensional analysis." *Communication Monographs* 47 (June 1980):132–148.

Combs, A. W. *Florida studies in the helping professions.* Gainsville, FL: University of Florida Press, 1969.

Coogler, O. J. *Structured mediation in divorce settlement.* Lexington, MA: D. C. Heath and Co., 1978.

Coser, L. A. *The functions of social conflict.* New York: The Free Press, 1956.

Coser, L. A. *Continuities in the study of social conflict.* New York: The Free Press, 1967.

Cromwell, R. E., and D. H. Olson. *Power in families.* Beverly Hills: Sage, 1975.

Cuber, J. F., and P. B. Haroff. *The significant americans: a study of sexual behavior among the affluent.* New York: Appleton-Century, 1955.

Cupach, W. R. *Interpersonal conflict: relational strategies and intimacy.* Paper presented to the Speech Communication Association Convention, New York, 1980.

Dahl, R. A. *Modern political analysis.* Englewood Cliffs, NJ: Prentice-Hall, Inc., 1963.

Dahl, R. A. "The concept of power." *Behavioral Science* 2 (1957):201–215.

Delia, J. G., and R. A. Clark. "Cognitive complexity, social perception and the development of listener-adapted communication in six-, eight-, ten-, and twelve-year-old boys." *Communication Monographs* 44, no. 4 (November 1977):326–345.

Deutsch, M., and R. M. Krauss. "The effect of threat upon interpersonal bargaining. *Journal of Abnormal and Social Psychology* 61 (1960):181–189.

Deutsch, M. "Trust and suspicion." *Journal of Conflict Resolution* (1958):265–279.

Deutsch, M. "Conflicts: productive and destructive." In *Conflict resolution through communication.* Edited by F. E. Jandt. New York: Harper & Row, Publishers, 1973.

Donohue, W. A. "Development of a model of rule use in negotiation interaction." *Communication Monographs* 48 (1981a):106–120.

Donohue, W. A. "Analyzing negotiation tactics: development of a negotiation interact system." *Human Communication Research* 7, no. 3 (Spring 1981b):273–287.

Druckman, D., ed. *Negotiations.* Beverly Hills: Sage, 1977.

Duhl, F. A., D. Kantor, and B. S. Duhl. "Learning, space and action in family therapy: a primer of sculpture." In *Techniques of family psychotherapy.* Edited by D. Bloch. New York: Grune and Stratton, 1973.

Duke, J. T. *Conflict and Power in Social Life.* Brigham Young University Press. Provo, Utah 1976.

Elliott, G. C. "Components of pacifism: conceptualization and measurement." *Journal of Conflict Resolution* 24, no. 1 (March 1980):27–54.

Ellis, D. G. "Relational control in two group systems." *Communication Monographs* 46, no. 3 (August 1979):153–166.

Emerson, R. M. "Power-dependence relations." *American Sociological Review* 27 (1962):31–41.

Etzioni, A. "On self-encapsulating conflict." *Journal of Conflict Resolution* 8, no. 3. (September 1964).

Falbo, T. "Multidimensional scaling of power strategies." *Journal of Personality and Social Psychology* 35 (1977):537–547.

Ferreira, A. J., and W. D. Winter. "Information exchange and silence in normal and abnormal families." *Family Process* 7 (1968):251–276.

Filley, A. C. *Interpersonal conflict resolution.* Glenview, IL: Scott, Foresman, & Co., 1975.

Filsinger, E. E., P. McAvoy, and R. A. Lewis. "An empirical typology of dyadic formation." *Family Process* 21, no. 3 (September 1982):321–335.

Fink, C. "Some conceptual difficulties in the theory of social conflict." *Journal of Conflict Resolution* XII (1968):412–460.

Fisher, B. A. *Small group decision making: communication and the group process.* New York: McGraw-Hill Book Company, 1974.

Fisher, B. A., and L. C. Hawes. "An interact system model: generating a grounded theory of small groups." *Quarterly Journal of Speech* 57 (1971):444–453.

Fisher, L. "Transactional theories but individual assessment: a frequent discrepancy in family research." *Family Process* 21 (September 1982):313–320.

Fisher, R., and W. Ury. *Getting to yes: negotiating agreement without giving in.* Boston: Houghton Mifflin Co., 1981.

Fisher, R. J. "Third party consultation: a method for the study and resolution of conflict." *Journal of Conflict Resolution* (March 1972):67–94.

Fitzpatrick, M. A. "A typological approach to communication in relationships." In *Communication yearbook I.* Edited by B. Ruben. New Brunswick, NJ: Transaction Books, 1977.

Folger, J. P., and M. S. Poole. *Working through conflict: a communication perspective.* Glenview, IL: Scott, Foresman and Co., 1984.

Frank, J. D. *Psychotherapy and the human predicament: A Psychosocial Approach.* New York: Schocken Books, 1978.

Frentz, T., and J. H. Rushing. *A communicative perspective on closeness/distance and stability/change in intimate ongoing dyads.* Unpublished manuscript, Boulder, CO: University of Colorado, 1980.

Friedman, P. H. A., and E. Yarbrough. *Designing and conducting training and retraining programs and workshops.* Englewood Cliffs, NJ: Prentice-Hall, 1984.

Gallessich, J. *The profession and practice of consultation.* San Francisco, CA: Jossey-Bass, 1982.

Galvin, K. M., and B. J. Brommel. *Family communication: cohesion and change.* Glenview, IL: Scott, Foresman and Company, 1982.

Garfield, P. *Creative dreaming.* New York: Ballantine Books, Inc., 1974.

Gaughan, L. D. "Toward a structural theory of family mediation." In *Therapy with remarriage families.* Edited by J. Hansen and L. Messinger. Rockville, MD.: Aspen System Corporation, 1982.

Gibb, J. R. "Defensive communication." *Journal of Communication* (September 1961):141–148.

Glick, B. R., and S. J. Gross. Marital interaction and marital conflict: a critical evaluation of current research strategies. *Journal of Marriage and the Family* 37, no. 3 (August 1975):505–512.

Goldberg, A. A., M. S. Cavanaugh and C. E. Larson. "The meaning of 'power.' " *Journal of Applied Communication Research* (Fall 1983) 11 (2), 89–108.

Goldhaber, G. M. *Organizational communication.* 3rd ed. Dubuque, Iowa: Wm. C. Brown Company Publishers, 1983.

Goldman, R. B., ed. *Roundtable justice: case studies in conflict resolution.* Boulder, CO: Westview Press, 1980.

Goodrich, D. W., and D. S. Boomer. Experimental assessment of modes of conflict resolution. *Family Process* 2 (1963):15–24.

Gottman, J., C. Notarius, J. Gonso, and H. Markman. *A couple's guide to communication,* Champaign, IL: Research Press, 1976.

Gottman, J. M. "Emotional responsiveness in marital conversations." *Journal of Communication* 32, no. 8 (Summer 1982):108–120.

Gray, F., P. S. Graubard, and H. Rosenberg. "Little brother is changing you." *Psychology Today* (March 1974).

Gray-Little, B., and N. Burks. "Power and satisfaction in marriage: a review and critique." *Psychological Bulletin* 93, no. 3 (1983):513–538.

Gray-Little, B. "Marital quality and power processes among black couples." *Journal of Marriage and the Family* 44, no. 3 (August 1982):633–646.

Guggenbuhl-Craig, A. *Power and the helping professions* Translated by M. Gubitz. Dallas, TX: Spring Publications, 1971.

Gulliver, P. H. *Disputes and negotiations: a cross-cultural perspective.* New York: Academic Press, 1979.

Gurman, A. S. *Questions and answers in the practice of family therapy.* New York: Brunner/Mazel, 1981.

Gurman, A. S., and R. W. Knudson. "Behavioral marriage therapy: A psychodynamic systems analysis and critique." *Family Process* 17 (1978):121–138.

Hale, C. L. *A conversational analysis of communication during negotiation.* Paper presented at the Western Speech Communication Association Convention, Denver, Co., February 1982.

Haley, J. "An interactional description of schizophrenia." *Psychiatry* 22 (1959):321–332.

Haley, J. *Strategies of psychotherapy.* New York: Grune and Stratton, 1963.

Haley, J. "Development of a theory: a history of a research project." In *Double bind. The Foundation of the Communicational Approach to the Family,* C. E. Sluzki and D. C. Ransom, ed. New York: Grune and Stratton, 1976.

Hansen, C. "Living in with normal families." *Family Process* 20 (March 1981):53–75.

Harre, R. "Some remarks on 'rule' as a scientific concept." In *Understanding other persons.* Edited by T. Mischel. Oxford: Basil Blackwell, 1974.

Harre, R., and P. F. Secord. *The explanation of social behavior.* Totowa, NJ: Littlefield, Adams & Company, 1973.

Harsanyi, J. C. "Measurement of social power, opportunity costs, and the theory of two-person bargaining games." *Behavioral Science* 7 (1962):67–80.

Harsanyi, J. C. "Measurement of social power in n-person reciprocal power situations." *Behavioral Science* 7 (1962):81–91.

Hart, R. P., and D. M. Burks. "Rhetorical sensitivity and social interaction." *Speech Monographs* 39, no. 2 (June 1972):75–91.

Hatfield, E., M. K. Utne, and J. Traupmann. "Equity theory and intimate relationships." In *Social exchange in developing relationships.* Edited by R. L. Burgess and T. L. Huston. New York: Academic Press, 1979.

Hawes, L. C. and D. Smith. "A critique of assumptions underlying the study of communication in conflict." *Quarterly Journal of Speech* 59 (1973):423–435.

Hayakawa, S. I. *Language in thought and action.* 4th ed. New York: Harcourt, Brace, Jovanovich, 1978.

Heer, D. M. "The measurement and bases of family power: an overview." *Marriage and Family Living* 25 (1963):133–139.

Herbst, P. C. "The measurement of family relationships." *Human Relations* 5 (1952):3–35.

Himes, J. S. *Conflict and conflict management.* Athens, GA: University of Georgia Press, 1980.

Hobart, C. W., and W. J. Klausner. "Some social interaction correlates of marital role disagreement and marital adjustment." *Marriage and Family Living* 21 (1959):256–263.

Hocker, J. *The implications of conflict theories of rhetorical criticism.* Unpublished dissertation, University of Texas, 1974.

Hocker, J. L., and B. W. Bach. "Functions of metaphor in couples' descriptions of conflicts." Unpublished paper, University of Montana, 1981.

Hocker, J. L. *Change in marital satisfaction and positive communication behavior in enrichment couples using a self-help manual: a multiple baseline study.* Dissertation in progress, Department of Psychology, University of Montana, 1984.

Hoffman, L. *Foundations of family therapy: a conceptual framework for systems change.* New York: Basic Books, 1981.

Hops, H., T. A. Wills, G. R. Patterson, and R. L. Weiss. *Marital interaction coding system.* Eugene, OR: University of Oregon & Oregon Research Institute, 1972.

Howard, A. M., J. L. Hocker. *Youths' descriptions of their place in the family: a qualitative study using metaphorical data.* Paper presented to the Language Behavior Interest Group, Western Speech Communication Association Convention, San Jose, CA, 1981.

Irving, H. H., and P. E. Bohm. "A social science approach to family dispute resolution." *Canadian Journal of Family Law* 1, no. 1 (January 1978):39–56.

Ivie, R. L. "The metaphor of force in prowar discourse: the case of 1812." *Quarterly Journal of Speech* 68 (1982):240–253.

Jamieson, D. W., and K. W. Thomas. "Power and conflict in the student-teacher relationship." *Journal of Applied Behavioral Science* 10 (1974):321–333.

Jandt, F. E., ed. *Conflict resolution through communication.* New York: Harper & Row, Publishers, 1973.

Johnson, P. "Women and power: toward a theory of effectiveness." *Journal of Social Issues* 32 (1976):99–110.

Johnson, B. *Communication: the process of organizing.* Boston: Allyn and Bacon, 1977.

Karrass, C. L. *Give and take: a complete guide to negotiating strategies and tactics.* New York: Thomas Y. Crowell Co., 1974.

Keltner, J. (Sam). *You are the mediator.* Unpublished guide, Dept. of Speech Communication, Oregon State University, 1983.

Kenkel, W. W. "Influence differentiation in family decision making." *Sociology and Social Research* 43 (1957):18–25.

Kifer, R. E., M. A. Lewis, D. R. Green, and E. L. Phillips. "Training predelinquent youths and their parents to negotiate conflict situations." *Journal of Applied Behavior Analysis* 7, no. 3 (Fall 1974):357–364.

Kilmann, R., and K. Thomas. "Interpersonal conflict-handling behavior as reflections of Jungian personality dimensions." *Psychological Reports* 37 (1975):971–980.

Kipnis, D. *The powerholders.* Chicago: University Press, 1976.

Knudson, R. M., A. A. Sommers, and S. L. Golding. "Interpersonal perception and mode of resolution in marital conflict." *Journal of Personality and Social Psychology* 38, no. 5 (1980):751–763.

Kochan, T. A., and T. Jick. "The public sector mediation process: a theory and empirical examination." *Journal of Conflict Resolution* 22, no. 2 (June 1978):209–240.

Koile, E. *Listening as a way of becoming.* Waco, TX: Regency Books, 1977.

Kolb, D. M. "Strategy and the tactics of mediation." *Human Relations* 36, no. 3 (1983):247–268.

Kressel, K., N. Jaffee, B. Tuchman, C. Watson, and M. Deutsch. "A typology of divorcing couples: implications for mediation and the divorce process." *Family Process* 19, no. 2 (June 1980):101–116.

Laing, R. D., H. Phillipson, and A. R. Lee. *Interpersonal perception.* Baltimore, MD: Perrenial Library, 1966.

Lakoff, G., and M. Johnson. *Metaphors we live by.* Chicago: University of Chicago press, 1980.

Langer, E. J. "Rethinking the role of thought in social interaction." In *New directions in attribution research.* Vol. 2. Edited by Harvey, W. Ickes & R. F. Kidd. Hillsdale, NJ: Lawrence Erlbaum Associates, Publishers, 1978.

Laue, J. and G. Cormick. *The ethics of social intervention: community crisis intervention programs.* St. Louis: Community Crisis Intervention Center, Washington University, Mimeo.

Lawrence, P. R., and J. W. Lorsch. *Organization and environment.* Homewood, IL: Irwin, 1969.

Leas, S., and P. Kittlaus. *Church Fights: Managing Conflict in the Local Church.* Philadelphia: Westminster Press, 1973.

Lederer, W. J., and D. D. Jackson. *Mirages of marriage.* New York: W. W. Norton & Company, Inc., 1968.

Locke, H. *Predicting adjustment in marriage.* New York: Holt, Rinehart and Winston, 1951.

Lustig, M. W. and S. W. King. "The effect of communication apprehension and situation on communication strategy choices." *Human Communication Research* 7, no. 1 (Fall 1980):74–82.

Mace, D., and V. Mace. "Marriage enrichment: a preventive group approach for couples." In *Treating relationships.* Edited by D. H. L. Olson. Lake Mills, Iowa: Graphic Publishing, 1976.

Mack, R. M. and R. C. Snyder. "The analysis of social conflict—toward an overview and synthesis." In *Conflict resolution through communication.* Edited by F. E. Jandt. New York: Harper & Row Publishers, 1973.

Madanes, C. *Strategic family therapy.* San Francisco: Jossey-Boss, 1981.

Mager, R., and P. Pipe. *Analyzing performance problems: or you really oughta wanna.* Belmont, CA: Fearon Publishers, Inc., 1970.

Mager, R., and P. Pipe. *Goal analysis.* Belmont, CA: Fearon Publishers, Inc., 1972.

Margolin, G. "Behavior exchange in distressed and nondistressed marriages: a family cycle perspective." *Behavior Therapy* 12 (1981):329–343.

Margolin, G. "A social learning approach to intimacy," in *Intimacy* Ed. by M. Fisher and G. Stricker. New York: Plenum, 1982, 175–201.

Marks, M. A. *The suing of America.* New York: Seaview Books, 1981.

Marwell, G. and D. Schmitt. "Dimensions of compliance-gaining behavior: an empirical analysis." *Sociometry* 39 (1967):350–364.

May, R. *Power and innocence: a search for the sources of violence.* New York: Dell Publishing Co., Inc., 1972.

McCall, G. J., and J. L. Simons. *Issues in participant observation: a text and reader.* Reading, MA: Addison-Wesley Publishing Co., Inc., 1969.

McCall, M. W., Jr. "Power, authority and influence." In *Organizational behavior.* Edited by S. Kerr. Columbus, OH: Grid Publishing Co., 1979.

McClelland, D. C. "The two faces of power." *Journal of International Affairs* 24 (1969):141–154.

McDonald, G. W. "Family power: the assessment of a decade of theory and research." *Journal of Marriage and the Family* 42, no. 4 (1980):841–854.

McGillis, D. "Conflict resolution outside the courts." *Applied Social Psychology Annual* 2 (1981):243–262.

Metcoff, J., and C. A. Whitaker. "Family microevents: communication patterns for problem solving." In *Normal family processes.* Edited by F. Walsh. New York: The Guilford Press, 1982.

Mettetal, G., and J. M. Gottman. *Affective responsiveness in spouses: investigating the relationship between communication behavior and marital satisfaction.* Paper presented at Speech Communication Association, New York, November 1980.

Miller, G., F. Boster, M. Roloff, and D. Siebold. "Compliance-gaining message strategies: a typology and some findings concerning effects of situational differences." *Communication Monographs* 44 (1977):37–54.

Miller, G. R., and M. Steinberg. *Between people: a new analysis of interpersonal communication.* Chicago: Science Research Assoc., 1975.

Miller, S., D. Wackman, E. Nunnally, and C. Saline. *Straight talk.* New York: New American Library, 1981.

Minuchin, S. *Families and family therapy.* Cambridge: Harvard University Press, 1974.

Minuchin, P., B. Biber, E. Shapiro, and H. Zimilies. *The psychological impact of school experience.* New York: Basic Books, 1969.

Mishler, E. G., and N. E. Waxler. *Interaction in families: an experimental study of family processes and schizophrenia.* New York: Wiley, 1968.

Moos, R. H., and B. S. Moos. "A typology of family social environment." *Family Process* 15 (1976):357–371.

Musetto, A. P. *Dilemmas in child custody: family conflicts and their resolution.* Chicago: Nelson-Hall, 1982.

Napier, A., and C. Whitaker. *The family crucible.* New York: Harper and Row, 1978.

Navran, L. "Communication and adjustment in marriage." *Family Process* 6 (1967):173–184.

Neill, John R., and D. P. Kniskern. *From psyche to system: the evolving therapy of Carl Whitaker.* New York: Guilford Press, 1982.

North, R. C. et al. "Some empirical data on the conflict spiral." *Peace Research Society (International) Papers* 1 (1964):1–14.

Olson, D. H., and H. I. McCubbin. *Families: what makes them work.* Beverly Hills: Sage, 1983.

Olson, D. H., and C. Rabunsky. "Validity of 4 measures of family power." *Journal of Marriage and Family* 34, no. 2 (May 1972):224–233.

Olson, D. H., and R. G. Ryder. "Inventory of marital conflict (IMC): an experimental interaction procedure." *Journal of Marriage and the Family* 32 (1970):443–448.

Olson, D. H., D. H. Sprenkle, and C. Russell. "Circumplex model of marital and family systems. I: cohesion and adaptability dimensions, family types and clinical applications." *Family Process* 18 (1979):3–28.

Olson, D. H. and M. A. Strauss. "A diagnostic tool for marital and family therapy: the SIMFAM technique." *Family Coordinator* 21 (1972):251–258.

Ortony, A. "Why metaphors are necessary and not just nice." *Educational Theory* 25, no. 1 (1975):45–53.

Osgood, C. E. "Graduate unilateral initiatives for peace." In *Preventing World War III.* Edited by Q. Wright, et al. New York: Simon and Schuster, 1962.

Ottaway, R. N. "The change agent: a taxonomy in relation to the change process." *Human Relations* 36, no. 4 (1983):361–392.

Papp, P., O. Silberstein, and E. Carter. "Family sculpting in preventive work with 'well' families." *Family Process* 12, no. 1 (1973):197–212.

Patterson, G. R. "Some procedures for assessing changes in marital interaction patterns." *Oregon Research Institute Bulletin,* Whole No. 16, 1976.

Patterson, G. R., H. Hops, and R. L. Weiss. "Interpersonal skills training for couples in early stages of conflict." *Journal of Marriage and the Family* 37, no. 2 (May 1975):295–302.

Pearson, J., N. Thonnes and L. Vanderkooi. "The Decision to Mediate Profiles—Individuals Who Accept and Reject the Opportunity to Mediate Contested Child Custody and Visitation Issues" *Journal of Divorce,* Winter 1982 pp. 17–35.

Peterson, D. R. "Conflict." In *Close relationships.* Edited by H. H. Kelley et al. New York: W. H. Freeman and Co., 1983.

Phillips, E., and R. Cheston. "Conflict resolution: what works?" *California Management Review* 2 (1979):76–83.

Phillips, G. M., and N. Metzger. *Intimate communication.* Boston, MA: Allyn & Bacon, Inc., 1976.

Pruitt, D. G., and D. F. Johnson. "Mediation as an aid to face saving in negotiation." *Journal of Personality and Social Psychology* 14, no. 3 (1970):239–246.

Pruitt, D. G. *Negotiation behavior.* New York: Academic Press, 1981.

Putnam, L. L., and T. S. Jones. "The role of communication is bargaining." *Human Communication Research* 8 (1982):162–280.

Putnam, L. L., and C. E. Wilson. "Communicative strategies in organizational conflicts: reliability and validity of a measurement scale." In *Communication yearbook 6.* Edited by M. Burgoon. Beverly Hills, CA: Sage Publications-International Communication Association, 1982.

Raiffa, H. *The art and science of negotiation.* Cambridge, MA: Belknap Press of Harvard University Press, 1982.

Rands, M., Levinger, G. and G. D. Mellinger. "Patterns of conflict resolution and marital satisfaction." *Journal of Family Issues* 2, no. 3 (September 1981):297–321.

Raush, H. C., W. A. Barry, R. Hertel, and M. A. Swain. *Communication, conflict and marriage.* San Francisco: Jossey-Bass, 1974.

Raven, B. H., and J. R. P. French, Jr. "A formal theory of social power." *Psychological Review* 63 (1956):181–194.

Raven, B. H., and A. W. Kruglanski. "Conflict and power." In *The structure of conflict.* Edited by P. Swingel. New York: Academic Press, 1970, 69–109.

Ray, L., ed. *Alternative dispute resolution: bane or boon to attorneys?* Washington, D.C.: Special Committee on Alterative Means of Dispute Resolution of the Public Services Activities Division, American Bar Association, 1982.

Resick, P. A., J. J. Sweet, D. M. Kieffer, P. K. Barr, and N. L. Ruby. *Perceived and actual discriminations of conflict and accord in marital communication.* Paper presented at the Eleventh Annual Convention of the Association for Advancement of Behavior Therapy. Atlanta, December 1977.

Resick, P. A., B. Welsh-Osga, E. A. Zitomer, D. K. Spiegel, J. C. Meidlinger, and B. R. Long. *Predictors of marital satisfaction, conflict and accord: Study I, a preliminary revision of the marital interaction coding system.* Unpublished manuscript, University of South Dakota, 1980.

Reychler, L. "The effectiveness of a pacifist strategy in conflict resolution: an experimental study." *Journal of Conflict Resolution* 23, no. 2 (June 1979):228–260.

Rogers, C. *Client centered counseling.* Boston: Houghton Mifflin, 1951.

Rogers, L. E., and R. Farace. "Analysis of relational communication in dyads." *Human Communication Research* 1, no. 3 (1975):222–239.

Rogers, M. F. "Instrumental and infra-resources: the bases of power." *American Journal of Sociology* 79 (1974):1418–1433.

Rogers-Millar, L. E., and F. E. Millar, III. "Domineeringness and Dominance: a transactional view." *Human Communication Research* 5 (1979):238–246.

Rogers-Millar, L. E., and F. E. Millar. *A transactional definition and measure of power.* Paper presented to the Speech Communication Association, Washington, D.C., 1977.

Rollins, B. C., and S. Bahr. "A theory of power relationship in marriage." *Journal of Marriage and the Family* 38 (November 1976):619–627.

Roloff, M. E. "Communication strategies, relationships, and relational change." In *Explorations in interpersonal communication.* Edited by G. R. Miller. Beverly Hills, CA: Sage, 1976.

Ross, R. and S. DeWine. *Interpersonal conflict: measurement and validation.* Paper presented to the Interpersonal and Small Group Communication Division, Speech Communication Association Convention, Louisville, KY: November 1982.

Rubin, J. A., and B. R. Brown. *The social psychology of bargaining and negotiation.* New York: Academic Press, 1975.

Rummel, R. J. *Understanding conflict and war: The conflict helix.* Vol. 2. New York: Sage Publication, 1976.

Rushing, J. H. *Rhetorical criticism as analogic process.* Paper presented at the SCA/ AFA Summer Conference on Argumentation, Alta, UT: July 1983.

Rusk, T., and R. Gerner. "A study of the process of emergency psychotherapy." *American Journal of Psychiatry* 128 (1972):882–886.

Ryder, R. G., and D. W. Goodrich. "Married couples' response to disagreement." *Family Process* 5 (1966):30–42.

Safilios-Rothschild, C. "The study of family power structure: a review 1960–1969." *Journal of Marriage & Family* 32, no. 4 (November 1970):539–549.

Sander, F. E. A. *Report on the national conference on minor disputes resolution.* Washington, D.C.: American Bar Association Press, 1977.

Satir, V. *Conjoint family therapy.* Palo Alto, CA: Science and Behavior Books, 1967.

Satir, V. *Peoplemaking.* Palo Alto: Science and Behavior Books, 1972.

Scanzoni, J. "Social processes and power in families." In *Contemporary theories in the family.* Edited by E. Burr. 1979.

Schelling, T. C. *The strategy of conflict.* Cambridge, MA: Harvard University Press, 1960.

Schmidt, S. M., and T. A. Kochan. "Conflict: toward conceptual clarity." *Administrative Science Quarterly* 17 (1972):359–370.

Schroer, C. *Reconciliation, transcendence and nonviolence.* Sermon delivered at University Congregational Church, Missoula, MT, February 22, 1981.

Schuetz, J. "Communicative competence and the bargaining of Watergate." *Western Journal of Speech Communication* 41 (1978):105–115.

Schuetz, J. E. *A contingent model of argumentation based on a game theory paradigm.* Unpublished dissertation, University of Colorado, 1975.

Schutz, W. C. *The interpersonal underworld.* Palo Alto, CA: Science and Behavior Books, 1966.

Scott, M. B., and S. Lyman. "Accounts." *American Sociological Review* 33 (1968):46–62.

Selye, Hans. *Stress Without Distress.* New York: Lippincott & Crowell, 1974.

Sherif, M., and C. W. Sherif. *An outline of social psychology.* rev. ed. New York: Harper and Brothers, 1956.

Shimanoff, S. B. *Communication rules: theory and research.* Beverly Hills: Sage Publications, 1980.

Siegel, S., and L. E. Fouraker. *Bargaining and group decision making: experiments in bilateral monopoly.* New York: McGraw-Hill, 1960.

Sillars, A. L. "Attributions and communication in roommate conflicts." *Communication Monographs* 47 (1980):180–200.

Sillars, A. L. "Attributions and interpersonal conflict resolution." In *New directions in attribution research.* Vol 3. Edited by J. H. Harvey, W. Ickes, & R. F. Kidd. Hillsdale, NJ: Lawrence Erlbaum Associates, 1981.

Sillars, A. L. "The sequential and distributional structure of conflict interactions as a function of attributions concerning the locus of responsibility and stability of conflicts." In *Communication yearbook IV.* Edited by D. Ninno. Edison, NJ: Transaction Books, 1980.

Sillars, A. L., S. F. Coletti, D. Parry, and M. A. Rogers. "Coding verbal conflict tactics: nonverbal and perceptual correlates of the 'avoidance-distributive-integrative' distinction." *Human Communication Research* 9, no. 1 (Fall 1982):83–95.

Simmel, G. *Conflict and the web of the group affiliations.* Translated by K. H. Wolff. New York: The Free Press, 1953.

Simons, H. "Persuasion in social conflicts: a critique of prevailing conceptions and a framework for future research." *Speech Monographs* 39 (1972):227–247.

Simons, H. W. *The management of metaphor.* A paper presented at ASILOMAR '79, Conference on Human Communication from the Interactional View, Asilomar, CA: February 16, 1979.

Smith, M. J. *When I say no, I feel guilty.* New York: Bantam Books, Inc., 1975.

Soloman, L. "The influence of some types of power relationships and game strategies upon the development of interpersonal trust." *Journal of Abnormal and Social Psychology* 61 (1960):223–230.

Spector, B. I. "Negotiation as a psychological process." *Journal of Conflict Resolution* 21, no. 4 (December 1977):607–618.

Sprey, J. "Family power structure: a critical comment." *Journal of Marriage and the Family* 33 (May 1972):722–733.

Steinglass, P. "The conceptualization of marriage from a system theory perspective." In *Marriage and marital therapy.* Edited by T. J. Paolino Jr. and B. S. McCrady. New York: Brunner/Mazel, 1978.

Stewart, J. "Foundations of dialogic communication." *The Quarterly Journal of Speech* 64 (1978):183–201.

Strauss, M. A. "Wife beating: causes, treatment and research needs." In *Battered women: issues of public policy.* U.S. Commission on Civil Rights, Washington, D.C., January 30–31, 1978.

Strauss, M. A. "Measuring intrafamily conflict and violence: the conflict tactics (CT) scales." *Journal of Marriage and the Family* 41 (1979):75–88.

Strauss, M. A., R. J. Gelles, and S. K. Steinmetz. *Behind closed doors: violence in the American family.* Garden City, NY: Doubleday, 1980.

Strodtbeck, F. L. "Husband-wife interaction over revealed differences." *American Sociological Review* 16 (1951):768–473.

Stuart, R. B. *Helping couples change: a social learning approach to marital therapy.* New York: Guilford Press, 1980.

Sundberg, N. D., J. R. Taplin, and L. E. Tyler. *Introduction to clinical psychology: perspectives, issues and contributions to human service.* Englewood Cliffs, NJ: 1983.

Taylor, W. R. "Using systems theory to organize confusion." *Family Process* 18 (1979):479–488.

Tedeschi, J. T., and P. Rosenfeld. "Communication in bargaining and negotiation." In *Persuasion: new directions in theory and research.* Edited by M. E. Roloff and G. R. Miller. Beverly Hills, CA: Sage Publishing, 1980.

Tedeschi, J. T. *The social influence processes.* Chicago: Aldine Publishing Co., 1972.

Tedeschi, J. T. "Threats and promises." In *The structure of conflict.* Edited by P. Swingle. New York: Academic Press, Inc., 1970.

Thomas, K. "Conflict and conflict management." In *Handbook of industrial and organizational psychology.* Edited by M. D. Dunnette. Chicago: Rand McNally, 1976.

Thomas, K. W., and L. R. Pondy. Toward an 'intent' model of conflict management among principal parties. *Human Relations* 30 (1977):1089–1102.

Thomas, M. T., II. *A critique of the two-dimensional model of conflict styles.* Paper for Interpersonal Communication 485: Interpersonal Conflict, University of Montana, 1982.

Toulmin, S. *The uses of argument.* Cambridge, MA: Cambridge University Press, 1958.

Tournier, P. *The violence within.* Translated by E. Hudson. New York: Harper and Row, 1978.

Turk, J. L., and N. W. Bell. "Measuring power in families." *Journal of Marriage and Family* 34, no. 2 (1972):215–222.

Van de Vliert, E. Siding and other reactions to a conflict. *Journal of Conflict Resolution,* September 1981, *25,* No. 3, 495–520.

Varney, G. H. "Strategies for designing an intervention." *The 1978 Annual Handbooks for Group Facilitators.* San Diego, CA: University Associates, 1978.

Vinacke, W. E., and A. Arkoff. An experimental study of colations in a triad. *American Sociological Review,* 1957, *22,* 406–414.

Vincent, J. P. *Problem-solving behavior in distressed and nondistressed married and stranger dyads.* Unpublished doctoral dissertation, University of Oregon, 1972.

Vincent, J. P., R. L. Weiss, and G. R. Birchler. A behavioral analysis of problem solving in distressed and nondistressed married and stranger dyads. *Behavior Therapy,* 1975, *6,* 475–487.

Vroom, P., D. Fassett, and R. A. Wakefield. Mediation: the wave of the future? *American Family,* June–July 1981, *4,* No. 4, 8–15.

Vroom, P., D. Fassett, and R. A. Wakefield. Winning through mediation: divorce without losers. *The Futurist,* February 1982, 28–34.

Wall, J. A., Jr., Mediation: an analysis, review, and proposed research. *Journal of Conflict Resolution,* March 1981, *25,* No. 1, 157–180.

Waller, W. *The family: a dynamic interpretation.* New York: Gordon, 1938.

Waln, V. *Interpersonal conflict interaction: an examination of verbal defense of self.* Paper presented to Speech Communication Association Convention, Anaheim, Calif., 1981.

Walsh, F., *Normal family processes.* New York: The Guilford Press, 1984.

Walton, R. E. *Interpersonal peacemaking: confrontation and third party consultation.* Reading, Mass.: Addison-Wesley Publishing Co., Inc., 1969.

Walton, R. E., and R. B. McKersie. *A behavioral theory of labor negotiations: an analysis of a social system.* New York: McGraw-Hill, 1965.

Warner, C. T., and T. D. Olson. Another view of family conflict and family wholeness. *Family Relations,* October 1981, *30,* No. 4, 493–504.

Watzwalick, P., J. H. Beavin and D. D. Jackson. *Pragmatics of human communication: a study of interaction patterns, pathologies and paradoxes.* New York: W. W. Norton and Co., Inc., 1967.

Wehr, P. *Conflict resolution.* Boulder, Colo.: Westview Press, 1979.

Weick, K. E. *The social psychology of organizing.* Reading, Mass.: Addison-Wesley Publishing Co., Inc., 1969.

Weick, K. E. *The social psychology of organizing* (2nd ed.). New York: Addison-Wesley Publishing Co., 1979.

Weiss, R., and G. Birchler. "Adults with marital dysfunction." In *Behavior therapy in the psychiatric setting.* Edited by M. Hersen and A. S. Bellack. Baltimore: Williams and Williams, 1978.

Weiss, R. L., H. Hops, and G. R. Patterson. A framework for conceptualizing marital conflict: a technology for altering it, some data for evaluating it. In L. A. Hammerlynck, L. C. Handy and E. J. Mash (Eds.), *Behavior change: methodology, concepts and practice* (The Fourth Banff International Conference on Behavior Modification). Champaign, Illinois: Research Press, 1972.

Weiss, R. L., H. Hops, and G. R. Patterson. A framework for conceptualizing marital conflict: a technology for altering it, some data for evaluating it. In F. W. Clark and L. A. Hammerlynck (Eds.), *Critical issues in research and practice. Proceedings of the Fourth Banff International Conference on Behavior Modification.* Champaign, Ill.: Research Press, 1973.

Weiss, R., and G. Margolin. Marital conflict and accord. In A. R. Ciminero, K. S. Calhoun, and H. E. Adams (Eds.), *Handbook for behavioral assessment.* New York: John Wiley & Sons, 1977.

Weiss, R. L., and B. A. Perry. *Assessment and treatment of marital dysfunction.* Eugene, OR: Oregon Marital Studies Program, 1979.

Welch-Osga, B., P. A. Resick, and E. A. Zitomer. *Revising the marital interaction coding system: Study II, extension and cross-validation.* Paper presented at the meeting of the American Psychological Association, New York, September 1979.

Wilmot, W. W. *The influence of personal conflict styles of teachers on student attitudes toward conflict.* Paper presented to Instructional Communication Division, International Communication Association Convention, Portland, Oregon, April 15, 1976.

Wilmot, W. W. *Dyadic communication* (2nd ed.). Reading, Mass.: Addison-Wesley, 1979.

Wilmot, W. W. Metacommunication: a re-examination and extension. In D. Nimmo (Ed.), *Communication yearbook 4.* New Brunswick: Transactions Books, 1980.

Yarbrough, E. *Rules of observation.* Unpublished monograph, Department of Communication, University of Colorado, 1977.

Yelsma, P. Conflict predispositions: differences between happy and clinical couples. *The American Journal of Family Therapy,* 1981, *9,* 57–63.

Yelsma, P. "Functional conflict management in effective marital adjustment." *Communication Quarterly* vol. 32, No. 1 (Winter 1984) 56–61.

Young, O. R. Intermediaries: additional thought on third parties. *Journal of Conflict Resolution,* March 1972, *16,* 51–65.

Zartman, W. I. "Negotiation as a joint decision-making process." *Journal of Conflict Resolution* 21, no. 4 (December 1977):619–638.

Author Index

Aldous, J., 149
Alper, B. S., 204, 205, 206
Altman, I., 32, 33
Apfelbaum, E., 86
Applegate, J. L., 125
Argyris, C., 182, 186
Arkoff, A., 145
Arnett, R. C., 162, 163
Arnold, W. E., 192
Bach, B. W., 139
Bach, G. R., 28, 31, 65, 82, 84, 114
Bahr, S., 83
Barnicott, J., 111
Barry, W. A., 147
Bartunek, J. M., 195
Bateson, G., 7, 27, 131, 140
Baucom, D. H., 173
Baxter, L., 33
Baxter, L. A., 29, 49, 107, 108, 148
Beavin, J. H., 72
Bell, J., 6
Bell, N. W., 80, 82, 148
Berger, C. R., 79, 82, 148
Berne, E., 17, 65
Berscheid, E., 75
Berstein, L., 35
Betnon, A. A., 195
Bienuenu, M. J., 148
Birchler, G. R., 32
Blake, R. R., 203, 204
Blau, Peter M., 74
Blood, R. O., 80, 149
Bochner, A. P., 11, 29, 80, 81
Bohn, P. E., 201
Boomer, D. S., 147
Boulding, K., 164, 185, 209

Bowers, J. W., 83, 111
Braiker, H. B., 26, 32
Brammer, L. M., 192
Brockriede, W., 113, 117, 122
Brommel, B. S., 29, 55, 79, 131, 148, 178
Brown, B. R., 145, 172, 182
Brown, C. T., 50, 53, 147, 163
Brown, L. D., 85, 159, 180, 190
Brown, P., 98, 111, 149
Buber, M., 163
Bullis, C. B., 110, 111
Burke, K., 10, 13, 65
Burks, D. B., 62
Burks, N., 149
Buzzard, L. R., 199, 207
Cahill, M., 68
Capella, J. N., 164
Carkhuff, R., 192
Carnes, P. J., 178
Carter, E., 131, 139
Cavanaugh, M., 67, 148
Chafetz, J. S., 149
Cheston, R., 43
Christensen, A., 148
Clark, R. T., 203
Cody, M. S., 111
Colletti, S. F., 112, 115, 116, 121, 125
Combs, A. W., 192
Conkhite, G., 93
Coogler, O. J., 199, 201, 203
Cormick, G., 88
Coser, L. A., 22, 32, 33
Cromwell, R. E., 148
Cuber, J. F., 53
Cupach, W. R., 111, 125

Dahl, R. A., 76, 83
Deutsch, M., 22, 29, 30, 76, 145
DeWine, S., 111
Donahue, W. A., 149, 172
Duhl, F. A. and Duhl, B. S., 139
Eck, L., 199, 207
Elliott, G. C. 163
Ellis, D. G., 80, 149
Emerson, R. M., 76, 77
Etzioni, A., 166
Falbo, T., 111
Farace, R., 80, 116, 149
Ferreira, A. J., 173
Filley, A. C., 121, 196
Filsinger, E. E., 55
Fink, C., 22
Fisher, B. A., 9, 166
Fisher, L., 53
Fisher, R., 91, 99, 102, 106, 111, 121, 173, 192, 205
Fitzpatrick, M. A., 55
Folger, J. P., 30, 50, 72
Fouraker, L. E., 145
Frank, J. D., 162, 163
Freidman, P. H. H., 182
French, J. R. P., Jr., 72, 79
Frentz, T., 29
Gallessich, J., 180, 182
Galvin, K. M., 29, 55, 79, 131, 148, 178
Garfield, P., 75, 164
Gaughan, L. D., 56, 57, 58
Gerner, R., 192
Gibb, J. R., 108
Glick, B. R., 147
Goldberg, A. A., 67
Goldberg, H., 82
Golding, S. L., 110, 111, 145, 147
Goldman, R. B., 208
Goodrich, D. W., 147
Gottman, J., 173, 175, 177, 178
Gottman, J. M., 20, 111, 125, 148
Graubard, P. S., 158
Gray, F., 158
Gray-Little, B., 81, 149
Gross, S. J., 147
Guggenbuhl-Craig, A., 84
Gulliver, P. H., 172
Gurman, A. S., 148
Hale, C. L., 172
Haley, J., 11, 20, 68, 100, 133
Hall, 148

Hansen, C., 12
Haroff, P. B., 53
Harre, R., 63
Harsanyi, J. C., 76, 119, 120
Hart, R. P., 62
Hatfield, E., 86
Hayakawa, S. I., 10
Heer, D. R., 80, 149
Herbst, P. C., 86
Hobart, C. W., 148
Hocker, J. L., 117, 119, 139, 173
Hoffman, L., 131, 132, 136
Hops, H., 148, 173
Howard, A. M., 139
Howes, L. C., 7, 94
Irving, H. H., 201
Jackson, D. D., 53, 65, 72, 175
Jamieson, D. W., 84, 85
Jandt, F. E., 23
Jick, T., 205
Johnson, B., 131
Johnson, D. F., 204
Johnson, M., 10, 13, 14
Johnson, P., 75
Jones, T. S., 172
Kantor, D., 139
Karass, C. L., 111
Keller, P. W., 50, 53, 147, 163
Kelley, H. H., 26, 32
Keltner, J., 204
Kenkel, W. W., 80, 149
Keys, C. B., 195
Kifer, R. E., 173
Kilmann, R., 40, 41, 66, 148
King, S. W., 111
Kipnis, D., 67, 68, 72, 79, 111, 149, 166
Kittlaus, P., 185, 207
Klausner, W. J., 148
Kniskern, D. P., 131
Knudsen, R. M., 110, 111, 145, 147, 148
Kochan, T. A., 23, 205
Koile, E., 87
Kolb, D. M., 205
Kressel, K., 58, 207
Kruglanski, A. W., 84, 85
Laing, R. D., 96
Lakoff, G., 10, 13, 14
Langer, E. J., 107
Laue, J., 88
Lawrence, P. R., 148

Leas, S., 185, 207
Lederer, W. J., 53, 65, 175, 178
Lee, A. R., 96
Levinger, G., 148
Levinson, S., 98, 111, 149
Lewis, R. A., 55
Liska, J., 93
Locke, H., 32
Lorsch, J. W., 148
Lustig, M. W., 111
Lyman, S., 183
Mace, D. and Mace, V., 178
Mack, R. M., 23
Madanes, C., 68, 85
Mager, R., 95, 105
Margolin, G., 148, 173
Marks, M. A., 201
Marwell, G., 111, 149
May, R., 72, 76, 83, 84
McAvoy, P., 55
McCall, M. W., Jr., 79, 148
McClelland, D. C., 68
McDonald, G. W., 80, 81, 88, 148, 149
McGillis, D., 182
McKersie, R. B., 111, 115, 121, 172
McLaughlin, M. 111
Mellinger, G. D., 148
Metcoff, J., 65, 66, 142, 143
Mettetal, G., 20
Metzger, N., 92, 105, 107
Millar, F. E., III, 80, 149
Miller, G. R., 25, 71, 111
Mishler, E. G., 80, 149
Moos, R. H. and Moos, B. S., 55
Mouton, J. S., 203, 204
Musetto, A. P., 208
Napier, A., 131
Nauran, L., 32
Neill, John R., 131
Nichols, L. W., 204, 205, 206
Nies, D. C., 148
North, R. C., 30
Ochs, D. J., 83
Olson, D. H., 29, 55, 56, 57, 80, 81, 132, 147, 148, 149
Olson, T. D., 129
Ortony, A., 10, 11, 12
Osgood, C. E., 166, 168, 169
Ottoway, R. N., 182
Papp, P., 131, 139
Parry, D., 112, 115, 116, 121, 125

Patterson, G. R., 148, 173
Pearson, J., 207
Perry, B. A., 148
Peterson, D. R., 26
Phillips, E., 43
Phillips, G. M., 92, 105, 107
Phillipson, H., 96
Philpott, J., 107, 108
Pipe, R., 95, 105
Pondy, L. R., 49
Poole, M. S., 30, 50, 72
Pruitt, D. G., 164, 172, 204, 205
Putnam, L. L., 40, 50, 52, 111, 148, 149, 172
Rabunsky, C., 80, 81, 149
Rands, M., 54, 55, 148
Raush, H. C., 93, 110, 111, 123, 145, 147, 148, 149, 169
Raven, B. H., 72, 79, 84, 85
Ray, L., 201
Resick, P. A., 148
Reychler, L., 164
Rogers, L. E., 80, 116, 149
Rogers, M. A., 112, 115, 116, 121, 125
Rogers, M. F., 76
Rogers-Millar, L. E., 80, 149
Rollins, B. C., 83
Roloff, M. E., 111
Rosefeld, P., 172
Rosenberg, H., 158
Ross, R., 111
Rubin, J. A., 145, 166, 172, 182
Rummel, R. S., 83, 86, 172
Rushing, J. H., 10, 29
Rusk, T., 192
Russell, C., 55, 56, 57, 132
Ryder, R. G., 147
Safilios-Rothschild, C., 80, 86, 149
Sander, F., 201
Satir, V., 100, 132, 136, 137, 139
Scanzoni, J., 80
Schelling, T. C., 27, 119
Schmidt, D., 111, 149
Schmidt, S. M., 23
Schuetz, J. C., 38, 125, 172
Schutz, W. C., 71
Scott, M. B., 183
Secord, P. F., 63
Selye, H., 106
Shepard, A., 203, 204
Sherif, C. W., 102
Sherif, M., 102

Shimanoff, S. B., 140, 141
Siegel, S., 145
Silberstein, D., 131, 139
Sillars, A. L., 111, 112, 115, 116, 121, 125, 149
Simmel, G., 7
Simons, H., 7, 10, 23
Smith, D., 7, 94
Smith, M. J., 187
Snyder, R. C., 23
Solomon, L., 76
Sommers, A. A., 110, 111, 145, 147
Spector, B. I., 172
Sprenkle, D. H., 55, 56, 57, 132
Sprey, J., 80
Steinberg, M., 25, 71
Steinglass, P., 131
Stewart, J., 29, 163
Strauss, M. A., 34, 80, 149, 172, 173
Strodtbeck, F. L., 145
Stuart, R. B., 105, 109, 110, 169, 171, 179
Sundberg, N. D., 182, 186
Taplin, J. R., 182, 186
Taylor, D., 32, 33
Taylor, W. R., 130
Tedeschi, J. T., 118, 172
Thannes, N., 207
Thomas, K. W., 40, 41, 44, 49, 66, 84, 85, 100, 110, 116
Thomas, Milt, 51
Toulmin, S., 98
Tournier, P., 161, 163
Traupman, J., 86
Turk, J. L., 80, 81, 148
Tyler, L. E., 182, 186

Ury, W., 91, 99, 102, 106, 111, 121, 173, 205
Utne, M. K., 86
Vanderkooi, C., 207
Van De Vliert, 74, 180, 187, 188
Varney, G. H., 182
Vinacke, W. E., 145
Vincent, J. P., 32, 173, 182
Wall, J. A., 205
Waller, W., 84
Waln, V., 163
Walsh, F., 131
Walster, E. H., 75
Walton, R. E., 24, 86, 111, 115, 118, 121, 159, 160, 172, 181, 182
Watzlawick, P., 72, 145
Warner, C. T., 129
Waxler, N. E., 80, 149
Wehr, P., 5, 6, 29, 33, 87, 88, 150, 163, 164, 190, 191, 200, 201, 205
Weick, K. E., 10, 12, 14, 55, 98, 129, 131, 205
Weiss, R., 8, 32, 145, 148, 173
Welsh-Osga, B., 148
Whitaker, C. A., 65, 66, 131, 142, 143
Wilmot, W. W., 7, 20, 29, 30, 85, 96, 101, 113, 136, 137
Wilson, E. E., 40, 50, 52, 111, 148, 149
Winter, W. D., 173
Wolfe, D. M., 80, 149
Wyden, P., 28, 31, 65, 84, 114
Yarbrough, E., 182
Yelsma, P., 50, 53, 147
Young, O. R., 205
Zartman, W. I., 172

Subject Index

Accommodation, 43, 48
Action planning, 104
Adjudication, 199
Arbitration, 203
Assessment, conflict, 129
  Metaphors, 133–136
  Microevents, 142
  Quantitative, 145
  Rules, 140–142
  Sculpting, or Choreographing, 139
  System, 130–133
  Triangles, 136–139
Assessment, power, 79
Avoidance, 43, 47, 109, 112. *See also*
        Nonconfrontation

Choreographing, 139
Collaboration, 42, 45, 120
Collaborative goals, 102–106
  Criteria, objective, 103
  Interests, not positions, 102
  Options, 103
  People, separation from problem, 102
Communication
  Conflict expression, 19–24
  Perspective, 24
  Transactional, 96
Competition, 41, 44, 116
Compromise, 42, 46
Conciliatory set, 169
Conflict
  Assumptions about, 4–9
  Chinese character for, 3
  Common images, 12–19

Elements of, 22–29
  Expressed struggle, 23
  Interdependence, 26
  Interference, 26
  Perceived incompatible goals, 24
  Perceived scarce rewards, 25
Expression by communication, 19–24
Intervention, see Intervention
Metaphors, 9–12, 133–136
Productive, 32–33
Tactics, *see* Strategy
Content goals, 99, 100
Crises, 175
  Editing, 175
  Leveling, 176
Criteria, objective, 103
Currencies, 72
  Expertise, 73
  Interpersonal linkages, 73–74
  Intimacy, 73, 75
  Personal qualities, 73, 75
  Resource control, 73

Family meeting, 173
Fractionation, 166

Goals
  Clarity of, 91
  Collaborative, 102–106
  Content, 99–100
  Prospective, 94
  Relationship, 99–100
  Retrospective, 98
  Short-term, 104
  Superordinate, 197
  Transactive, 95
GRIT, 168

Hocker-Wilmot Conflict Assessment
    Guide, 153

Individual view of conflict, 37
    Adapting and unfreezing, 60–64
    Identification, 39–49
    Limitations, 49–53
Interests, separation from positions, 102
Intervention, 127
    Adjudication, 199
    Arbitration, 203
    Assessment, 129
    Mediation, 204
    Process, 184
    Self-regulation, 157
    Tactics, 191
    Third-party, 179

Mediation, 204
Metaconflict, 109
Metaphors, 9–12, 133–136
Microevents, 65, 142
Mid-range conflict, 159

Negotiation, 172
Nonconfrontation, 52, 111
Nonviolence, 161

Options, 103

People, separation from problem, 102
Planning, action, 104
Power
    Assessment, 79
    Balancing, 86
    Currencies, 72
    Imbalances, 83
    Relational view, 76
Process control, 195
Prospective goals, 94

Quantitative assessment, 145

Relationship goals, 99, 100
Retrospective goals, 98
Rules, system, 140–142

Satyagrahc movement, Ghandi's, 164
Sculpting, see Choreographing
Self-regulation, 158
    Conflict containment, 169
    Fractionation, 166
    GRIT, 168
    Negotiation, 172
Spirals, 30, 125, 151
Strategy in conflict
    Avoidance, 109, 112
    Collaboration, 120
    Competition, 116
    Control, 52, 111
    Description, 122
    Engagement, 109, 115
    Escalation, 123
    Maintenance, 123
    Non-confrontation, 52, 111
    Process, 107
    Reduction, 123
    Solution-orientation, 52, 111
Stuart's Conflict Containment Model, 169
Styles of conflict
    Adapting and unfreezing, 60
    Individual, 37
    System, 53, 130–133
Superordinate goals, 197
System view of conflict, 53–59, 130–133
    Adapting and unfreezing, 64
    Identification of, 53–59, 133
    Limitations, 59–60
    Rules, 132, 140–142

Tactics, see Strategy
Third party intervention, 179
Toxic triangle, 132, 137
Transactive goals, 95
Triangles, 132, 136–139
    Toxic, 132, 137

Wehr's Conflict Map, 150